A Spiritual Life

Also by Allan Hugh Cole Jr. from Westminster John Knox Press

Good Mourning: Getting Through Your Grief

The Life of Prayer: Mind, Body, and Soul

Losers, Loners, and Rebels: The Spiritual Struggles of Boys
(with Robert C. Dykstra and Donald Capps)

A SPIRITUAL LIFE

Perspectives from Poets, Prophets, and Preachers

Allan Hugh Cole Jr.

Editor

WESTMINSTER
JOHN KNOX PRESS
LOUISVILLE • KENTUCKY

First edition
Published by Westminster John Knox Press
Louisville, Kentucky

11 12 13 14 15 16 17 18 19 20—10 9 8 7 6 5 4 3 2 1

Unless otherwise indicated, Scripture quotations are from the New Revised Standard Version of the Bible, copyright © 1989 by the Division of Christian Education of the National Council of the Churches of Christ in the U.S.A., and are used by permission. Scripture quotations marked RSV are from the Revised Standard Version of the Bible, copyright © 1946, 1952, 1971, and 1973 by the Division of Christian Education of the National Council of the Churches of Christ in the U.S.A., and are used by permission.

Excerpts from Barbara Crooker, "In the Middle," from Radiance bry Barbara Crooker, Word Press, Cincinnate, OH, 2005. Reprinted by permission. Excerpts from Madeline DeFrees, "Skid Row" from *Blue Dusk: New & Selected Poems, 1951-2001.* Copyright © 1964, 2001 by Madeline DeFrees. Reprinted with the permission of Copper Canyon Press, www.coopercanyonpress.org. Excerpts from Gerard Manley Hopkins, "As Kingfishers Catch Fire," lines 5–10 only, cited on p. 129 from *Oxford Authors: Gerard Manley Hopkins,* edited by Catherine Phillips, copyright by permission of Oxford University Press on behalf of The British Province of the Society of Jesus. Excerpts from Rainer Maria Rilke, translated by Babette Deutch, from *Poems from the Book of Hours,* copyright © 1941 by New Directions Publishing Corp. Reprinted by permission of New Directions Publishing Corp. Excerpts from Rainer Maria Rilke, "Gott spricht zu jedem . . . / God speaks to each of us . . . ," "Du bist die Zukunft . . ./You are the future," from *Rilke's Book of Hours: Love Poems to God* by Rainer Maria Rilke, translated by Anita Barrows and Joanna Macy, copyright © 1996 by Anita Barrows and Joanna Macy. Used by permission of Riverhead Books, an imprint of Penguin Group (USA) Inc., and reprinted by permission of the translators. Excerpts from Rainer Maria Rilke, "Imaginary Biography," "You See I Want a Lot," "My Eyes Already Touch the Sunny Hill" from Selected Poems of Rainer Maria Rilke, a translation from the German and commentary by Robert Bly, copyright © 1981 by Robert Bly. Reprinted by permission of HarperCollins Publishers.

Chapter 10, "A Spiritual Person," by Donald Capps was published first in the *Journal of Religion and Health.* Reprinted by permission. Chapter 14, "Nursing, Eucharist, Psychosis, Metaphor" by Kerry Egan was first published previously in *From the Pews in the Back: Young Women and Catholicism,* ed. Kate Dugan and Jennifer Owens (Collegeville, MN: Liturgical Press, 2009). Reprinted by permission. Chapter 18, "Reading St. Therese," by Stephanie Paulsell was originally published in the *Harvard Divinity Bulletin,* Summer/Autumn 2010, Vol. 38, Nos. 3 and 4. Reprinted by permission.

Book design by Sharon Adams
Cover design by designpointinc.com
Cover illustration: © konradlew/istockStockphoto.com

Library of Congress Cataloging-in-Publication Data

A spiritual life : perspectives from poets, prophets, and preachers / Allan Hugh Cole, Jr., editor.
   p. cm.
   ISBN 978-0-664-23492-8 (alk. paper)
   1. Spiritual life—Christianity. I. Cole, Allan Hugh.
BV4510.3.S67 2011
248.4—dc22

2010038789

PRINTED IN THE UNITED STATES OF AMERICA

∞ The paper used in this publication meets the minimum requirements of the American National Standard for Information Sciences—Permanence of Paper for Printed Library Materials, ANSI Z39.48-1992.

Westminster John Knox Press advocates the responsible use of our natural resources. The text paper of this book is made from 30% post-consumer waste.

To Jon L. Berquist,
colleague and friend

Contents

Contributors

Homer U. Ashby Jr. is a clinical psychologist and pastoral counselor at Triangle Pastoral Counseling in Raleigh, North Carolina. For twenty-seven years he taught pastoral care and counseling at McCormick Theological Seminary in Chicago. He is an experienced clinician with a special interest in working with persons across the life span who are experiencing stress as they adjust to changes in their lives. A minister in the United Methodist Church, he is author of *Our Home Is over Jordan: A Black Pastoral Theology* (2003).

Deborah A. Block is pastor and head of staff at the Immanuel Presbyterian Church in Milwaukee. She was ordained to the ministry of Word and Sacrament in the Presbyterian Church (U.S.A.) in 1977. She is a trustee of Carroll University in Waukesha, Wisconsin, and of McCormick Theological Seminary in Chicago, where she has been chair of the board of trustees and the recipient of the Distinguished Ministry Award. Currently, she serves as chair of the board of the Presbyterian Publishing Corporation. She has been a teacher and preacher at many conferences and has contributed to several recent publications, including *Proclaiming the Great Ends of the Church* (2010), *Celebrating Our Call: Ordination Stories of Presbyterian Women* (2006), and the *Feasting on the Word* lectionary series, Years A and C.

Brad R. Braxton is Distinguished Visiting Scholar at McCormick Theological Seminary in Chicago. He is an ordained Baptist minister and a leading voice among today's progressive religious leaders. His publications include three books: *Preaching Paul* (2004), *No Longer Slaves: Galatians and African American Experience* (2002), and *The Tyranny of Resolution: I Corinthians 7:17–24*

(2000). He is a member of a team of scholars who have created *The African American Lectionary*, the first online ecumenical African American preaching and worship lectionary.

Donald Capps was professor of pastoral theology at Princeton Theological Seminary from 1981 until his retirement in 2009. Previously, he taught at the University of Chicago Divinity School, the University of North Carolina at Charlotte, and the Graduate Seminary at Phillips University in Oklahoma. He is the author of numerous books reflecting his dual interests in pastoral care and psychology of religion, including *Jesus the Village Psychiatrist* (2008), *A Time to Laugh: The Religion of Humor* (2005), *Men and Their Religion: Honor, Hope, and Humor* (2002), *Jesus: A Psychological Biography* (2000), *Men, Religion, and Melancholia* (1997), *Agents of Hope: A Pastoral Psychology* (1995), *The Child's Song: The Religious Abuse of Children* (1995), *The Poet's Gift: Toward the Renewal of Pastoral Care* (1993), and *Reframing: A New Method in Pastoral Care* (1990). He served as president of the Society for the Scientific Study of Religion from 1990 to 1992 and was awarded an honorary doctorate from the University of Uppsala in 1989. He has also received the American Psychological Association's William F. Bier Award for Contribution to Psychology of Religion in 1994 and the College of Pastoral Supervision and Psychotherapy's Helen Flanders Dunbar Centennial Award in 2002.

Allan Hugh Cole Jr. is academic dean and the Nancy Taylor Williamson Professor of Pastoral Care at Austin Presbyterian Theological Seminary. He is the author of *The Life of Prayer: Mind, Body, and Soul* (2009), *Good Mourning: Getting through Your Grief* (2008), and *Be Not Anxious: Pastoral Care of Disquieted Souls* (2008), as well as a coauthor of *Losers, Loners, and Rebels: The Spiritual Struggles of Boys* (2007) and editor of *From Midterms to Ministry: Practical Theologians on Pastoral Beginnings* (2008). An ordained minister in the Presbyterian Church (U.S.A.), he has served congregations in Upstate New York and on Long Island.

Kerry Egan is a mother, hospice chaplain, and author of *Fumbling: A Pilgrimage Tale of Love, Grief, and Spiritual Renewal on the Camino de Santiago* (2004). She works for Home and Hospice Care of Rhode Island and lives in Massachusetts with her family.

Ismael García is professor emeritus of Christian ethics at Austin Presbyterian Theological Seminary. Previously he taught at McCormick Theological Seminary in Chicago. A native of Puerto Rico, he has been a leading voice among Protestant Hispanics in the United States and beyond for more than two decades. He is author of *Introdución a la Etica Cristiana* (2005), *Dignidad: Ethics through Hispanic Eyes* (1997), and *Justice in Latin American Theology of Liberation* (1987). He is a member of the United Church of Christ.

Greg Garrett is professor of English at Baylor University, writer in residence at the Episcopal Seminary of the Southwest, and a licensed lay preacher in the Episcopal Church. He is the author of three acclaimed novels, *Shame* (2009), *Cycling* (2003), and *Free Bird* (2002), which was nominated for the Pulitzer Prize, and numerous books on religion, narrative, and culture, including *We Get to Carry Each Other: The Gospel according to U2* (2009), *Stories from the Edge: A Theology of Grief* (2008), and *The Gospel according to Hollywood* (2007). In addition, he is coauthor of *The Gospel Reloaded: Exploring Spirituality and Faith in* The Matrix (2003). He is a past winner of the Pirate's Alley William Faulkner Prize for Fiction and a CASE Gold Medal for Nonfiction, and he is a member of the Texas Institute of Letters.

Elizabeth Damewood Gaucher graduated Davidson College as a scholar in the Kendrick K. Kelley Program in Historical Studies. She has served as executive director of two nonprofit organizations, the West Virginia Alliance for Sustainable Families and the West Virginia Land Trust, that work in child advocacy and land conservation, respectively. Previously, she served as special assistant to the governor of West Virginia for various projects in economic development and education, was acting director of the Governor's Cabinet on Children and Families, and held a position on the citizens' advisory council to the Department of Health and Human Resources. She is also a founding board member for the West Virginia Center for Budget and Policy. As a writer, she has contributed frequently to *Corporate Idealist* and maintains a blog about honoring authenticity in life choices: www .essediemblog.com.

Gail Godwin is the author of thirteen novels, three of which were finalists for the National Book Award. Her novels include *Unfinished Desires* (2010), *Queen of the Underworld* (2006), *Evenings at Five* (2003), *Evensong* (1999), *The Good Husband* (1994), *Father Melancholy's Daughter* (1991), *A Southern Family* (1987), and *The Finishing School* (1984). Volume 2 of her book *The Making of a Writer* will be published in 2011. She has received a Guggenheim and two National Endowment grants, one for fiction writing and one for libretto writing, and has taught literature and fiction writing at Vassar College, Columbia University, and the University of Iowa. She lives in Upstate New York. Her Web site is www.gailgodwin.com.

Albert Y. Hsu is an acquisitions and development editor at InterVarsity Press. He is the author of *The Suburban Christian* (2006), *Grieving a Suicide* (2002), and *Singles at the Crossroads* (1997). He has been a columnist for *Christianity Today* magazine and is working on his PhD in educational studies at Trinity Evangelical Divinity School in Deerfield, Illinois. He is a member and worship leader at an Anglican church, and he lives with his wife and two sons in the western suburbs of Chicago.

Deborah van Deusen Hunsinger is the Charlotte W. Newcombe Professor of Pastoral Theology at Princeton Theological Seminary. An ordained Presbyterian minister, she is interested in educating clergy and laypeople to offer theologically sound and psychologically informed pastoral care in the church. A Fellow in the American Association of Pastoral Counselors, she is the author of *Pray without Ceasing: Revitalizing Pastoral Care* (2006) and *Theology and Pastoral Counseling: A New Interdisciplinary Approach* (1995). She is coeditor of *Healing Wisdom: Depth Psychology and the Pastoral Ministry* (2010) and *The New Dictionary of Pastoral Studies* (2002).

Michael Jinkins is president of Louisville Presbyterian Theological Seminary in Kentucky, where he also teaches theology. Previously he served as academic dean and professor of pastoral theology at Austin Presbyterian Theological Seminary. A minister in the Presbyterian Church (U.S.A.), he has served as pastor in several congregations in Texas and Scotland. He is the author of many articles and books, including *Called to Be Human* (2009), *Letters to New Pastors* (2006), *Christianity, Tolerance, and Pluralism* (2004), *Transformational Ministry: Church Leadership in the Way of the Cross* (2003), *Invitation to Theology* (2001), and *The Church Faces Death: Ecclesiology in a Post-Modern Context* (1999).

Elizabeth Liebert, SNJM, serves as dean of the seminary, academic vice president, and professor of spiritual life at San Francisco Theological Seminary. She is the author or coauthor of four books: *The Way of Discernment: Spiritual Practices for Decision Making* (2008), *A Retreat with the Psalms: Resources for Personal and Communal Prayer*, (2001), *The Spiritual Exercises Reclaimed: Uncovering Liberating Possibilities for Women* (2001), and *Changing Life Patterns: Adult Development in Spiritual Direction* (revised edition, 2000). When not serving in seminary administration, she teaches in the areas of spiritual formation, discernment, and prayer.

Michael L. Lindvall is the senior minister of the Brick Presbyterian Church in New York City. He is the author of two novels, *The Good News from North*

Haven (2002) and *Leaving North Haven* (2002), as well as several volumes of accessible theology, including *Knowing God's Triune Story* (2010), *A Geography of God* (2007), and *What Did Jesus Do?* (2007). He and his wife, an artist, live in Manhattan.

Bonnie J. Miller-McLemore is E. Rhodes and Leona B. Carpenter Professor of Pastoral Theology at the Divinity School and Graduate Department of Religion of Vanderbilt University. Ordained by the Christian Church (Disciples of Christ), a leader in pastoral theology, and recognized for her work on families, women, and children, she is the author of numerous articles and books, including *In the Midst of Chaos: Care of Children as Spiritual Practice* (2006), *Let the Children Come: Reimagining Childhood from a Christian Perspective* (2003), and *Also a Mother: Work and Family as Theological Dilemma* (1994). She is currently working on several projects in pastoral and practical theology, including an edited volume, *The Blackwell Companion to Practical Theology* (2011).

Richard R. Osmer is the Thomas W. Synnott Professor of Christian Education at Princeton Theological Seminary. An ordained minister in the Presbyterian Church (U.S.A.), he is the author of several books, including *Practical Theology: An Introduction* (2008), *The Teaching Ministry of Congregations* (2007), *Confirmation: Presbyterian Practices in Ecumenical Perspective* (1996), *Teaching for Faith* (1992), and *A Teachable Spirit* (1990). A leading voice in practical theology and religious education, he is the former editor of the *International Journal of Practical Theology* and past president of the Association of Practical Theology.

Stephanie Paulsell is the Amory Houghton Professor of the Practice of Ministry Studies at Harvard Divinity School and an ordained minister in the Christian Church (Disciples of Christ). The author of *Honoring the Body: Meditations on a Christian Practice* (2002) and coeditor of *The Scope of Our Art: The Vocation of the Theological Teacher* (2002), she also writes regularly for the *Christian Century*. She lives in Cambridge, Massachusetts, with her husband and daughter.

Sheri Reynolds is the author of the novels *The Sweet In-Between* (2008), *Firefly Cloak* (2006), *A Gracious Plenty* (1998), *The Rapture of Canaan* (1996)—an Oprah Book Club selection and *New York Times* best seller—and *Bitterroot Landing* (1995). Her play *Orabelle's Wheelbarrow* won the Women Playwrights' Initiative award in 2005. She's been the recipient of a Virginia Commission for the Arts grant in playwriting and also received the Outstanding Faculty Award from the State Council for Higher Education of Virginia. Sheri teaches creative writing and literature at Old Dominion University in Norfolk, Virginia, where she is the Ruth and Perry Morgan Chair of Southern Literature. She lives in the town of Cape Charles on Virginia's eastern shore.

Marjorie J. Thompson has been engaged in an ecumenical ministry of spiritual formation retreats, teaching, and writing for over twenty-five years. She is the author of *Soul Feast: An Invitation to the Christian Spiritual Life* (1995/2005), *Family, the Forming Center* (1989/1996), and several volumes in the small-group resource series Companions in Christ, including *The Way of Blessedness* (2003) and *The Way of Forgiveness* (2002). Ordained in the Presbyterian Church (U.S.A), she has served as associate pastor for the First Presbyterian Church in Stamford, Connecticut, and as director of Pathways in Congregational Spirituality for Upper Room Ministries.

Theodore J. Wardlaw is president and professor of homiletics at Austin Presbyterian Theological Seminary. He has served on the board of trustees at Union Presbyterian Seminary in Richmond, Virginia, and on the board of visitors at Johnson C. Smith Theological Seminary in Atlanta, Georgia, and Presbyterian College in Clinton, South Carolina. He has served as pastor of congregations in Tennessee, Texas, and Long Island. Most recently, he served for almost twelve years as senior pastor at Central Presbyterian Church in Atlanta, Georgia. He has been active for many years in the Presbyterian Church (U.S.A.) at local, regional, national, and international levels.

William H. Willimon, former dean of the chapel at Duke University, is bishop of the United Methodist Church's North Alabama Annual Conference (Birmingham area). He is also research professor at Duke Divinity School and is the author of many books, including *The Early Sermons of Karl Barth* (2009), *Conversations with Barth on Preaching* (2006), *Thank God It's Friday: Encountering the Seven Last Words from the Cross* (2006), *Sinning Like a Christian: A New Look at the Seven Deadly Sins* (2005), *Pastor: The Theology and Practice of Ordained Ministry* (2002), and *Worship as Pastoral Care* (1979), and he is a coauthor of *Resident Aliens: Life in the Christian Colony* (1989).

Lauren F. Winner, an Episcopalian, teaches at Duke Divinity School. She has written several books, including *A Cheerful and Comfortable Faith: Anglican Religious Practice in the Elite Households of Eighteenth-Century Virginia* (2010), *Mudhouse Sabbath: An Invitation to a Life of Spiritual Discipline* (2003), a book about what Christians can learn from Judaism about spiritual practices, *Real Sex: The Naked Truth about Chastity* (2006), and a memoir called *Girl Meets God* (2003). Her Web site is www.laurenwinner.net.

J. Philip Wogaman, longtime professor, and now professor emeritus, of Christian ethics at Wesley Theological Seminary, also served as pastor of Foundry United Methodist Church in Washington, D.C. He was interim president of Iliff School of Theology in Denver and served as interim dean of Claremont School of Theology in Claremont, California. A past president of the American Theological Society and of the Society of Christian Ethics, he is the author or editor of more than twenty volumes, including *Moral Dilemmas: An Introduction to Christian Ethics* (2009), *Faith and Fragmentation: Reflections on the Future of Christianity* (2004), *An Unexpected Journey: Reflections on Pastoral Ministry* (2004), *Christian Perspectives on Politics* (2000), *From the Eye of the Storm: A Pastor to the President Speaks Out* (1998), and *Christian Ethics: A Historical Introduction* (1993).

Preface

This book explores the spiritual life. Its approach assumes that people live this life in diverse forms with various emphases and that this life fosters a range of personal and corporate commitments. As a result, understandings of what makes for a spiritual life, which many people these days seem eager to discover, differ among people. Differences exist for people of different religious faiths but also for people who adhere to the same faith. Each contributor to this book looks to Jesus of Nazareth in order to discern and live a spiritual life, which is to say that although they represent a range of perspectives within a broad religious tradition, these contributors offer various perspectives on a spiritual life tethered to Christianity.

In light of these essays and drawing from my own experiences—as a seminary professor, former pastor, and one seeking to discern and live a more faithful and authentic spiritual life himself—I have identified three ways of discerning and living this life: as *poets*, *prophets*, and *preachers*. Grouping these essays accordingly, I have sought to highlight ways that contributors have reflected on the notion of a spiritual life themselves. I do not mean to suggest that these three descriptions—poets, prophets, and preachers—exhaust how we might discern or live a spiritual life. Nor do I mean to suggest that every contributor would self-identify with the description to which I have tied him or her. For example, I suspect that some might resist being called a prophet, perhaps even appealing to an old adage: "I am neither a prophet nor a prophet's child!" Others might prefer not to be called a poet or preacher, suggesting that these descriptions simply do not fit. I recognize the limits of my using these three descriptive terms for how we might discern and live a spiritual life and for how best to arrange these essays. Nevertheless, using some editorial license, I have assigned each contributor a place in this descriptive mix—at least for this particular project—because the contributor's vocational life, the content of his or her essay, or both, seem to fit with the description I've assigned. I ask for pardon if I have erred.

One may read these essays in any order, for each one stands as a discrete work. However, I believe that the essays cohere as I have arranged them and that reading them in sequential order may prove helpful.

Acknowledgments

I enjoyed editing this book, a privilege that allowed me to invite some of the most creative, generous, and wisest people among us to share their experiences and perspectives on the spiritual life. My gratitude extends to every contributor for the hard work done in these pages. I admire each of them. They have taught me and will continue to do so. I believe that they will teach you too.

The opportunity to work once again with Westminster John Knox Press, an author's press par excellence, brings its own rewards. The leadership of Marc Lewis, the editorial vision provided by David Dobson, the efficiency and attention to detail offered by Julie Tonini and the entire production staff, the efforts of Jennifer Cox and her staff to market and to sell books, and the solid work of Emily Kiefer as publicist make me proud and thankful to be associated with this group. I am also grateful to Don Parker-Burgard for his fine copyediting.

I owe a special word of gratitude to Jon L. Berquist, who served as my editor for most of the time it took to write this book. We have been friends for over a decade now. Jon's counsel continues to help me get better at conceptualizing and writing books even as his friendship helps me get better as a person. I am also thankful for Jana Riess, a longtime friend and trusted colleague, who subsequently served as my editor when the book was put into production. Her contributions made this book better.

I want to note, too, how satisfying it has been to work on this project with Sheri Reynolds and Elizabeth Damewood Gaucher. The three of us first became friends twenty-five years ago at Davidson College, and I'm delighted that our paths have converged again in this book. Sheri has been a special writing friend in recent years and has given me loads of sound and helpful input regarding my work. Her extraordinary talent is matched by her generosity.

I continue to find joy in teaching at Austin Presbyterian Theological Seminary. I remain grateful for the vision and leadership of our board of trustees and President Ted Wardlaw, for the professional support offered by our previous academic dean, Michael Jinkins, and our interim dean, David H. Jensen, and for faculty and staff colleagues and students who represent excellence in theological education.

I am also honored that three of my foremost teachers at Princeton Seminary—Donald Capps, Deborah van Deusen Hunsinger, and Richard Osmer—have contributed to this book. Each has played a role in how I think and write about many things, including the spiritual life, though none should be held responsible for my views.

My parents, Allan and Jeri Cole, introduced me to God's love as a child and thus to a spiritual life. They did so as much by their actions as through their words, which is as it should be. I am grateful for this enduring gift and for the many others they have given me and my family.

All that I know and experience in the spiritual life, especially its deepest joys, values, and hopes, connects to living daily with my wife, Tracey, and our daughters, Meredith and Holly. The loves of my life, they nurture my spirit. As the Scriptures declare: "God is love, and those who abide in love abide in God, and God abides in them" (1 John 4:16).

1

More Religious than Spiritual

ALLAN HUGH COLE JR.

I was only four years old on April 16, 1972—the day of my baptism—but I remember this day. Momma, Daddy, and I stand in front of the sanctuary doors at the little Holy Cross Episcopal Church in Simpsonville, South Carolina. Daddy bends down to wipe dew that glistens atop my black dress shoes, a sheen picked up from the thickening grass. Two acolytes not much older than me take their places in front of us. One of them carries a shiny processional cross high in the air, his bent elbows pointing slightly upward as if to nudge heaven. The other one holds a large Bible out in front of him. It hides the bottom third of his face. Our kind priest, Father Henry Summerall, who still practices law part-time in order to support his young family, gets in line behind us. He smiles and offers a slight but deliberate nod of the head, as if to say, "Here we go," but says nothing. Closing his eyes, he appears to pray. As often happens, his white-laced surplice and satin stole draped over a black cassock draw my fixed gaze. Who he is and what he does fascinates me.

The organ begins to play—or was it a piano? The sanctuary doors open, and I turn to face the music. The people gathered there stand and face us, and they begin to sing. About fifty feet ahead I glimpse the wall-bound altar still common among southern Episcopalians in those days. It captivates me too, despite my not understanding its significance or use. I enjoy walking by it, which I do as often as I can. Sometimes I think I tingle inside when I do. Beautiful tapestries—later I would learn to call them paraments—bathe this centerpiece. Today they are white; at other times they are red or green or purple. A large shiny cup and plate, along with an opened black-leather-bound *Book of Common Prayer* (1928 edition), rest there too.

1

My family and I walk down the center aisle and take our places in front of the congregation. I'm still too young to feel self-conscious. The acolytes bookend the altar. Father Summerall faces it and begins reciting the liturgy.

After what seems like a long wait "down front," he turns to Momma and Daddy. He asks, "Hath this child been already baptized, or no?" "No," they reply. He then continues with more prayers and questions. I know that at some point he will look at me, and he does. He gestures for me to climb the two steps of the little wooden stool placed before the baptismal font, which I do with appropriate aplomb.

Nearly four decades later, my two young daughters, Meredith and Holly, ages five and three, climb a similar stool several times a day to wash hands and brush teeth. Sometimes when they do, I think back to the stool before the baptismal font, where a different kind of washing took place, and I picture the little boy who climbed it and consider his spiritual journey in the years since. At times I also think of the journeys that Meredith and Holly may make—perhaps they have already begun making them—and of the ministers and faith communities that might serve as beacons along the way.

"Name this child," Father Summerall says, almost chanting.

"Allan Hugh Cole Jr.," say Momma and Daddy.

I lean over the silvery bowl of water, in whose mirror I see my reflection. Every now and then I can still see it if I squint hard enough. I'm careful to keep my burgundy clip-on tie out of the way so that it stays dry. I think I'd practiced this part at home.

"I baptize thee in the name of the Father," proclaims Father Summerall. Cool water begins to flow over the crown of my head. I keep looking at my reflection in the bowl, which, though refracted now, is still there. "And of the Son." A second watery stream crosses the path of future sideburns. I feel warm inside despite the cool water. I lean forward, slightly closer to my future. "And of the Holy Ghost." With a final pouring, a few drops slide across one corner of my mouth onto my lips, so that I taste the occasion—hints of brassiness crossing my palate.

"Amen."

Father Summerall places his hand on my forehead. He makes the sign of a cross there while he continues to pray. The remaining water drips off of me, back into the bowl. I take in the host of aromas lingering in the air. The smell of this place is like no other I know—flowery and leathery and spicy and woodlike, all at once. Like the lives of church members, these assorted smells collide to create an aroma that's distinctive and mostly inviting but never exactly the same with every whiff.

"Amen."

Father Summerall pats my forehead with a white handkerchief that looks clean and smells cleaner. He puts his arms on my shoulders, gently helps straighten me up, and guides me down from the stool. He then hands the handkerchief to me so that I may wipe some more, and I put it in the side pocket of my navy blue polyester sport coat. Momma and Daddy smile and hug me. I hug them back. I hear Momma say, "I'm proud of you." Smiles and nodding heads proliferate around the sanctuary. Were this not an Episcopal church, folks may have clapped too.

Staring at the prayer book with his hands extending upward, Father Summerall once again faces the altar and begins to pray. When he finishes, music plays and one of the acolytes extinguishes candles on each side of the altar. As the congregation begins to sing, we all get back into line, file back through the sanctuary, and pass quickly across the narthex, both acolytes leading the way. One of them throws open the church's double doors, the other peels off to the side, deliberate and dutiful. I squint into southern April breezes and a piercing blue, almost cobalt, sky. Though not understanding this occasion, I have a sense of its significance, for me and for others. Welcomed officially into the church and charged to follow Jesus, my life is to be different.

Somehow, I think I knew this.

Thirty-eight years later, now a seminary professor, I sit at my campus desk and ponder a painting that hangs above it. The painting depicts Jesus washing Peter's feet as described in the Gospel of John (13:1–17). I find this story simultaneously beautiful and challenging, which I suppose is the point. Beautiful because of Jesus' tender care for those he loved; he washed the feet of many disciples on this occasion, a humble and generous act. Challenging because he tells Peter and the rest who profess to follow him to go and do likewise to others: "I have set you an example, that you also should do as I have done to you" (John 13:15). I've long thought that this story sums up the Christian life.

Rather ordinary, the painting's inexpensive frame cost more than the print itself. I picked it up years ago in a squishy religious bookstore in Myrtle Beach, South Carolina, where I lived. It was the kind of bookstore that sold bumper stickers that said things like "Christians Don't Burn in the Son" (a clever turn of phrase, especially in a beach town), "My Boss Is a Jewish Carpenter," "Christians Aren't Perfect, Just Forgiven," and "In Case of Rapture, This Vehicle Will Be Unmanned." During my high school and college years, long before the age of Amazon.com and its kin, this was the only place I knew of in my town to find religious books and potpourri. Waldenbooks in the Myrtle Square Mall had a few religious titles, but nothing close to what this other store stocked. Anyway, my trips to the mall were usually made with my friends to meet girls. Religion was not on my mind.

This religious bookstore was something altogether different. Located not far from my home, I'd stop in every now and then to peruse the bookshelves and listen to the cassette tapes on display. While I never purchased a bumper sticker there, I remember listening to bands like White Heart and Petra, and to Amy Grant and Steven Curtis Chapman. This bookstore also stocked a few U2 tapes, as I recall, its owners evidently putting U2's music in the genre of "contemporary Christian." The independent record store in town, a place called Sounds Familiar, had a much better selection of U2 and of many other artists I enjoyed. It also attracted more girls.

A friend I played sports with introduced me to this religious bookstore and to these Christian artists. He had joined a Bible church and, in his words, "caught fire" for Jesus. He wanted others to catch fire too, and he began to see himself as a kind of accelerant if not the fire starter itself. As a cradle Episcopalian, I could recite the Holy Eucharist, Rites I and II, in my head, but I knew next to nothing about contemporary Christian music and even less about human infernos fueled by the Lord, so I was intrigued.

Incidentally, this same friend also introduced me to smokeless tobacco, which of course required no fire at all. He used a brand called Skoal but suggested that I try something different, one called Hawken. It was a milder, wintergreen-flavored tobacco for lightweights. Many of us boys experimented with smokeless tobacco during various high school sports seasons, a rite of passage for male teens in low-country South Carolina. But try as I did, neither my taste for Hawken nor for contemporary Christian music ever took hold. I preferred listening to Led Zeppelin and chewing Hubba Bubba.

I believe I was in college when I bought the Jesus painting, perhaps while on one of the spiritual junkets I took in those years, one of which carried me to the Presbyterian Church. But it was several years later before I had it framed and hung it on a wall. I was finished with seminary and serving as pastor of a congregation when I first displayed it.

I kept the painting, and I display it in a prominent place these days because it speaks to me. It speaks differently to me now than it did when I bought it, which I attribute to years of study, questioning, pondering, and seeking to live out the Christian faith—all of which I continue to do, and every now and then with a measure of faithfulness. Illustrative of a life lived in service to God and others, the painting depicts the life that Jesus embodied and charged his followers to emulate, a life for which footwashing—offering it and receiving it—serves as a guiding metaphor.

This painting reminds me, at least in part, of who I am, and thus, of why I do what I do. In other words, it reminds me of my identity: one who follows

Jesus. The psychologist Erik H. Erikson claimed that adolescence prompts one to give more psychological energy to figuring out one's identity than ever before—to figuring out the type of person that one wishes to be. Adulthood seems to call for the same intensity of figuring with regard to one's spiritual life. For many people, including those interested in reading a book such as this one, I suppose, questions of who one is in relation to God, the divine, the transcendent, the spiritual—however one might express it—become hallmarks of adulthood experience and occupy us like never before. We want to know what kind of person we shall be, spiritually speaking.

Pondering the painting while thinking about what kind of person I want to be, I remember who I already am: I am one who follows Jesus. This is not my only identity. I am other things too, some of which I want. For example, I'm a husband, father, son, friend, writer, teacher, colleague, neighbor, and New York Jets fan. I'm also a devotee of the music of Dwight Yoakam, Dale Watson, and Lyle Lovett, and of the writings of Wallace Stegner, Wendell Berry, Gail Godwin, and Sheri Reynolds, among others. I like these aspects of who I am, these ways that my identity gets expressed. But when I allow my identity as a follower of Jesus not simply to figure into the mix of my identities but rather to lead the way and become the *primary* identity that shapes the other identities I claim, I have discovered that it enriches these other identities in ways that I'm proud of and, I hope, ways conducive to enriching the lives of others. When any enrichment happens, however minor in scope, I think it's precisely because I am more faithful to this Jesus and his example, and thus to my identity as one who follows him.

I say all of this only to add that much of the time I don't follow Jesus very well, which is to note that a good deal of my life passes with me not being true to myself. In fact, my faithfulness to the example that Jesus offers, which is to say the quality of my spiritual life, rarely exceeds the quality of the painting over my desk—that is, nothing extraordinary, average at best. But this is who I am, nonetheless, or who I mostly am; I'm a follower of Jesus. As I follow him I look to him, the one that the Scriptures describe as a man "in whom the fullness of God was pleased to dwell" (Col. 1:19). I look to him in order to glimpse divine love and its purposes, including its purposes for me and my life but not *only* for me and my life. God's love and purposes reach well beyond me. Jesus' washing the feet of others reminds me of that, and following Jesus means that I try to go and do likewise. I often encourage students to ponder the notion that the Christian life is lived as much horizontally as vertically, as much in terms of relationships with other persons—including intimates and strangers, friends and foes alike—as in terms of one's relationship with God. In other words, a Christian life resists so-called private religion or spirituality, which means a Christian life resists being reduced to no more than one's personal relationship with God. Most of those bumper stickers in that bookstore missed this point, I think. So seeking to practice what I preach, I try to think, relate, love, forgive, hope, and act in ways that Jesus did, not only as regards God but as regards other people too. I learn about all of these aspects of faithful living in the writings that bear witness to Jesus' life: the Bible.

I am one who needs regular reminders of Jesus and of who I am as his follower. I am also one who needs encouragement to read the Bible regularly. So I cheat by hanging this painting front and center over my primary workspace. It speaks to me of Jesus' life, and thus of my life too. It serves as an icon of the Christian life well lived, which remains my goal, and I have to look at it anytime I come to work, whether I feel like it or not.

Looking at the painting today, with water flowing over a washbasin onto the floor and Jesus on his hands and knees washing Peter's dirty feet, I remember how Peter resisted Jesus' offering. I also think about my own resistances that hamper my following Jesus. Thinking about my identity turns to thinking about the spiritual life, including some questions: What marks this life? How does one cultivate it? What typically hinders it? What makes it worthwhile anyway? But try as I may, I can barely think about these questions, much less hope to answer them, without once again harking back to that spring morning at the Holy Cross Episcopal Church, where my path toward following Jesus began with baptism.

Sometimes, I can still smell that sanctuary.

In order to say more about my postbaptismal path, on which I have trod my spiritual journey, I first have to say something about my vocational life. By this I mean my calling to teach, write, and lead in a mainline Protestant seminary that educates men and women for various forms of Christian ministry. To some ears, the term "calling" may be religious racket, the kind that blares from self-righteous folks on fire for Jesus. But I appreciate the term "calling" precisely because it has particularly religious overtones. I learned about it first while in seminary, when reading the works of John Calvin, a minister and key thinker in Geneva, Switzerland, during the Protestant Reformation of the sixteenth century. I'd heard the term "vocation" before, and I suspect that I'd heard people mention their "callings," but I think the only association I had with vocation was the alternative high school in my town. The vo-tech school was where students less academically inclined went to learn a trade, anything from automotive repair to culinary arts. And because I was ignorant, I never put "vocation" and "calling" together.

Calvin taught me that one's vocation is one's calling. He believed that God fills every person with particular gifts that may (and should) be used to God's glory. Whatever one's gifts, however simple or seemingly insignificant, she has a duty to make use of them faithfully. In doing so, she honors God and participates in God's purposes. Calvin taught me that at the heart of a spiritual life lies a vocational life, a "called" life. Who one is remains tethered to what one does, even though what one does never exhausts who one is.

I spend much of my time and energy thinking, reading, writing, and teaching about matters relating to God, specifically the God of the Christian story. Jesus of Nazareth, the one who washes feet above my desk, knew this God intimately. Jesus also worshiped and sought to lead others to this God through both his words and actions. As a seminary professor, much of what I try to do, my calling, relates to Jesus' work. I seek greater wisdom concerning theology, religion, deep existential concerns, and an array of human experiences and problems, along with trying to discern how God may be present in their midst and how God may assuage them. I do all of this because I hope to help others gain wisdom on these matters too, so that they, in turn, may help still others in similar ways. Much of my work issues from a desire to help present and future ministers, including pastors, chaplains, counselors, and lay leaders, thrive in their own callings to serve God and others, and thus to honor both their gifts and the One who gives them. The cultivation and sharing of wisdom becomes the crop work that teachers carefully undertake, or hope to, to feed others and themselves.

I love my work. I feel privileged to do it. This work chose me before I chose it, which may be the case with any true vocation that marks a spiritual life. My work contributes to my living a rich and meaningful life as long as I do not allow it to insulate me from the lives and world beyond it, an ongoing risk in academia. Furthermore, although one's vocation is forever being revealed *as* it is lived (because callings, like identities, are dynamic in nature), I have come to believe in recent years that what I do—that, indeed, who I understand myself to be because of what I am called to in life (to follow Jesus)—traces directly to that April morning at Holy Cross Episcopal Church when I was four years old.

That day, the day of my baptism, simultaneously routine for the church and life-changing for me, issued a particular life course stretching from boyhood to manhood. Every baptism issues a life course, whether the person baptized knows it or not. At the time, I was much too young to know the meaning or lasting significance of this day for me, and of course, not every baptism begins the path that I have traveled. God is much too interesting and creative for that. Furthermore, not every person drawn to a vocational life marked by overt religious and spiritual interests will link her path so explicitly (if at all) to her baptism. Different strokes for different folks! But as I survey my own journey, the one that I know the most about, it's clear that my experience of baptism—including the fact that I remember it so clearly—set an enduring spiritual and vocational tone in my life, albeit one that has changed pitch from time to time.

I have observed that when people speak of the spiritual life they describe it in various forms and with a range of emphases. This observation, among others, spawned my interest in this book.

People talk about the spiritual life in terms of a desire to live in closer relationship to God. They muse about life's meaning, purpose, and the human values that follow. Sometimes they speak in terms of wanting more insight or wisdom regarding this or that problem or option. For some, a desire for healing and a newfound inner or relational peace remains bound to their views of and need for a spiritual life. Whatever the specifics, however, I often sense that when people speak about the spiritual life, they have in mind a kind of life notably different from a life *absent* the spiritual, and sometimes a life at least somewhat different from the one they currently live.

I also get a sense that whatever the spiritual life is to them, it's important; so I want to know more of what they know and certainly to gain knowledge that comes by way of experience, whether my own, others', or both. Another reason I sought to do this book is that, selfishly, I want some of the wisest people I know to teach me what they know about the spiritual life, especially by virtue of their experiences. If that's not possible, I want at least to know how they approach the questions relating to the spiritual life as they seek to know and experience more of it themselves. In this way, I am spiritually hungry.

I say all of this only to add that despite my best efforts, I admit to knowing rather little about the spiritual life: what it is, what marks it, how to cultivate it, what gets in the way of it, or why it matters. My lack of knowledge becomes most apparent when the descriptive term "spiritual" becomes a catchall, genre term with little to no specificity, which seems a rather common way of using it.

The closest I come to knowing about the spiritual life happens when I appeal *not* to the general category of "the spiritual" but, rather, to a particular Spirit, the Holy Spirit of Christian faith and life. I claim no uniqueness or innovation here. For more than two millennia, Christians have derived "the spiritual" from the Spirit—at least they have at their best. I also don't pretend to understand this Spirit any more than I understand the spiritual life. And when I hear people convey confidence in their knowledge and experience of the Holy Spirit, I get uncomfortable. This is *my* problem, not theirs, but when I hear "Spirit-talk" I usually hark back to my friend who "caught fire" for Jesus or to earlier childhood experiences with a Pentecostal distant cousin, or to both. This cousin's self-proclaimed "Spirit-filled" life scared the wits out of me and sent me running for nonspiritual sanctuaries for too many years.[1] I still avoid people who make similar proclamations.

I also usually assume that confident talk of the Holy Spirit will fairly soon be overly sentimental if not self-indulgent, sort of like those bumper stickers in that religious bookstore in Myrtle Beach. While I'm on the subject, I worry especially when the Holy Spirit becomes a cipher for propping up oneself and one's own desires and ambitions. I have in mind when people say things like "The Spirit is leading me to this or that decision or conclusion" or "The Spirit spoke to me." Honestly, much Spirit-talk fosters an ethos akin to one created by a popular antiphonal cheer at ball games when I was in high school: "We got spirit, yes we do; we got spirit, how 'bout you?"

My tacit suspicions about the Holy Spirit were pointed out to me in 1994, my last year of seminary. My friend and neighbor, the late Michael Girolimon, had the honors. Mike was working on his PhD at Princeton Seminary when I was completing my MDiv degree there. He died too young from cancer just a few years after graduation, and I miss him. I was preparing for ordination in the Presbyterian Church (U.S.A.). Crafting a required statement of faith to include with my ordination materials and to read when examined by my presbytery (the governing judicatory), I asked Mike to read it. A kind and thoughtful soul, he consented. He read it with care and offered suggestions on how to improve it, structurally and stylistically, which were relatively minor. He also made an observation that called for more substantive editorial work. "It's a good statement, Allan," he said, "of a Binitarian." Assuming he was simply showing off with PhD words, I asked what he meant. He said, "You fail to mention at all the Holy Spirit. You do just fine with God and Jesus, but you're one short of a Trinity."

The fact that he was raised a Pentecostal does not mean that he was wrong. In fact, he was right, and that experience prompted me to work harder to become a Trinitarian. I still work at this, but I got ordained and I've come a long way with the Spirit since then. At the same time, being in some measure a Calvinist, I also know that old habits die hard.

I think that the twentieth-century theologian Karl Barth was right in urging that we recognize and honor God's transcendence, God's "wholly otherness," by not presuming that we know all that much about this God directly. Somewhat ironically, Barth went on to write tens of thousands of pages about this unknowable God, but that he did so does not undermine his point, one that needs stressing today in North American Christian circles, especially when talk turns to spirituality. One mark of Christian spirituality as commonly

---

1. I have written about this experience previously. See Robert C. Dykstra, Allan Hugh Cole Jr., and Donald Capps, *Losers, Loners, and Rebels: The Spiritual Struggles of Boys* (Louisville, KY: Westminster John Knox Press, 2007), 107–12.

conceived of these days is that one can encounter God directly, tap the Divine for all manner of needs, and even snuggle up to God for a friendly back rub if need be. Sometimes this way of relating to God gets framed in terms of one's "personal relationship" with God, a relationship seemingly cultivated as readily in a coffeehouse as in a house of worship. Other times it gets framed in terms of God being "everywhere" and "in everyone and everything." Sometimes the way one relates to God gets expressed between these two relational poles. But for Barth, and for me, what we know about God comes to us in Jesus, and we do well to look first to his life as we seek to know God most fully. We also do well to look to him to know more about the spiritual life.

If Barth is correct, we also do well to tread lightly when presuming to know the Holy Spirit. So on my better days I work to create space for this Spirit in my life, which unfolds against the backdrop of the Christian story. On my better days I want that Spirit to shape and lead my life, which Jesus said happens among those who seek to follow him. This shaping and leading occur especially in prayer, worship, Scripture reading, service to others, and when playing with my children, among other ways, but always indirectly and never in a way that makes me catch fire. Thanks be to God.

Another aspect of Barth's thinking about baptism has been particularly important to me. He makes a persuasive case for delaying baptism until a person requests it, which means that Barth discourages infant baptism. With this line of thinking, he swims against the prevailing tides of Christianity, past and present. I do not mean to take issue here with parents who choose to baptize their children. For the most part, the church practices baptism in this fashion, which may be reason enough to embrace it. At the same time, I find Barth's rationale for delaying baptism compelling, and particularly when I remember my own baptism. In fact, the meaningfulness of my memories, along with Barth's insights, has prompted my wife and me to delay our children's baptisms until they are old enough to remember them.

In the final volume of his *Church Dogmatics*, Barth reflects on what he terms "the foundation of the Christian life," which we may also call a spiritual life: "The first step of this life of faithfulness to God, the Christian life, is a [person's] baptism with water, which by [one's] own decision is requested of the community and which is administered by the community, as the binding confession of one's obedience, conversion, and hope, made in prayer for God's grace, wherein [one] honors the freedom of this grace."[2] Barth might be guilty sometimes of understating what human nature and agency may contribute to God's work, but not so with regard to baptism. He recognizes the

2. Karl Barth, *Church Dogmatics*, IV/4, trans. Geoffrey W. Bromiley (Edinburgh: T. & T. Clark; Grand Rapids: Wm. B. Eerdmans, 1981), 47.

value of a person's request for baptism and, implicitly, of the opportunity to remember one's own baptism throughout life. Although I was not the one who requested my baptism (my parents did that), I do remember it, and it remains a powerful, life-shaping memory even today. Remembering my baptism helps me make more sense of the spiritual life because it helps me make more sense of following Jesus.

When I think of the spiritual life, I'm back to where I began this essay and back to where my Christian life began—at my baptism. When attempting some provisional answer to questions of the spiritual life—and I think the *only* responses we appropriately offer must have provisional status, else we think more highly of ourselves and of our knowledge of the Divine than we should—I struggle to find sets of images or memories that grab hold of me with a more lasting grip than those that trace to that windy April morning in Simpsonville, South Carolina, when the people of Holy Cross ushered me into a new kind of living.

Wendell Berry's writings convince me that he and I are in some ways kindred spirits, especially about matters spiritual. I say this wishing I were more like him and knowing that when I read anything he's written that I can get my hands on I'm attempting to be just that—which could mean that one way to discern the spiritual life and to live it is to know Wendell Berry. Of course, he would be the first to reject such a claim as ludicrous. Humility marks any true spiritual life, including his.

Berry writes of living (for the most part willingly) "under the influence of the Bible, especially the Gospels, and of the Christian tradition in literature and the other arts," and he states that he is "by principle and often spontaneously, as if by nature, a man of faith."[3] He makes this admission right after noting that "anybody half awake these days will be aware that there are many Christians who are exceedingly confident in their understanding of the Gospels, and who are exceedingly self-confident in their understanding of themselves in their faith."[4] Berry has a different perspective: "[My] reading of the Gospels, comforting and clarifying and instructive as they frequently are, deeply moving or exhilarating as they frequently are, has caused me to understand them also as a burden, sometimes raising the hardest of personal questions, sometimes bewildering, sometimes contradictory, sometimes apparently outrageous in their demands. This is the confession of an unconfident reader." So Berry remains intentionally modest with regard to what he claims to know about his faith, which always involves loads of questions and

---

3. Wendell Berry, "The Burden of the Gospels," *The Way of Ignorance and Other Essays* (New York: Shoemaker & Hoard, 2005), 127–28.
4. Ibid., 127.

concomitant burdens that "are not solvable but can only be lived with as a sort of continuing education."[5] He then describes "the burden of the Gospels"—namely, that if we read them in a way that leads us to take them seriously, then our lives get changed, often in ways that seem to bring as much discouragement as affirmation, as much cost as reward.

The same is true for the spiritual life, it seems to me, and especially when this life begins with and remains tethered to the baptized life. In saying this, I also recognize that this way of viewing the spiritual life offers nothing new or innovative. Lodged in a premodern worldview and way of living, this view of the spiritual life may struggle to find its place among postmodern sensibilities, many of which I welcome and embrace. But this is what I can say about the spiritual life: it links to a life in which one seeks to follow Jesus, and that life begins, at least formally, in the waters of baptism. About the spiritual life I can say nothing more or less.

I should add that I envy those who know more definitively what the spiritual life is and, more importantly, who confidently (but not overconfidently) live it in more innovative ways. More power to them. I've discovered, however, that I actually come closer to understanding and, on my better days, to living, more of a *religious* life than a spiritual one. I find religion less nebulous than spirituality, particularly when grounded in a set of religious practices that give concrete expression to beliefs, values, and purposes tied to the religion. Right-brained though I am, I struggle with the abstractness of "the spiritual," which, for me, can quickly dissolve into the disembodied ether before it ever hangs around long enough for me to encounter it in any fleshy sort of way. I need these kinds of encounters, which is probably why Holy Cross remains such a part of me, and also why I need to stare at Jesus washing another person's feet.

St. Augustine described baptism, among the oldest Christian practices, as a visible sign of an invisible grace. I like that way of putting it, and I've staked my life, vocationally and spiritually, on its being true.

5. Ibid., 130.

PART I

Poets

2

The High Note

SHERI REYNOLDS

One stormy night when I was driving home from work, a rogue wave hit my car. I had already been a writer for a long time; I'd also been a teacher for a long time. Then a wave hit my car, and I became something else.

If there's a word for what I became, I do not know it yet.

There'd been a tropical system far away—I think her name was Wilma— and she'd blown in around the Yucatan, then backtracked across the Gulf and crossed Florida. On this night, she'd veered out into the Atlantic, weakening. Along the coast of Virginia we were only getting residual rains and wind. Though conditions weren't ideal for driving, they weren't severe enough to close the Chesapeake Bay Bridge-Tunnel, an eighteen-mile stretch that connects the Norfolk/Virginia Beach Area (where I work) to the Eastern Shore of Virginia (where I live). At the tollbooth, police were restricting traffic, stopping the eighteen-wheelers, turning around campers, trucks with ladders, cars with luggage racks. But regular cars like my old Subaru were deemed safe to cross. So I paid my toll and gratefully headed home.

I've driven across that bridge in all kinds of conditions. Sometimes the winds make it hard to hold the car in the lane. Sometimes the bay churns so fiercely that looking at it makes me seasick. I've driven across in fog and snow and ice, in milky hazes that blur the line between water and sky. Regardless of weather, all the days seem glorious to me. It's as beautiful a drive as I've ever seen, with all that water and all that sky. Some nights there's no moon at all; other nights the moon looms otherworldly, psychedelic, low, and orange. I love the drive, regardless of the time of year, day, or night. The bridge-tunnel is my favorite transition and best metaphor. Even when the drive is difficult, I enjoy it.

15

But that doesn't mean I'm not scared. When driving conditions are rough, I turn up the music and sing along. It's what I've always done in hard times. I lose myself in a song and let the drive become secondary, hiding in familiar melodies. When I sing loudly, I take deep breaths, and the extra oxygen off-sets some of my anxiety. Each song clicks minutes off my journey, and in a while, I'm safe and all sung out.

So I was singing that night on the bridge, creeping north, headlights on. My windshield wipers put up a decent-enough fight, and there was hardly any traffic at all.

I used to be afraid of tunnels, but traveling this long bridge in a storm helps me appreciate them. They seem perfectly spaced to provide breaks from bad weather and fear. The Chesapeake Bay Bridge-Tunnel has two tunnels, each about a mile long and forty feet underground, deep enough for Navy ships and merchant vessels heavy with cargo to pass overhead. These tunnels are two-lane and can seem especially narrow through their middles. They remind me of throats, and I can't stand to look at the ceiling because I feel like I'm being swallowed. But when I look at the road and remind myself that it's the same road as the bridge, and when the bridge ends, I'll be on Route 13 that takes me home, then I can be grateful for the tunnels.

On this night I took solace in the tunnel, where my hands could relax on the wheel and my eyes no longer had to strain to see through rain. I don't recall if I passed any vehicles at all. I don't know if I was singing, but I'd guess I was probably singing, and when the light appeared up ahead I probably shifted my wipers from intermittent to full speed. I probably tightened my grip on the wheel.

As you emerge from the tunnel, wind gusts sometimes surprise you. They can be strong, and it's startling when the car suddenly tugs in a direction you don't intend. So I've learned to keep both hands on the wheel as I transition from tunnel to bridge. But on this night, I don't remember any gusts. On this night, I came up and into the rain, and in spite of the darkness, I was aware of something white off to my right.

As my car climbed higher, there seemed to be a whiteness, and when I glanced over, what I saw was a wave hovering there. There's no other way to describe it. It seemed almost to hesitate. It was all I could see, and it lingered. It curved at the top, like it was saying "Hi," like a hand caught in the first impulse of a greeting. It was white, and it hovered, a trembling pause before it toppled.

It crashed, that wave—or it seemed like a crash. When it shattered against my car, it sounded like a whip. And I ducked, because in that instant, I didn't remember that the car was there at all, or maybe I couldn't distinguish my body from the car. I ducked like that wave was about to smack me flat, my whole body crouching as low as I could get, and in that gesture, without mean-ing to—without even knowing it—I stomped the accelerator to the floor.

I wish I knew a name for those moments so tiny and loaded that they open into entire universes of their own. The wave crashed fast, but there are stages and steps inside those short seconds. I didn't know my eyes were closed until I told myself to open my eyes. Somehow I remembered that it's bad business to operate machinery with closed eyes. My foot cramped in its strain against the gas pedal, and I decided to leave it there on the floor, thinking if I let it up, the car could take on water and flood out. And I knew that I was inside a wave. It was the most exhilarating experience of my life, and also the most terrifying. My windshield wipers passed over the glass—once, twice, three full times—water beyond water, thick, opaque weight. Then, finally, I was out of the wave and back in the rain.

I was still on the bridge, still driving. I'd wound up in the left lane but never even grazed the side rails. Far ahead, taillights from another car pointed the way to land, and I wondered if that driver had seen the wave crash over me from his rearview mirror. (Would I have noticed if a wave crashed over him?) Behind me, another car came up out of the tunnel, and I wondered if that driver could tell that my car had been hit. Was I dented or smoking? Would my car break down before I got off the bridge?

The wave couldn't have been as big as it seemed. It must have splashed more than it smacked. Then again, for the wave to have hit my car at all, it had to be sizable. I've been sprayed by waves on the bridge before, but never before or since has a wave come anywhere close to the one that taught me what it meant to *be* a wave.

I'm not a water person, though I like water in metaphor and theory. In col-lege, I kept signing up for my swimming test and not showing up to take it—until my final semester, when I had no choice, and I passed by simply not drowning. I can float and tread water and awkwardly make it where I need to go next, but that's the extent of my swimming. Every morning I walk the two blocks down to the bay just to admire it. I love most the place where water and land overlap. Sometimes in the summers, I wade through the shallows, kayak in deeper water, or float on an inner tube, but I don't swim. Only in the bathtub do I enjoy full submersion.

Since I travel the Chesapeake Bay Bridge-Tunnel regularly, I've often thought of what I'd do if my car went over the side. In all my fantasies, I survive. Sometimes I remember to roll down the window as I'm airborne. I release my seatbelt on impact, and I swim safely out and hug a concrete bridge-support until help arrives. The only casualties in my fantasies are my

book bag, student papers, and sometimes my laptop. If I have passengers or
my dog in the car, I rescue them too. Sometimes no one knows I've driven off
the bridge, but miraculously, in spite of my limited abilities, I swim to shore.
I crawl out of the waves half-drowned but fine, and news crews marvel that I
could survive such a thing.

In reality, I know that if I went off the bridge, I'd be a goner. In all my
memory, I don't recall anyone who went over surviving. Knowing that my
fantasies are born of fear and are a kind of preparation against catastrophe
doesn't stop them. But on the day the wave broke over my car, I didn't resist
it. There was no opportunity to resist. There was only instinct—ducking—
and then there was one other thing: understanding how powerless I was, how
no amount of human preparation or fast thinking could help me in the face of
something so large and unforeseen. Then there was the resignation, a sense
that I'd been consumed, taken in by the wave, and that it was all okay. In spite
of my fear of the water, I wasn't afraid. There was no time to pray, and in that
instant, that wasn't my impulse anyway. There was no *need* to pray, nothing
to pray for, no one to pray to. I wasn't just inside the wave—I *was* the wave. I
had to think like a wave, which meant not to think, but to give in.

I had to roll. I had to tumble. I had to turn myself to liquid and spray in
droplets, laced in air and froth.

My car didn't stall. I waited for it to break down, but it didn't. Slowly I
became aware of the music playing on my stereo. How could my car get hit
by a wave and my stereo not even know it?

The song playing was one I'd known for a long time, a classic, recorded by
crooners through the ages. This particular version had a note I couldn't hit.
I'd never hit it, though I'd aimed to often enough on my bridge rides. When
no one was there to hear me shriek, I'd roll down the windows and belt it out
to the seagulls.

But this time, when the high note came, I hit it without even thinking. No
straining, no problem. It wasn't until the high note was over that I realized I'd
even done it. I backed the music up and hit the note again. I played that song
the rest of the way home and hit the high note over and over.

The rogue wave gave me that note. The rogue wave opened my throat.
I don't know what surprised me more—the wave or hitting that impossible
note. I realized then that I'd had my throat closed all my life. For that one
night, it was open. By the next day, my throat was closed again, and I haven't
hit the note since. But I know now that I have the capacity to hit it, and when
I sing it, if I am ever brave enough to make myself a wave, I can break above
the note, above the tightness in my throat and in my life.

There are sopranos all over creation hitting high notes every day, and surfers who'd find my wave no more than average. And there are people who seek big notes and big waves all their lives, not realizing that the seeking becomes the barrier, because seeking goes against being. In the same way that you can't extract oxygen from water, you can't extract Godness from creation. You can't label one thing holy and another thing not, because what is holy exists all the while inside its opposite.

Though I like my baptisms dry, deep down I know that if I'd been washed off the bridge that night, it would have been perfect, an adventure to the end and beyond—one I couldn't practice for or predict. I'd have drowned, and crabs would have eaten out my eyeballs, and then I'd go traveling over the floor of the Chesapeake Bay inside the bellies of the crabs. So be it.

If I'd never hit that high note, if I'd lived my whole life with my throat never opening, not even for one short night, I would be no less awake. I'd awaken in some other way. Maybe I'd have opened my ears instead, or my eyes. What was profound had nothing to do with the note itself. There are infinite ways to perceive what is sublime, available in every instant. But if we felt them in every instant, surely we'd burst into flames, or melt into our loafers, explode, implode, fizzle out in a flash. It is nothing to worry about when the high note doesn't come. We're never separated from God. We *can't be* separated. After all, it is only through closing that we recognize opening.

I spend much of my life writing and teaching, and these are the labels I put on myself, ways I recognize myself, and ways I'm recognized in the world. But I'm not what I do. I *do* what I do, but I am what I *am*—a spiritual being, no better or worse than all the other spiritual beings sharing the planet with me in this season: people, animals, trees, fruits. In birth, in growth, in rot, we are always living the spiritual life. Can we do better? Of course we can. Can we make choices that bring good things to the planet and to those we share it with? Absolutely. But our choices don't change our essence, and there is nothing to resist, whether we are washed away or whether we just fade out into the silence.

3

Musings on the Spiritual Life

GAIL GODWIN

I had a gardener who saw Christ once. She was working in a garden and sensed someone behind her. She turned, and there he was. After the vision she made changes to her life. She kept on working in gardens because that was her livelihood, but she learned to write icons. That's how we had met. I had bought her icon of St. George and the dragon at a local gallery. Later I bought a small head of Christ, which looks down on me in my study as I write this.

The nearest I have come to a vision was when I was four years old. I was walking along the sidewalk in front of my house in Weaverville, North Carolina, and looked up to see an overwhelming cumulus cloud bearing down on me. I knew it was called a cloud but knew nothing of its provenance. I hadn't yet learned that it was "just" vapor. And what I felt was holy dread. I knew this thing was beyond anything I could control or understand, bigger than anyone could protect me from, and I felt it wanted something from me. I turned and ran for the safety of the house.

My shelves are full of evidence of my decades of grappling toward the holy, yet I have never desired to be one of those who turn around and find themselves face-to-face with God. I'm not sure I could survive it. I'm definitely in the Jonah camp and must have known it by the time I was four. If something too big comes after you, run for the house.

Yet, paradoxically, I have been a pursuer of that "something" all my life, so here I sit, facing my shelves (so many books on God!), gazed down upon by a Christ evoked by an iconographer who once saw him face-to-face in a garden.

Some years ago, I became addicted to the Jesus Seminar's assessments of what Jesus really said and did. Internationally recognized biblical scholars had

gotten together and color-coded their collective votes: red for the words and
actions most probably his; pink for those that "may have suffered modifica-
tion in transmission," gray for "did not originate with him but may reflect
his ideas," and black for "inauthentic." I would look up the Gospel stories
that meant most to me in *The Five Gospels: The Search for the Authentic Words
of Jesus*[1] and *The Acts of Jesus: The Search for the Authentic Deeds of Jesus*[2] and
hope I was going to see red or at least pink. My biggest letdown was their con-
sensus for John 21:1–14 (fishing instructions, breakfast on shore, and Jesus'
third appearance after being raised from the dead). Not only was the dialogue
assigned to Jesus color-coded in black, but it was deemed in a note by the
scholars to be "the result of the storyteller's imagination."

I continued on in this obsession for a while until I realized I was probably
committing a form of book abuse. Now the Jesus Seminar's volumes are having a rest on my shelves along with other past engrossments: mysticism and
varieties of religious experience, liturgies and patterns of worship, handbooks
of contemplation and prayer, saints' lives, and Jungian psychology.

God, help me. I am going straight to hell.

This I penned at the top of a page in my diary on the morning of May 12,
2009. It was the first time I had committed this prayer to paper. The thing
was, I knew, even as I was still writing the words, that *it had been taken care of.*

Now all I had to do was live with the results of the instant rescue for the
remainder of my life. That was going to be the hard part, and it is.

I had tried everything else but desperately addressing God to break a drinking habit begun sixty-one years ago when my eleven-year-old best friend and
I sat down at the kitchen table, experimentally polished off a pint of my new
stepfather's Kentucky Tavern, and then, infused with a powerful "spirit" new
to both of us, flew into a fighting frenzy. I sustained bites and scratches, but I
made her head bleed and ripped all the buttons off her blouse. Back at school,
we attempted it once more on the playground, without alcohol this time, until
the nuns separated us. After that, we became adversaries but remained fasci-
nated with each other to the end. When she was dying of cancer (we were in
our fifties by then) we sat in her den putting away the white wine, and I asked
her to visit me in dreams after her death. She has done so and our relationship
continues to evolve.

---

1. Robert W. Funk, Roy Hoover, and the Jesus Seminar, *The Five Gospels: The Search for the
Authentic Words of Jesus* (New York: Macmillan, 1993).
2. Robert W. Funk, ed., *The Acts of Jesus: The Search for the Authentic Deeds of Jesus* (New York:
HarperSanFrancisco, 1998).

The dreadful cloud at age four, from which I fled, and the instant removal, at age seventy-two, of the affliction that was well on its way to destroying my life—these have been my two religious experiences.

But we, who have undertaken God, can never finish.

Nonetheless, being one of those who have undertaken God, I go on composing utterances and collecting the utterances of others that bolster me in this passion.

"I prefer the mystery of what is beyond my ken." That is C. G. Jung, late in life, replying to a correspondent who was trying to pin him down about his beliefs.

Or a Woodstock, New York, priest confiding to his congregation on a Sunday morning: "We just have to accept our inseparability from God."

Or a diary entry when I was twenty-eight: "A polarity in me wants to bestow a blessing on him [a cynical, amoral boyfriend] and let him go his way, but equally to want wholeness, direction, God, for myself. It has nothing to do with my church upbringing or convent school training. It is something built into my system and I am responsible for replenishing it and keeping it intact."

As a novelist, I send out characters as emissaries, to see how they go about making sense of their lives. In some cases, this means discovering how they relate to God. Margaret Bonner, the Episcopal priest in *Evensong*, steps outside in the darkness to pray.[3] "What are you, anyway?" she muses aloud. "And yet how close you are."

Margaret addresses her God at a wary slant. Whereas Mother Suzanne Ravenel, the Catholic headmistress in *Unfinished Desires*, teases and argues God down in her daily dialogues: "Of course, You know best, Lord, but I would never advise my girls to begin a project the way you're suggesting."[4] She always assumes God will be there for their dialogues—until one day he isn't.

I am drawn to those voices in novels that express complex relationships with their God as they go about their soul-making, voices that are comfortable squinting at vistas "beyond their ken."

Saul Bellow's Mr. Sammler confides to a fellow philosopher that what he would miss most in his life, if they were to be taken away, are his "God-adumbrations" in their many daily forms.[5]

---

3. Gail Godwin, *Evensong* (New York: Ballantine, 1999).
4. Gail Godwin, *Unfinished Desires* (New York: Random House, 2009).
5. Saul Bellow, *Mr. Sammler's Planet* (New York: Penguin Twentieth Century Classics, 2004), 236–37.

The young narrator of Rainer Maria Rilke's *The Notebooks of Malte Laurids Brigge* reflects to himself, "But we, who have undertaken God, can never finish."[6]

In a related passage, Malte speculates about the passionate inner life of his Aunt Abelone.

> I had sometimes wondered why Abelone did not use the calories of her magnificent feeling on God. I know she yearned to remove from her love all that was transitive, but could her truthful heart be deceived about God's being only a direction of love, not an object of love? Didn't she know that she need fear no return from him? Didn't she know the restraint of this superior beloved, who quietly defers delight in order to let us, slow as we are, accomplish our whole heart?[7]

Just now, as I revisited this passage, I thought maybe I am one of God's wary mystics, conscious every day of his restraint while I slowly accomplish my whole heart.

But when the morning was now come, Jesus stood on the shore; but the disciples knew not that it was Jesus.

In the first chapter of *Evensong*, Margaret and Adrian, the man she will marry, are visiting Dr. Stroup, a professor at General Theological Seminary. The three of them are discussing a new piece of art acquired by the professor, an acrylic rendering of "Cast your nets," done in the iconic style by a Staten Island painter:

> Out of a dark blue and purple nighttime seascape, some of the disciples were returning to shore with their surprise harvest of fishes. The single area of brightness comes from the glow of the charcoal fire on shore where Jesus, returned from the dead, is cooking their breakfast. All three of us were drawn to the painting and continued to talk about it over lunch, along with the mysterious final chapter of the Fourth Gospel on which it was based.[8]

Professor Stroup tells them, "There's an interesting Greek word, *kalchaino*. Literally it means 'to search for the purple fish.' Either of you heard of it?"

Adrian, a therapist as well as a priest, says, "No, but I like the idea already."

"Well, of course you do, dear boy," says Stroup. "It's your favorite element, those waters where the purple fish swims."

6. Rainer Maria Rilke, *The Notebooks of Malte Laurids Brigge*, trans. M. D. Herter Norton (New York: W. W. Norton & Co., 1949), 199.

7. Ibid., 208–9.

8. Godwin, *Evensong*, 27–28.

The professor explains that the purple fish was a shellfish so highly prized by the Greeks for its rich purple dye that divers went to the bottom of the sea in search of it, and that was how "searching for the purple fish" came to be a Greek expression for plumbing the depths of one's mind. When Stroup had asked the artist, of Greek descent, if he had known this, the artist had told him that was why he made his sea predominantly purple, and why the fish Jesus is cooking are the purplest of all.

"That makes sense," Adrian comments, "because in the language of the unconscious, when the dreamer is about to eat something, it's often a signal that there is submerged content ready to be assimilated."

The professor then asks Margaret for her thoughts on the painting, and when she admits to being most moved by "someone returning from the dead to give advice and sustenance to loved ones when they are most in need of it," Stroup tells her, "My dear, you provide the crucial third element of this luncheon triad. I'm the old academic. Adrian is the deep-sea diver, but you remind us what it's all about in the first place."

"And what's that?" Adrian asks Professor Stroup, who had been his teacher.

"Love, old fellow, love. He's out there cooking their breakfast because he *loved* them, and they knew it."

A WALK WITH AN OLD NUN

She had been my eighth-grade teacher, and we became friends for life. I sent her Mother's Day cards because I considered her my spiritual mother. Her given name was Kathleen, the same as my mother's. Later she became close friends with my mother, and the two Kathleens would go out to lunch and argue theology. ("I can't go along with women priests," says my mother. "Didn't Jesus himself come to us as a man?" "But, Kathleen," the other Kathleen protests, "he couldn't very well have come as both.")

On the day of that walk I'm remembering, it's suddenly chilly, and I insist she wear my black wool cape. She is eighty-three to my fifty-nine. "I don't see how you can be so sure God loves you," I say. We are climbing a hill. "Well, you have to love yourself first, Gail," she replies, hugging the cape closer. "Because if you don't, you'll never be able to accept that God loves you."

She's not among the characters in my nun-populated novel *Unfinished Desires*. Her solidity in my life is not easily broken up into fictional fragments. She comes across better in memoir-type offerings—essays like this, for example.

WRITING AS A FORM OF PRAYER

When you write as much as I do, and when you have been "undertaking God" for as long as I have, there is no way that writing can escape becoming a form of prayer. You get used to struggling with words to sneak up on the unknown. The more you develop and play with your craft, the more things you didn't know you knew find their way into the material. The act of *writing faithfully* allows answers to slip through.

I didn't realize it at the time, but I see now that my "purple fish" scene in *Evensong* allowed me to explore in fictional safety, and at several removes (the painting itself and three different characters approaching it from different angles), my emotional longing for that scene in John's Gospel to have "really happened." Approaching something from an unexpected angle can suddenly reveal its life to you. Recall those elementary drawing classes in which you were instructed not to draw the chair but to draw the spaces around the chair.

THE DREADFUL TUMBLE OF INFINITY

For me, the worst hour of the nondrinking life is five p.m., or thereabouts. In winter, "thereabouts" can start as early as three in the afternoon, and in high summer it can last until after dark.

Five p.m., or thereabouts, has always meant for me that the day's work is over. The work part of it has not changed. Work always has been my main protection.

But then comes the sunset hour when, with a companion and then later without one, you unstop the bottle or open a new one and let it assist you in parachuting gently to earth. You revel in all you have done during the day, you let go of all that has been left undone, and, sip by sip, you sink gently into oblivion's welcoming container.

But when there is no container to count on at the close of a working day, what then?

In early childhood I ran from the cloud. This spring I caught myself hurriedly exiting the terrace on the first beautiful March evening, driven inside by—what? Too much time and space? Too much consciousness? It seemed as though I was being threatened by the sheer tumble of infinity.

Threatened how? What might it ask of me? What could it do to me? And whatever it did, so what? I'd had a life, hadn't I?

Nevertheless, I fled the terrace. The angle of the hill on which this terrace is set makes it seem eye-level with the sky. The sky was all around me; it was in my face. I was right back in my four-year-old dread.

Now we are almost into May and the sky stays lighter longer, but I'm still having trouble with sticking it out on the terrace. After a few minutes of forced sitting (covering myself with a blanket helps), something drives me inside. It's too much. Too much what? What would happen if I stayed? Would I be enveloped by infinity, lost in something too big to imagine?

In one of those surprising zigzags the mind is capable of, I suddenly find myself being offered a form of containment through the example of one of my own characters. "Being offered," I say, because I haven't taken her up on it yet.

Toward the end of *Unfinished Desires*, a young teacher and the school infirmarian at Mount St. Gabriel's Academy are reflecting on their vocations as nuns. The infirmarian had been a nurse until the day she decided not to turn on the radio while driving to the hospital, and "the connection with God was made in that first silence." She has just asked the teacher if she will mind very much if she has to be transferred back to Boston because of suspected heart disease.

"I had known, from the day I put on my ring, that my 'minding' something was going to be beside the point for the rest of my life, and that I had chosen this," the young nun tells the infirmarian. "The practice closest to me now, the practice I find central to everything I do, is living every day and night as fully as I can in consultancy with God. The questions I ask and the insights that come out of the listening—I'm not saying this very well—but the more I live this way, the more I want to—to—*pray my life* rather than stumble through it."[9]

What would happen if I sat out there on the terrace, under the blanket, totally and soberly conscious, until dark? Would I become one of those who discovers she is praying her life rather than stumbling through it? Or, like the young nun in my novel, would I die that very night?

What would the chances of my survival be? What do I even mean by "survival"? Where is the line between "my survival" and "my eternal life"?

And what difference does it make, the exact hour of my death, if, at that hour, I am living in consultancy with God? That's the sort of question in which you may at last find some respite, after musing for decades on the spiritual life.

9. Godwin, *Unfinished Desires*, 305.

4

What I Do and Why I Do It; Or, the Writing Life and the Spiritual Life

GREG GARRETT

> But this too is true: stories can save us.
> Tim O'Brien, *The Things They Carried*

WHAT I DO

I am a writer.

Although it is an essential truth about me, it is not necessarily something you will hear me say out loud without a stutter, stammer, or pause. Sometimes my girlfriend glares at me, tells people whom she has just introduced me to that I am a writer and a teacher, maybe tells them about my latest project with meaningful glances that I should join in the conversation at any time.

A part of me—not, perhaps, a spiritually healthy part of me, but a part nonetheless—tries to deny that I am a writer. Because it is denying an essential part of me for inessential reasons, it is a little like Peter's denying Christ, and like Peter, maybe with some cursing added for emphasis. Some of this denial comes simply because I, paradoxically, am really uncomfortable with the attention that such a claim automatically draws in many circles. Some of the discomfort grows out of the false "Aw shucks, it's nothing, ma'am" humility with which I was raised, although it is false modesty—the worst kind— because I happen to think that writing is a pretty important thing. But I was raised to deflect interest and praise of any sort, and that is a hard habit to break. Writing is what I do and who I am; leading a conversation by talking about it sometimes feels to me a little like informing a new acquaintance, "I'm a bipedal humanoid who converts oxygen to carbon dioxide." It feels that obvious, although, of course, it isn't obvious to anyone but me.

Part of this denial, though, is social, because I anticipate the direction that conversation often turns when people discover my secret identity, and am not so sure I want to be pastoral about what is coming. Calling yourself a writer attracts attention. Whether worthily or not, unlike the everyday lives of priests or plumbers, the lives of writers are sometimes seen as romantic, exotic even: *Wow, isn't that great? Honey, Greg here is a writer! Books and everything!*

And also unlike the lives of priests or plumbers, people often imagine that this life could be emulated with just a little bit of effort—if they just turned their mind to it. "I've always wanted to write," people often sigh. "I think I could be pretty good at it."

Stephen King says that when people at parties tell him they've always wanted to be a writer, he responds, "I've always wanted to be a brain surgeon," and then he stands there watching them blink. I feel a vocational calling to something a little nobler than the easy joke, so I generally offer in return an encouraging "Well, I hope you will." Then I settle in to hear their story about the story they would write if they could only find the time.

I nod my head politely when I hear people talk about their understanding of what I do, then nod my head encouragingly when they talk about how they would and could do it themselves if they could find a few spare hours to type.

And I offer sincere encouragement, because, sincerely, the world does need more true stories. As my friend Jack Butler says, "Stories are a gift to the tribe," and stories have always been the best way for us to make sense of this hard world, or try to.

Without stories, we wither and die.

And when I hear these people suggest that the practice to which I've devoted my life is something easily done, that all that might be keeping them from fame and fortune and appearances on *Oprah* or whatever replaces her is a little bit of time, I never say the two most obvious things out loud, although I generally think them, and sometimes—as right now—write them down.

One: if you were really a writer, nothing in the world could stop you from telling your stories.

My Grandma Irene—my Pentecostal grandma, not my Methodist one— has a file of stories I wrote and illustrated when I was four years old, most of them about clowns and firefighters. I have been writing about funny men and those who rescue people ever since, through chronic depression, through three marriages and two kids and three divorces, through economic difficul- ties, and on into my recent run of joy and modest success that could be just as distracting as heartache.

Stephen King wrote his novel *Carrie* late at night in a closet, during time pulled away from the baby, after working his shift at the laundry.

Anne Lamott wrote through addiction and bulimia and an unplanned pregnancy and on into monumental success.

My former teacher, the Pulitzer Prize-winning fiction writer Robert Olen Butler, wrote bad novel after bad novel in longhand on yellow legal pads on a commuter train to and from New York City, until the gates flew open and he finally wrote one that actually worked.

Like all of these folks, if you were truly a writer, you wouldn't be telling people at cocktail parties how much you've always wanted to write.

You'd be writing, wherever you were, whatever the circumstances of your life.

In the Gospels, Jesus said that where your treasure is, there will be your heart; this is one of the wisest sayings I know. If your heart were for the writing life, that's what you'd be doing, however hard. A spiritual director once told a friend of mine that if you want a relationship with God, you may have to lose a little sleep. I've been telling people the same thing about writing: if it's important to you, you don't just wish you were doing it; you find a way to do it, regularly.

The second misconception about the writing life is perhaps worse than the first: if you imagine that you want into this writing thing because it leads to a positive outcome, you're barking up the wrong tree; you have your money on the wrong horse.

WHY I DO IT

There are lots of reasons to write, the most compelling of which have nothing whatsoever to do with wealth and celebrity: the joy of constructing a good sentence or entertaining a friend (or stranger), the desire to preserve family stories or to explore your own history, the compulsion to see what happens next in the story, the faithful belief that when we create we are participating in the life of God. Since fame and fortune come to so few writers, if what matters most to you is the chance of achieving something external instead of something eternal, of a big reward rather than the hard-earned but genuine joy of making something beautiful, you might just as well spend your time and effort systematically playing the lottery, or in front of your computer trading foreign currencies or hog futures. Be honest about it; if this is what you want, then writing is a means to an end, and a direct contradiction of this truth: writing is a practice, not an outcome.

You are a writer because you write, not because you publish, or win awards, or sell books to the movies.

So if it is a practice, then it is something you do faithfully and regularly and with a focus away from what you might get out of it and toward the practice itself.

That idea seems to bring us back onto familiar spiritual ground, although I think that the way people misunderstand the writing life has a lot to say about the ways that we misunderstand the spiritual life. First, as with writing, it seems to me that many American Christians believe the spiritual life is easily attained—perhaps just by saying words of intent. In his book *Revolution*, religious pollster George Barna documents how lots and lots of Americans call themselves regular churchgoers, but in his polling he discovered that the spiritual lives of these confessing churchgoers was limited primarily to churchgoing, and that even there, many felt that they were not connecting with God in any meaningful way. They called themselves religious, but their lives didn't show them making any real effort to connect with God. As with my cocktail party acquaintances, it's entirely too easy to give lip service to something, to say we value it or even want it, but then to leave it at that.

What many modern American spiritual lives also seem to have in common with the writing life, as perceived by many folks I meet, is that often people are expecting to get something tangible and demonstrable from their faith and practice. Whether it's the American prosperity gospel, which holds that the faithful will be rewarded by God in tens, twenties, and hundreds, or specific prayer practices that promise that those who follow them will gain God's favor or that they will direct fortune their way as though God is the genie from *Aladdin*, or the pervasive myth that people should confess their faith in God because it will pay off big for them at the end, too many pursue the spiritual life for the wrong reasons—and for reasons that do not have lasting value, if in fact they even come to pass.

Year after year, I stand in front of classrooms and conference rooms full of students, talk to folks at cocktail parties and in bookstores and in parish halls, and many of them truly seem to believe that just a few short hours of typing at their keyboards is all that stands between them and hitting the bars with George Clooney and Matt Damon, hanging out with Madonna and her *paramour du jour*, or, at the very least, signing books for crowds at Barnes & Noble. They see themselves decked out in mysterious black, sipping expensive single malts as everyone laughs at their bon mots. Maybe they imagine themselves being carried around the town square on the shoulders of a cheering throng, or diving into pools of golden coins like Scrooge McDuck in those old Disney comics.

And year after year, I also watch as people who call themselves spiritual or even religious seem to hope primarily for individual payoffs, to care more about some triumphal parade at the end of things than they do about the rewards and hard work of daily practice.

So I think the writing life can teach us about the spiritual life because of the similar misconceptions people have about both. But I think the converse is also true: the writing life has enough spiritual qualities, and enough of a sacred dimension, that it can shed positive light on our quest for the holy.

Of all the many true things I know, this is one of the truest: the writing life, like any worthwhile existence where you are attempting to live faithfully and serve others in the process, is a life of discipline, a life dedicated to hard work, a life where you have to show up, not simply say that you would like to. It is a life filled with rewards, although many of the external benefits that come from this life are truly that—external—to the real reasons I pursue it.

Writing calls me to be present and to be silent. It calls me to watch and listen for the movement of God in my life and in the world. And it urges me to take what I see and hear and think and return it back to the world, so that my life and my observation of it isn't simply for my own benefit.

So the misconceptions—it's easy, you don't have to work at it, it pays off big if you do actually get around to it—are irksome. But the truths are profound.

I know who I am and what God wants of me primarily because I read and write. I understand my primary vocation in the world to be to write with honesty, candor, hope, and joy about a life that is beautiful and difficult and God-given, in the hope that the things I write will remind people that life is beautiful and difficult and God-given. I write fiction, personal essays, and critical essays, and in all of those different forms of writing, I find myself doing the same things I do when I work at my spiritual life.

I tell the truth, because as Walker Percy noted in one of his seminal essays, "The Man on the Train," telling the truth allows readers to know that they are accompanied in their own experiences, that however they might feel in the moment, they are not alone, even when times are tough.

I watch for how God might be moving in my life, in the lives of those around me, in the church, in the world, for I understand our purpose to be best fulfilled when we are most attuned to what God is and does and desires, and I look especially for those places where God might be present even if at first I don't expect to find God there.

This means, incidentally, that in fiction and nonfiction both I tend to acknowledge despair and difficulty—and to suggest the possibility of grace and hope in the hardest of times and darkest of places that might lead to joy. Like many writers, I have suffered experiences that have bent me to the breaking point. Sometimes, as Ernest Hemingway wrote, you can become stronger at the place where you were bent; sometimes, as with Hemingway himself, you can be bent so far that you cannot be put right again, at least without the miraculous grace of God. But as a person of faith who writes, I recognize a responsibility to both reality and possibility; Advent and Lent have taught me that hope in the One who loves us will someday be answered, and my own life has taught me that the community who believes in that One can be the support that those who are bent and broken most need to go on living.

My life has also taught me that stories themselves can be a part of the healing of individuals and of the world.

This is a substantial claim to make, but if a writer doesn't argue for the sacred importance of what he does, who will? In my own life, the novels of Lee Smith, Walker Percy, Graham Greene, and Harper Lee, the poetry of Billy Collins, Scott Cairns, and Jane Hirschfield, the spiritual autobiographies of Anne Lamott, Dennis Covington, and Kathleen Norris, and the lyrics of Bruce Springsteen, Bono, and Patti Griffith have all been sacred touchstones in my life. It is no exaggeration to say that there have been times when their words have carried me over chasms in my life I thought I could not cross, pulled me out of depths I feared I could never overcome. And I hear from my readers, more often than I ever expected, how a novel or a book or a memoir or an essay that I wrote arrived in their lives at the moment they needed it most, and I believe that this is how the Spirit moves.

Stories too can save us.

The work the writer does is sacred—as, I think, all work is that is entered into on behalf of others and practiced with reverence.

I have said that in whatever I write, my aesthetic is realism; I do try to be conscious about reproducing what I see and hear, reflecting the way people act, think, consume, believe, and deny. But if I had to claim an exact aesthetic, I would call it, perhaps, *hopeful realism*, or *faithful realism*, for while I have promised to tell the truth as I see and understand it, I have also promised not to write a book in which there is not movement toward possibility, hope, and redemption.

Sometimes there would be no book without that promised hope. When I wrote *Crossing Myself*, the book about my battle with chronic depression, the happy ending was already apparent to anyone reading, since if I had not found healing from the pain and despair that was eating me like runaway cancer, I would not have been alive to write. With my first published novel, *Free Bird*, even as I was in the middle of that horrible despair, I wrote a story about a man coming through pain to the possibility of redemption, a man rediscovering the power of love and community after years of building walls around himself. An early reader e-mailed me to say that in the midst of his own despair, *Free Bird* had pulled him up out of the darkness for a few days and given him hope. I understood that, for the writing of the book had done the same for me.

The Jewish poet and nonfiction writer Rodger Kamenetz and I have often been paired on panels on spirituality and writing over the years, and much of what I have come to understand about the intersection of these two comes from his wisdom and faithful example. I remember him once describing the rabbinical tradition as being a tradition of wise storytellers, which is a story that itself gets at the heart of how writing might function in the lives of writers and readers. "The great rebbes were all great storytellers," Rodger says. "They could look at you and see the story you needed to hear to be healed."

The writing life, like the contemplative spiritual life, is about taking a close look at oneself and at the world, and about trying to be completely truthful about what one sees there. Where there is brokenness it is acknowledged, mourned, held up for healing. Where there is joy it is claimed, celebrated, spread around. And in doing any of this honestly, without, as the Japanese film director Akira Kurosawa says, averting one's eyes, the writer is both faithful to a practice and faithful to a vocation.

Writers tell the stories people need to hear to be healed.

HOW I DO WHAT I DO

As I near the end of this exploration, I'm wondering if perhaps the writing life has some kinship to the monastic life. Certainly many writers live monastically, rising at odd hours to do their reflective work, shutting themselves away from the world for a while so that they can see that world more clearly. I myself tend to actually go away to cathedrals or retreat centers in the desert so that I can finish the particular writing that has been a part of my daily practice for the previous year or two or three. It is an odd withdrawal, and one not suited to all people or even to all writers. Dietrich Bonhoeffer observed that monasticism allowed common people to make the mistake of thinking that only people who had removed themselves from the world were called to Christian life and sacrifice, and I don't want to suggest that writers should always separate themselves from the world; most of my life does not look like that. During my daily routines of teaching, speaking, preaching, and being a committed boyfriend, father, and friend, I am also observing, journaling, writing essays, imagining scenes.

But by stepping away from the things and the people I love several times a year, even sometimes stepping away from the church that has saved me and entering into round-the-clock contemplation and focus, I am able to take what I am inspired to say and to say it with some beauty and grace.

Like the monastics, I find that I am at my best when I alternate prayer and work, something that Benedict knew long ago when he formulated his rule. So when I am away writing, several times a day I pray—or go to Evensong or to Communion when I am at or near a cathedral. Some might find it ridiculous that I would pray for hours while on retreat to write—it might reasonably be argued that this consumes a ridiculous amount of the time that already seems so limited—yet I find that everything comes together more easily when I am praying, that I write better, despite mathematically, at least, having fewer hours in which to do it.

This, incidentally, is a lesson that travels well away from monastery and cathedral. I do everything better when I am praying.

My embrace of retreat to write my books is not to say that a mother of three small children who cannot abandon her responsibilities or a person who is tied to a full-time job may not also be a great writer with stories to give the tribe. My experience is that both can be and have been, and I myself have written books while the baby was taking a nap—or after everyone else in the house was asleep. Here at the end, I come back to what I felt called to say at the beginning: those who are called to write are going to write, and the history of stories given to the tribe is a history of stories urged from lived lives, of writing that is practiced in whatever time that writers have set aside for it.

Here, as elsewhere, the writing life illumines the spiritual life: if you want to make your practice a priority in your life, you may have to lose a little sleep.

5

The Spiritual Life
as an Editorial Process

ALBERT Y. HSU

I work as an editor at a Christian book-publishing house. My job is to acquire and develop manuscripts, working with authors and shepherding them through the publishing process. As a project editor, I review proposals and manuscripts and interact with authors to shape the content at both a big picture level as well as in the smaller details. On any given day, I might restructure a table of contents, suggest that a chapter needs to be added or deleted, or identify weaknesses in an argument. I'll notice that "begging the question" is being used improperly, or I'll tell an author that "Dr Pepper" should not have a period. I might check an author's spelling of *"weltanschauung"* or suggest that a book be entirely reconceptualized for a different audience. My overall goal is to help authors hone and clarify their material to be as helpful and effective as possible for their intended readers.

Editors in the book-publishing industry often use various metaphors to describe our work. Sometimes we speak of ourselves as midwives that help birth books into the world. (And the long writing and publishing process means that authors can be pregnant for years before delivery!) One of my colleagues, an organist at his church, talks about the editor as accompanist. He prefers to accompany someone else musically rather than perform a solo. His role is not to be in the spotlight himself, but rather to help someone else take center stage and to highlight his or her gifts for the benefit of others.

Another colleague, whose primary focus is books on spiritual formation, says that the editor's role is similar to that of the spiritual director. A spiritual director helps people attune themselves to God's work in their lives. Similarly, an editor helps authors discern the directions in which a manuscript should be developed or revised.

I often tell potential authors that writing is not only a creative act in which we can participate with God in co-creation, but that it is also an exercise in expressing one's vocation and calling. No one can or should write anything and everything, but individuals may well be called to write out of the particularity of their calling to accomplish what they are uniquely gifted to address. Books often work best when authors discern how God is distinctively prompting them to write and contribute in ways that others cannot or do not.

All of this leads me to conclude that the editorial process is a spiritual process and that writing and editing are windows into the spiritual life. Moreover, my work as an editor gives me glimpses into how God may be editing my life for the sake of spiritual transformation.

GOD AS DIVINE EDITOR

One daily e-newsletter that I receive gives the etymologies of interesting words. One entry about "back-formation words" talked about words that are devised from what appears to be a derivative word. For example, the verb *beg* was actually derived from the noun *beggar*, and the noun *injury* preceded the verb form *injure*.

The verb *edit* is one of these back-formation words. The primary source word was the noun *editor*, from the Latin *edere*, "to give out." That word came first. Only later was the verb *edit* derived from the preexisting *editor*.[1]

Knowing this says something to me about the primary identity of the editor. Even before an editor actually edits, he or she has an editorial identity apart from any utilitarian function of editing. An editor is predisposed toward shaping and honing material even before a particular manuscript or project comes across the desk.

This understanding of editing points to an innate quality of the editorial personality—namely, the yearning for redemption. An editor looks at projects with an eye to bringing the best out of what might be currently an unreadable mess. An editor desires to make things better. The editor sees latent potential and draws the best out of an author. The editor prompts the author toward revision, sometimes with gentle encouragement, sometimes with heavier editorial direction. An editor has an eschatological hopefulness that in the end a manuscript can become much more than it presently is; that it can find fulfillment and fruition in new and unexpected ways.

1. Anu Garg, *A.Word.A.Day* (e-newsletter), April 26, 2010, http://wordsmith.org/words/cathect.html.

In some theological circles, narrative theology is done in such a way that God is presented as the sole author writing the story of human history. In this framework, God is a novelist who plots out every detail, and we humans are merely characters doing God's will in the drama. While narrative has been a fruitful way of doing theology, in some oversimplified versions God scripts the plot in such a way that human agency is minimized or eliminated.[2]

I think it might be more helpful to think of God not as a novelist but as an editor who shapes us as we write our lives. In this scenario, humans are not puppet actors but collaborative authors working with an editor who sees the bigger picture. Author and editor work together in partnership to shape the trajectory of a book. The author is still fundamentally responsible for his or her own work, but the editor guides and directs the author to bring out the best in both the author and the text.

God is the divine editor. Long before humanity came into being, God was already at work shaping the creation of the universe. God gave agency to humans to write and tell their own stories, setting the stage for narratives to be written and performed. And even in the midst of a fallen world, God has an editorial eye. God sees the tangled plotlines of damaged lives and yearns to bring redemption and resolution to them. Whether on an individual or a cosmic level, God collaborates with human actors to point them toward ultimate good.

This view retains the paradoxical balance of human responsibility and divine sovereignty. Some Christians are often too quick to move toward catch phrases and slogans like "It's all about God" or "My life is in God's hands," as if we have no say whatsoever about how our lives unfold. On the other hand, other Christians are "practical deists," living their lives as if God doesn't exist at all.[3] One group says it's all about God, and the other lives as if it's all about us. But the reality is that humans and God live together in interactive partnership.

That is the paradoxical tension depicted in the author-editor relationship. Author and editor journey together on a shared pilgrimage. God might not be a novelist but may well be an editor. Just as an editor commissions and acquires projects for development and publication, so too does God commission us to write our lives for the sake of others, editing us along the way.

---

2. On why God is not a novelist, see Bruce Reichenbach, "God Limits His Power," in *Predestination and Free Will: Four Views*, ed. David Basinger and Randall Basinger (Downers Grove, IL: InterVarsity Press, 1986).

3. See Craig M. Gay, *The Way of the (Modern) World: Or, Why It's Tempting to Live as if God Doesn't Exist* (Grand Rapids: Wm. B. Eerdmans, 1998).

THE PRACTICE OF
INCARNATIONAL REMEMBRANCE

One of the most valuable aspects of the publishing process is that it is an act of cultural production, or what Andy Crouch calls "culture making."[4] Writing creates artifacts. Publishing takes the abstract ideas of an author's mind and puts them into print in a physical, tangible object. This process preserves someone's insight and anchors it in space and time. The physical artifact of the book also makes an author's ideas portable and transferable to others.

How often have we woken up in the middle of the night with a brilliant thought that is lost in the dawn of the new day? Many writers and pastors keep a pad of paper on the nightstand to capture the fleeting thought that might otherwise evaporate. I am an occasional insomniac, and sometimes I wake up at two or three in the morning with random thoughts. I find that I often need to get up and write the ideas out of my head before I can get back to sleep. Even though the written ideas may not necessarily all make sense in the morning, I am frequently glad to have preserved some nuggets for further development.

I also practice the discipline of daily journaling. I have been doing this since high school, and I have filled up dozens of spiral notebooks with my reflections on each day. Sometimes my journal entries are little more than a daily log of what I did that day. But other times I have space for more spiritual reflection, especially when I am grappling with a decision or processing an emotional situation. Daily journaling parallels the spiritual practice of the daily examen, looking for how God has been present in one's day. Just as some people who process things verbally don't know what they think or feel until they explain it out loud to a friend, many who journal or write books don't discover what they truly believe until it is written on a page.

The act of writing is incarnational. When significant thoughts or events occur, the act of writing them down makes the abstract concrete. Whether for a book manuscript or for a personal journal, writing is a spiritual practice of remembrance and meaning-making that endures in a lasting form that allows for future engagement.

At one gathering of editors and publishers, one participant described his work as helping authors "capture the 'aha' moment." In other words, an editor guides the writer to practice the discipline of remembrance. In essence, the editor is saying to the author, "Don't lose this. Pay attention. This is important. Commit this to memory. Preserve it in print."

---

4. See Andy Crouch, *Culture Making: Recovering Our Creative Calling* (Downers Grove, IL: InterVarsity Press, 2008).

When I go back and review my journals, I am able to discover and rediscover time preserved.[5] I am able to reread my own story as an epic narrative, like a really long movie or perhaps a television series that has been unfolding for decades. Rereading journal entries can be like the recaps offered at the beginning of TV shows: "Previously in Al's life . . ."

Understanding my life as an unfolding narrative helps me look for recurring themes and developing plotlines. God as editor might call my attention to particular things in the past to help me understand what's going on in the present. For example, I lost my father to suicide some years ago. While grieving his death and trying to understand his actions, I later remembered that during my teen years I had gone through occasional periods of depression, one significant enough that counselors at a camp had put me on suicide watch. I had somehow forgotten that fact entirely, and recalling that part of my own story helped me identify with and better understand my father's despair.

Our lives are unfolding stories. Sometimes an unexpected event throws in a plot twist rife with pain. But these events need not define our stories as tragedies. As we write our lives, God the divine editor may nudge the story in certain directions. "Here is how the story is going," God might whisper. "Instead of moving toward calamity, we can steer it toward redemption." My father's suicide prompted me to reframe and redirect my own story toward suicide prevention and helping other survivors of suicide walk through their own grief and loss.

THE GRACE OF EDITORIAL REVIEW

One of the key aspects of the editorial process is outside review. Editorial review gives authors a space in the writing process to step away from their work and forget about it for a while, maybe up to a few months. I tell authors that while their manuscripts are being reviewed, their job is to forget about the book and to resist tinkering with the manuscript. Don't think about the book at all. That way, when the reports eventually do show up, the author may revisit the book and see it again with fresh eyes. Authors often discover areas of weakness that they may have been blind to when they were previously immersed in the writing.

After the author has written the first draft, the manuscript is sent to outside readers who review it. Most books get two or three readers, and those

5. See Bob Greene, *Be True to Your School* (New York: Atheneum, 1987), based on Greene's high school diary. He writes, "When I look at the diary after years had passed, I realized that what I had here was something money could not buy: time preserved" (vii).

readers may include a peer in the author's academic discipline, a professional writer or editor, or a general reader or layperson. These readers are invited to respond to the manuscript in whatever ways make sense for them. They might pay attention to big-picture issues of style and tone, or they might be concerned about details relating to content. "I don't get this point on p. 48," one might write. "You need to substantiate this better." Or "Page 102, good idea, but what does this look like in real life? Give me an example."

Once the reader reports are in, the editor sends this feedback to the author (anonymously). For example: "Reader #1 is a sociologist, reader #2 is a New Testament scholar, and reader #3 is a layperson who volunteers on a local church mission committee. The last report is from me." This feedback may result in quite a tall stack of paper. One of my authors was daunted when she received twenty-five single-spaced pages of editorial feedback in her reports. I myself have on occasion written reports that are over twenty pages long.

Many authors say that this part of the editorial process is by far the most painful. I know authors who have been reduced to tears by these reports. Some swear that they will never write anything for publication again. A few have bailed out on a book project at this point, when the feedback was too much to bear or seemed beyond the scope of their capacity to rework or revise a manuscript.

I've been on both sides of this process. As an author, I remember the sense of rebuke I got from one reader who critiqued my ideas, style, and use of language. I was somewhat immobilized and not sure how to go about revision. But then I had lunch with my editor, and we were able to process together how best to move forward. She guided me through the feedback, saying to listen to this suggestion but not to worry about that one. Like a wise spiritual director or pastoral counselor, she listened both to my angst and the editorial feedback to help get me unstuck and to move forward in the process.

As painful as it may be to receive such feedback, we are invariably better off for receiving it than not to hear it at all. Several years after my first book was published, I discovered that for some reason I had not received one particular editorial report on my draft manuscript. A departure from the usual situation, in which readers remain anonymous, I figured out that the report was from someone I highly respected, and his points of critique were insightful and perceptive. I wished I had received the report prior to publication, and I could have sharpened my points and addressed his concerns to make my book better.

Authors don't necessarily need to do everything that the readers suggest. But the very act of going through the editorial review process creates the opportunity for self-examination and reflection that almost always leads to a better manuscript. Even when authors choose not to follow a report's particular piece of advice, they often find other ways of rewriting the material that resolves the problem.

The external review process can also confirm that an author is headed in the right direction. I was nervous about writing *Grieving a Suicide* because I am not a professional psychologist or counselor.[6] So I made all sorts of disclaimers in the text about my status as a layperson. But I was encouraged when the reader reports came back and one psychologist said that I had gotten the psychology right.

In a similar way, we need outside voices speaking into our spiritual lives, to speak words of affirmation as well as critique. In many circles, spirituality is viewed as a private, individualistic thing. We tend not to ask one another about our spiritual experience, as this seems overly personal and intrusive, like asking about someone's weight, income, or sex life. But while most of us don't live so transparently to the whole world, all of us need at least a few "outside readers" who can give us occasional editorial feedback on how our lives are going. For some, a spouse or trusted friend serves in this role; for others, it may be a pastor, counselor, therapist, or small group. Classical Christian writers on spirituality speak of "soul friends" who are intentional companions on our spiritual journeys.

One of my high school friends and I have this kind of friendship. We don't talk to each other very often, but when we do, there's a level of depth and connectedness that we don't find with other, more casual acquaintances. We occasionally call or e-mail one another, especially in times of life transition, when we ask one another for guidance and discernment. It is tremendously helpful when someone can provide an outside perspective: "Hmmm, it sounds like you'd really like to head in this direction rather than that one."

Such external feedback can be received as a gift of grace. God's editorial work can provide a kind of outside review that shapes us with negative rebuke as well as constructive affirmation. Like a tumbler that polishes stones, the grace of editorial review smoothes off our rough edges to make us more what we ought to be, especially in God's eyes.

THE SIGNIFICANCE OF COMMUNITY

We often hold to a cultural myth of the solitary writer, the genius hermit who hides in a cave to produce a masterpiece. While many writers do tend to be

---

6. Albert Y. Hsu, *Grieving a Suicide: A Loved One's Search for Comfort, Answers, and Hope* (Downers Grove, IL: InterVarsity Press, 2002).

introspective and reclusive, the vast majority of books are written as the fruit of community.

That's why most books have extensive acknowledgments pages. Authors don't have one-line acknowledgments thanking themselves for their own intellectual brilliance. No, most authors take paragraphs to thank various friends, family, colleagues, and communities that have contributed to the book. One of my authors had twelve pages of acknowledgments, listing over a thousand people by name, some of them several times.

For one of my own books, I acknowledged every person in our publishing house, including editors, designers, publicists, marketers, accountants, and techies. It takes a whole village to publish a book. I always enjoy reading acknowledgment pages and seeing how the author thanks those who have helped develop the book and who have otherwise contributed to the author's life.

I once served as project editor for a book on Asian American churches that involved three coeditors and a dozen contributors and collaborators.[7] The group met annually to bounce ideas off of one another and give each other advice and encouragement about particular ministry situations. We also spent lots of time eating together and sharing personal stories. What I witnessed in these gatherings was an actual community writing a book together. Certain individuals were identified as the point person for each chapter, but people freely contributed stories and illustrations to each other's chapters with a spirit of mutuality and generosity. Once the book was published, the group reconvened to celebrate its publication, and everybody autographed everybody else's copy, including myself as editor and participants who weren't formally writers but nevertheless had helped generate the book.

Whether aware of it or not, we are all products of community and often of several overlapping and intersecting communities of family, friends, colleagues, students, and churches. One of the principal ways that God edits us is through locating us in communities where we rub shoulders with people who challenge us to grow in different ways.

In previous centuries, people tended to be located in homogenous communities with a single, static identity or societal role. These days, we often find ourselves in diverse multiple communities, wearing various and sometimes contradictory identities, depending on the context. One might be socially liberal but religiously conservative, or vice versa. One might be both parent and child, or care for children and parents simultaneously. And the diverse members of our communities challenge our biases and help us grow in different

---

7. Peter Cha, S. Steve Kang, and Helen Lee, eds., *Growing Healthy Asian American Churches* (Downers Grove, IL: InterVarsity Press, 2006).

directions. At the same time, these different identities and plotlines all con-verge in the narratives of our lives, with each playing an integral role in our spiritual formation.

The vision of the kingdom of God is one in which individual identities and larger communal identities are held together in dialectical tension. Christians understand themselves all to be parts of the body of Christ, with both indi-vidual identities and membership in the universal communion of saints that transcends time and space. The larger story of God's divine kingdom gives shape to our individual narratives. We are a people headed in a particular direction, with a certain vision for a world marked by God's shalom.

This larger story has helped me properly reckon with my place in the uni-verse. I am not an anonymous drop in an ocean of Nirvana, nor am I just an atomistic individual in American consumer society. I have an identity that neither overemphasizes nor underemphasizes who I am. I am a child in a family, a citizen in a kingdom. I have significance in my own right but also a corporate identity that is larger than myself and gives me a sense of calling and mission.

Over the centuries, the Christian church has had many different kinds of orders and guilds, tribes and subcultures. There have been Benedictines and Jesuits, Franciscans and Methodists, mystics and evangelicals. Some of these groups have focused on preaching and proclamation, while others have focused on acts of justice and mercy. As an editor at a Christian publishing house, I can locate myself in the tradition of the scribes in the scriptoriums, the makers and keepers of the books. Christians have always been people of the book.

It also seems to me that even the scriptoriums are missionary orders of a sort. Books are like little missionaries, going out into the world to places the authors could not go on their own. My work as an editor is to commission and send out books to herald their messages to those who need to hear them, to widen their readership and invite more people into God's kingdom commu-nity. Working with authors from various corners of the church, I am able to partner with people from many traditions, extending their ministries through the printed book, for the benefit of the church and the world.

Whatever communities we find ourselves in, whatever particular missional purposes we have, we all participate in some aspect of God's grand narrative. We do so not merely as actors but as collaborative authors in the unfolding redemptive drama. Thus, our individual lives are transformed by God's edito-rial vision of what C. S. Lewis called the Great Story, "in which every chapter is better than the one before."[8]

8. C. S. Lewis, *The Last Battle* (New York: Harper Collins, 1956), 211.

6

The Pie Social

I am asked, all the time it seems, why I am a Christian. What people mean is: why did you become a Christian? Sometimes they mean: how could you possibly have given up the beautiful rituals and compelling community of Judaism for the pale performances of Protestant Christianity? Sometimes they mean: tell us a story of drama, of God's arresting you on a road one fine afternoon, of voices from heaven and lights from the sky and certainty. Sometimes they mean: tell us about that dream you had, a million years ago, the dream about Jesus coming to rescue you from a kidnapping.

In all cases, they want an answer about something that happened to me almost half a lifetime ago.

But here's the truth: I can't really remember why I became a Christian. I can remember bits and pieces of the why, bits and pieces that you'd think might add up to a story, but they don't, not really. And here's the other truth: the events that happened to me fifteen years ago—the dream, the purchase of a Book of Common Prayer, the first shy church attendance—those vignettes have very little to do with why I am a Christian today. They are not wholly unrelated—they make a sort of genealogy, that dream and the prayer book. And perhaps they answer the question "Why did you become a Christian?" But they don't do much to answer the question "Why are you a Christian *today*?"

Think of it like this: If at your golden anniversary party someone asks you why you are married to your husband, to that particular balding, half-deaf man who fathered your children and once got fired from a job and loved you through the trauma of your mother's death and took you to Italy for your twentieth anniversary; that man who in midlife learned to cook and started hosting elegant dinner parties for all your friends on the first Friday of every month; that man who had the slightly annoying but slightly adorable habit of repeating what you just said before he responded to it; that man who stopped drinking for ten years and then started again and then stopped again; that man who always said that if you wanted to become a dolphin, he would find a way to make it happen, and he would get you the moon if he could—if your answer to the question "Why are you married to him?" were purely historical, about your first date and why you fell in love with him way back when, fifty-one years ago—that would be a sad and partial answer. Maybe it would be no kind of answer at all. What the question wants to know is why you are married to him now.

And so with Jesus: why are you still here with him? What sustains your spiritual life this week? What makes you a Christian today?

In church today the Gospel reading is the end of Luke 2, that story where the boy Jesus stays back in Jerusalem at the Temple and his parents don't know where he is and it takes them three days to find him. After church my friend Q says to me, "Of all the Gospel readings, that was the one that most got me as a kid. How on earth do parents lose a child?"

I tell Q that I have great sympathy for Mary and Joseph. How did they lose him? Haven't you? I lose Jesus all the time.

I suppose there are different kinds of loss that "losing Jesus" might name. There's losing Jesus in a kind of William James way—a change in religious experience; we sense Jesus' presence intimately, and then we don't. Or, again, there's losing Jesus because we have departed from his norm, from his *derech*: You begin to take for granted that he is next to you. You head home after some intense temple experience and just assume that the direction in which you're walking is the direction in which he's walking, and your assumption, it turns out, is wrong. Then perhaps there is a third kind of loss—the loss that comes when we notice the limits of our knowledge of God, when we feel bereft of guidance, when we feel the loss of God's saving power or of God's grace. This is the loss that notices, and mourns, the *Deus absconditus*, the hidden God. This is the loss you name when you ask why God does not answer your prayers. It is the loss entailed when we realize that Jesus is more mysterious and more inscrutable than we had at first understood.

Over spring break, I went to Washington, D.C. I was visiting a friend who grew up in the church and was for many years vitally involved in the church. Sometime in the last year, my friend began to realize that she had lost Jesus. She said he seemed to have withdrawn from her utterly. Last week I was sitting in her living room grading papers as she rested on the couch. I thought she was asleep, but later she told me she had been praying. Her prayer was beautiful and simple and heartbreaking: "God," she said, "I don't know who you are or what you are like, but I miss you."

I don't have a recipe for how to find Jesus when you've lost him. I didn't have a recipe to give my friend in D.C. I managed, when she told me of her prayer, to bite my lip and thus stop myself from saying something like "Oh, you're having a dry spell. We've all had them." I managed not to invoke, in a ham-fisted and patronizing way, the dark night of the soul. Days later I thought of the lovely snippet from the prayer book, the moment in the prayers for the people where we bid prayer "for all who seek God, or a deeper knowledge of God," saying "Pray that they may find and be found by God."

In her novel *Horse Heaven*, Jane Smiley writes about a horse trainer named Buddy Crawford.[1] He gets born again and is all fired up, and then one night he is praying and he sits down on the bed and looks "up to the full moon, in whose region he imagines Jesus to be," and to his Lord and Savior he says this: "Okay. Here's the deal. I thought I was saved. That was what was advertised. I would accept you as my personal savior, and there you were. And, you know, I felt it, too. I felt saved and everything. . . . But I find out all the time that I've got to keep getting saved. Am I saved? Am I not saved? What do I do now? . . . Are you talking to me? Are you not talking to me? Am I good? Am I a sinner? Still a sinner?" And then he bursts into tears. His wife—a "nice person" who had been "a good mother to all those ungrateful children"—comes into the room, gets undressed, and asks Buddy what has made him cry. "When the Lord came into me," Buddy tells his wife, "it was such a good feeling, I thought, Well, I can do anything because of this feeling, but there was all this stuff to do and to think about, and I don't remember the feeling all that well."

I know I had some feelings back in the day of the dream and the prayer book. I suspect they were feelings of closeness, maybe of rest, of knowing and being known by God—but I'm just guessing. I don't remember the feelings all that well. I don't actually remember them at all. Those feelings may have been the reason I asked a priest to baptize me. They may explain why I started wearing this little silver cross around my neck. They may explain why once, a long time ago, I gave up what felt like my whole life—all my community, all the ways I had theretofore known for how to know God—and entered this new life. They have almost nothing to do with why I'm a Christian this week.

The clearest way to tell you, I think, is to tell you about last Monday. A fine September Monday. The start of the school year. The season when churches

1. Jane Smiley, *Horse Heaven* (New York: Ballantine, 2001), 192–93.

come back to themselves after everyone's summer hiatus at the beach. The season of red leaves and almost, though not quite yet, apple cider.

We were having a pie social at church that night to kick off our fall adult education program. Homemade pies, a short video—I was assigned to be a table facilitator. Around three p.m. I asked three students—one of whom is our new intern and two of whom are quite new Episcopalians, also attending my church, students I adore—if they wanted to go to this pie social and have a quick bite of dinner with me beforehand. Then at four o'clock I had a really invigorating, really fabulous phone conversation with my new spiritual director, a woman who over and over seems very wise. At five o'clock, I headed to my car to go meet the three students for dinner. I was ecstatic, although that may seem odd given such an ordinary afternoon. The conversation with my spiritual director was thrilling, although I can't remember more than a sentence. (Already it has dissolved into tangled memory, the odd consonant or vowel floating around the air; I can only remember how I felt during it and after it.) And this gathering for adult education in the recently renovated fellowship hall—I love church happenings like this. They make me feel like my life is real, not floating away like a vowel in the air.

I got most of the way back to my car and realized that my car key—which is one of those black pads, not really a traditional key at all—had, at some point in the day, fallen off my key chain. I looked through my purse. I retraced my steps through Duke Gardens. I returned to my office, looked on my desk, then on my office floor. No key. This is the sort of quotidian, keeping-body-and-soul-together kind of thing that just undoes me. I knew these keys are very expensive to replace. And for a while I couldn't get my students on the phone, so they were waiting for me at a restaurant at which I never appeared, and this role I had looked forward to—Lauren as the sensitive professor who is involved in her students' lives and encourages their engagement in the local parish—dissolved. Finally, the new intern answered her phone, and I wound up asking her to pick me up, which she did, in perhaps her first act of service to our church, and then the other two students ordered dinner and brought a plate to me at church. When I walked through the doors of the newly renovated fellowship hall, they handed me a coffee mug filled with red wine. So there I was, being taken care of by these students, instead of enacting whatever cool professor role it was I had wanted to enact.

And then there was the video itself, the educational part of our adult ed evening. The sound (which thankfully I was not in charge of) was iffy, and half my table couldn't hear. As the video played, I realized that I knew several of the "talking heads"—Nora Gallagher, Phyllis Tickle, Tracey Lind. Two of them I count as pretty good friends. I managed mostly to silence the voice of insecure ego in my head, but occasionally it did speak up, asking, "How come Nora was invited to be in this film and I wasn't?"

And then—this is so typical of my beloved little ordinary church, the church that looks like a spaceship and whose parking lot has been under construction for what seems like three years—no one at my table would talk about what we were supposed to talk about. The rector had explained that while watching the video, we were to jot down things that struck us, things with which we agreed or disagreed. Then we were to discuss these things for twenty minutes. Well, everyone at my table wanted to discuss only the video as such—to critique it: "It used too much insider-y lingo," said one person. "All the featured people seemed to be well-educated and middle-class, not sufficiently diverse, all sporting expensive haircuts and long, dangly, artsy earrings," said another. "Did you see the promotional materials?" asked a third. The promotional materials were apparently very low-rent; they wouldn't do at all. This was one of the moments when I was trying to channel the rector: she would know how to get these people to actually talk about their reactions to the content of the video, to what Nora and others said about sin, Jesus, the Holy Spirit. For the most part, I failed at that task; we said maybe three minutes of things about Jesus, and seventeen about the promotional materials. The rector, another parishioner, and I talked about this later. They assured me that I am a good facilitator, and that even the rector herself couldn't have moved this conversation much further. We wound up having a good conversation about what this says about our parish: are we so wildly uncomfortable talking about Jesus and related topics that even when the priest has told us to, we stay in this more comfortable space of critiquing the video?

Taken together, this afternoon and evening are a first answer to the questions: Why am I a Christian this week? Why am I a Christian still?

There are other answers—more theological answers, more spiritual answers, answers that have to do with the Eucharist and prayer and God—but this is the first one, and it is about this spaceship building full of people who are not very comfortable talking about Jesus, and this is where I keep getting saved, which it turns out I have to do.

There was something about this pie social, something abundant. It was the kind of potluck where you take a little sliver of everyone's pie, because this was the offering of the people (well, mostly the women) of your church and you will eat too much rather than hurt anyone's feelings, and you might even fib a little and say the pecan cream pie (whoever heard of such a thing?) was better than you thought it was. (I thought it was gross.)

And that seems the very truest thing. In the midst of the lost car key, the failed cool-professor moment, the video no one could hear, and the endless conversation about promotional materials, still there was abundance at the heart of it, there in the groaning board full of pies, pies you taste beyond the point of necessity and hunger, because Mary Catherine made this and it is her offering even if she's not comfortable sitting around a circular table talking about sin, and you will taste her pie and remember that you are fed.

7

Habits of a Whole Heart

Practicing Life in Christ

MARJORIE J. THOMPSON

TWO VIGNETTES

Vignette 1

Lately I have begun practicing yoga again. I cannot claim to understand or espouse the spiritual foundations of this ancient path, but the physical benefits are excellent. Since my early twenties I have begun my day with a series of breathing and stretching exercises that limber and strengthen my energies for waking hours. Over the years these have evolved into a form of prayer as well. Now I embed these prayers in a sequence of yoga stretches that demand of me more precision and attention. The prayer expressing itself in these poses combines praise, self-offering, and receptivity to divine grace.

The poses themselves suggest to me postures of heart and mind. Breathe in: *Holy Spirit fill me, indwell my life this day.* Breathe out: *My God, I release to you my anxiety, tension, desire to control.* Stretch forward over crossed legs, forehead to mat: *Here am I, Lord; guide me as you will this day.* Hands stretching up from standing: *Praise to You, Holy Presence, Light of Life; I receive you gladly into my heart!* Prayer pose, hands pressed lightly together before heart: *Fill me with your love, Lord Christ; increase my love for you and all you love.* The precise words and sentiments vary from day to day, but the essence of such prayers I find readily embodied in the flow of physical movements.

Vignette 2

This morning I completed a twenty-minute period of centering prayer, a practice I am only now making regular as I struggle to find my way toward a satisfying pattern of life in the "freelance" lane. I found centering prayer a good aid in turning my intention toward "consent to God's presence and action within."[1] Centering prayer is a form of contemplative practice in which words, thoughts, feelings, and images (the usual content of our prayer, and of waking consciousness in general) are gently but resolutely turned aside so that we may receive a simple awareness of divine presence. This morning I was able to recognize when I was engaging in thoughts, seeking an insight, or desiring a feeling, and I could gently let each go without undue attachment. Moments of deeper availability broke through; a sense of interior opening and receptivity, like a deep-throated flower or vase, came over me for a time. On the whole I felt the release of effort and anxiety, and the ease of allowing God to be God. It was a practice from which I emerged with a deep sense of gratitude, freedom, and peace. Not every period of my centering prayer reflects these characteristics. That fact does not make this morning's prayer more or less "successful" than other times, merely more satisfying.

In describing these two vignettes, I see that the first represents the wider path of *kataphatic prayer*, in which grace is mediated through the embodied material and sensory world. It is prayer suited to the reality that in this world, spirit must be incarnated in form to be grasped. The second vignette represents the less traveled and culturally more alien way of *apophatic prayer*, in which the ordinary markers of human knowing and acting bow to the mystery of a God who cannot be adequately named, felt, or comprehended. Here is prayer that acknowledges the limits of incarnate form where matters of the Spirit are concerned, prayer that forever eludes our need to grasp truth in order to control life.

I find that I need both paths for a balanced experience of God's life in and beyond this world. One keeps me grounded, and the other stretches the horizons of my soul. I need both for a whole heart; together they lead me toward a more wholehearted love of God, others, self, and creation.

THE NATURE OF THE SPIRITUAL LIFE

The spiritual life is as broad and deep as the cosmos brought into being by God's living Word: "All things came into being through him, and without him

---

1. This is the basic content of this form of contemplative practice, as taught by Father Thomas Keating.

not one thing came into being" (John 1:3). The range of possibilities for growing in spirit and expressing life in Christ are as infinite as he is in himself, since
it is his desire to abide in us. To the extent that we die to our self-referential
posture and welcome the Holy Spirit in our inmost being, our life is "hidden
with Christ in God" (Col. 3:3). The Christ life takes various shapes within
individuals, depending on unique circumstances, gifts, and callings, yet the
spiritual marks of Christ's love are evident in each. These marks are recognized
in the lives of the saints though the ages, including those of our own time.

I understand the spiritual life to be the reality and vitality of the divine
Spirit indwelling and flowing out of human life, personally and corporately.[2]
It is as valid to speak of the spiritual life of a community as it is to speak of an
individual's spiritual life. When Paul exhorts the Philippian believers, "Let
the same mind be in you that was in Christ Jesus" (Phil. 2:5), he is addressing
the church as a whole in relation to its corporate witness to life in Christ—a
life lived by and through the power of the Holy Spirit.

The mystery of grace in community illumines a paradox. On the one hand,
the Spirit transcends individual faithfulness or failure. Where the Lord is present, the basic insight of gestalt applies: the whole is greater than the sum of its
parts. On the other hand, the strength of any faith community derives from
the integrity of its parts. If individuals within a community of faith are not living in the spirit of grace, their opacity clouds the transparency of the community to God's truth. Perhaps it can be said of this paradox that where there is
basic health in the leadership and underlying spirit of a faith community, it can
bear and lift its weaker members, maintaining faithful witness in the world.

Yet we are accustomed to framing the spiritual life in personal terms, and
each of us needs to take responsibility first of all for the state of our own
mind and heart before God. Since my task here is to reflect on the nature of
the spiritual life in relation to my own experience and practice, I will trust a
perspective my mentor Henri Nouwen never tired of repeating: that the most
personal truths are also most universal.[3]

MARKS OF THE SPIRIT

Early in my ministry, I had the freedom to structure my life around several
spiritual practices. I had tasted these as a research fellow at Yale Divinity
School while exploring ecumenical prayer traditions both academically and

2. See the first chapter of my book *Soul Feast: An Invitation to the Christian Spiritual Life* (Louisville, KY: Westminster John Knox Press, 1995) for my thoughts on biblical and theological
foundations. I hope to build upon rather than repeat those perspectives here.
3. Nouwen drew this wisdom from the psychologist Carl Rogers.

experientially. For a number of years I was able to set aside times for daily morning prayer with Scripture and journaling, to schedule periodic spiritual retreats, experiment with limited fasting, and share the daily office of Compline with my husband before going to bed.

These time-dependent practices laid excellent groundwork for my spiritual life, but I could not maintain them when I began a full-time commuting job. I found over the course of several years that my spiritual sustenance gradually shifted from "time-based" to "situation-based" practices. I made more effort to be mindful of how I lived my days in relation to central signs of God's presence and guidance. The circumstances of my work and family, the "accidents" of daily interaction, the ordinary activities of the day, were slowly becoming the altar of my sacrifice of praise and thanksgiving.

As work and family circumstances became more challenging with time, I found myself turning to those texts in the Gospels and Epistles that delineate the new life in Christ and describe the marks of a Christ-follower. Signs of the reality of God's Spirit alive in us are beautifully expressed in texts such as Colossians 3:12–15 and Ephesians 4:25–5:2. Over and over, the Gospels point to the centrality of divine love as the primary mark of the Spirit in human life. Divine love is *agape*, God-referential love in place of self-referential love. We see this love revealed with purest clarity in the person of Jesus Christ, God's life-giving Word made visible, tangible, and accessible to us in human form. Among the clearest marks of God's Spirit at work in us is the "fruit" described by the apostle Paul: "love, joy, peace, patience, kindness, generosity, faithfulness, gentleness, and self-control" (Gal. 5:22–23).

I have discovered that these character traits belong together, in the cluster that joins them as a unified "fruit" of the Spirit. They do not grow singly, since they are related expressions of God's love in human life. So each time I act with patience, the lungs of my love expand a little more. Each choice of constructive self-control brings a greater measure of balance to my love for others. Peace is the mantle that falls on my spirit when I have lived faithfully in the virtue of love—something I manage only in fits and starts. I look to the fruit of the Spirit for basic guidelines in discerning where I might be making some small measure of progress in my spiritual growth, as opposed to merely talking or writing about it—an occupational hazard in professional ministry that seems especially acute for those of us who earn our keep through work in spiritual formation!

SIGNS OF GROWTH

I am pondering a few examples of the way these central Scripture texts have informed and continue to shape my daily practice. According to Paul, the spiritual life means being transformed by the renewing of my mind. Evidence of its reality is found in not thinking more highly of myself than I should, but rather in acknowledging the gifts of every person in the community to build up the body of Christ or contribute to the common good (see Rom. 12:2–8). For me, this has entailed a growing awareness over time of how deeply rooted my competitive spirit was from early childhood, how much I wanted to distinguish myself from others by excelling in whatever ways I could. As an adult, I began to discover how striving for distinction led to making unfavorable comparisons between myself and others, and how easily professional jealousy could grow from this ingrained self-focus. Learning to celebrate with real delight the gifts of those far more gifted and accomplished than I, and coming to appreciate those with gifts vastly different from mine but equally if not more important to the good of the whole, has been—and continues to be—a healthy journey in self-acceptance, humility, and respectful appreciation of others. I have learned that I do not need to possess a gift I admire, and that joy comes in seeing how God has adorned another's life with grace for the sake of the beloved community.

"As God's chosen ones, holy and beloved, clothe yourselves with compassion, kindness, humility, meekness, and patience. Bear with one another" (Col. 3:12). I have returned time and again to this passage as an anchor for my spiritual life in relation to family. In the years when my mother-in-law visited us annually for a month at a stretch, I chafed increasingly at some of her traits and behaviors. Conversations with her were difficult, brief, and predictable, partly by virtue of her deafness. By the last week of her visit, I was usually past ready for her departure.

With time, prayer, and practiced patience, I have come to a different relationship with my mother-in-law. She has now lived in our home for more than eight years. Daily life with her has permitted my husband and me to see things we were blind to during her shorter visits. Like all of us, she has strengths along with her limitations. And like most elderly people I have known, she has strong reactions, preferences, and resistance to certain ideas and persons. I readily admit that even with increased understanding and appreciation for her, exercising patience can still be trying. A good dose of her stubbornness can elicit my immediate impatience. But in general, I have observed over the years that my capacity to bear with her limitations has grown. I have learned to reach out to her with little acts of love that she herself would probably never request but deeply needs. She accepts a kiss from me on the cheek each night, and I see that it feeds her heart. I touch her with care as often as seems natural, and she is openly grateful for a periodic neck or foot massage. I have learned that the very act of caring for her helps me grow in patience and tenderness toward her. As my friend Parker Palmer is fond of observing, sometimes "we live our way into new ways of thinking" rather than "thinking our way into new ways of living."

It is one thing to grow in patience and understanding with time, a universal aspect of emotional maturation. Understanding in itself can bring a welcome deathblow to my judging ego. But the greater dying to self, I believe, comes when I have no understanding at all of another person's repellant behavior or character traits. There are no doubt always reasons driving such behaviors, but I need not have access to those reasons to live in greater acceptance and kindness toward difficult people. I will never comprehend the impenetrable reaches of my mother-in-law's mind—nor should I, as that prerogative belongs to God alone. Her unique personhood stands as a mystery before which I bow in wonder. My love, patience, and tenderness toward her express the life of God's Spirit in me, and to whatever extent I open myself to the grace and blessing of that larger Spirit, I die a bit to my small self—even the self that needs to understand in order to act with love.

"Put away from you all bitterness and wrath and anger and wrangling . . . and be kind to one another, tenderhearted, forgiving one another, as God in Christ has forgiven you" (Eph. 4:31–32). A recent example of how life circumstances offer ready occasions for spiritual practice concerns my job loss of two years ago. A week before Christmas, my boss—also a personal friend—informed me that he was cutting my staff position, a position I had thought to be reasonably central to the purpose and mission of the organization I had served for nearly thirteen years. Indeed, only six months earlier my boss had affirmed the centrality of the chief work I was doing there. I felt a mix of shock, pain, betrayal, disappointment, and grief at the loss of my primary work community. Anger and resentment were not far behind. It seemed the work I had given myself to for so many years was sufficiently devalued that organizational decision-makers had not even made an effort to reshape my position, an effort they clearly had made for some other staff.

I have written and taught on the practice of forgiveness. Here was a call to walk the talk. It helped to know that my boss had not come to his decision lightly and had given careful consideration to my family as a whole. It gave him no pleasure to do what he felt was required by economic necessity. It helped even more to recognize that God was, through the medium of his decision, opening a door to me that I had seriously considered walking through myself for nearly two years. I could see the fingerprints of God all over this new circumstance, and I understood that the divine design was far more significant and gracious than the designs of human institutions. But the larger positive picture did not erase my need to work through painful feelings until I could come to a certain peace of freely felt forgiveness. While I readily admit that the inner tussle occasionally resurfaces, it heartens me to trust that my former boss and I will retain the friendship that long preceded our work relationship.

Questions of self-examination in my life abound. How available do I choose to make myself to someone seeking counsel when I am feeling pressed by multiple deadlines and preparations? Am I more accepting of those little habits of my truly dear husband that have sometimes driven me to distraction over our nearly thirty years of marriage? Do I check that immediate judgment of a person I have already labeled and allow myself to see or hear afresh? When do I exercise restraint in speaking, where "delicious gossip" is only a hair's breadth from slander? Conversely, when is failing to speak my mind clearly a failure of responsibility or conscience in the economy of God's justice and peace? How often does the day's news propel me into intercessory prayer? What is the most faith-filled act in a perplexing or threatening situation? How do I spend my time and treasure? (A review of my checkbook or credit card statement can offer a sobering window onto where actual values contradict supposed values.) My response to such daily situations is the ultimate test of the authenticity and maturity of my spiritual life.

To the extent that I notice marks of the Spirit in my thoughts, feelings, and responses in these ordinary circumstances, I may gratefully acknowledge that God's mercy and grace have slowly been resculpting my naturally ego-driven life into something that more closely resembles the Christ life.

PERSPECTIVES AND PRACTICES AIDING MY SPIRITUAL LIFE

I remember how energized and delighted I was to discover that the early Christian tradition held up two "books of revelation": Scripture and creation. As a young child growing up in Thailand, I felt close to the deep mysteries of life and death through creation. I harbored secret fantasies of living a hermit's life in a rice paddy under a flame of the forest tree, spent hours contemplating sky and clouds from a backyard tree perch, and marveled over the wonders of every creature I could see, smell, and touch. One of my friends from that era recently commented that she was struck by my sensitivity to fragrances as a child. When I moved with my family to the United States at age eight, I discovered a very different world of seasons and senses. I began writing poetry largely focused on natural beauty, colors, and their connection to my growing awareness of divine providence.

Perhaps for this reason, creation-centered spiritualities feel deeply native to me. Eastern Orthodox and Celtic Christian sensibilities echo strains deep in my own soul. The sacramental understanding of the created order I encountered in the theology and spirituality of the Orthodox East was perhaps the most energizing perspective imparted to me in my seminary years. The concepts of "spirit-bearing matter" and of creation as a medium of mutual divine-human blessing held out to me a healing of the split between nature and grace that underlay my experience of a largely rational Protestant theology. I now understand creation as sacrament in the context both of the originating creative Word and of Christ's sacrificial act in which the fallen created order is redeemed and resacralized by the incarnation.

My spiritual practice includes walking in places of natural beauty where I can absorb the energy and peace of creation. I am frequently drawn to contemplation of the Creator while marveling over the gift of creatures. Indeed, the more I learn about the creatures with whom we share this planet, the more amazing, complex, and mysterious they appear to be—animated by the same life from which we draw our own, and revelatory of divine being in their own distinctive ways. Nothing so deeply refreshes me in body and soul as a good walk in the woods around our home, or along the river that runs below the limestone bluff on which our house is perched. Insights, prayers, or poems often emerge spontaneously from such moments. And I find myself forcefully drawn into intercession for God's creation as I become more aware of how pervasively human excess, including my own, continues to destroy and degrade the environment on which all life depends. The vulnerability of the natural order prompts me to a thousand confessions, both personally and on behalf of my kind. It also compels me to choose simpler ways of living to conserve natural resources.

Scripture, kin to creation as a "book of revelation," also has a central role in my spiritual practice. The "Good Book" is equally mysterious, at times impenetrable, and both reveals and conceals the deeper truths of God. I have found two forms of praying with Scripture especially meaningful. The most enlivening is an Ignatian-style contemplation of the Gospels in which I enter their scenes and characters with sensory imagination, noticing my affective response. My preference is to bring as informed an imagination as I can to the stories, which entails some preliminary study of word meanings and historical context. The ancient Gospel stories come alive for me in this way, shaping my prayer life and the guided imagery I often use in leading retreats. Discovering common human dynamics between people of two thousand years ago and our own day is sometimes comforting, sometimes discouraging. Cultural differences can be both interesting and instructive.

The second form of prayer shaped by Scripture that I use frequently is simple *lectio divina*, which often yields a "word" for my daily life. I read a short text, allowing a word or phrase to rise to awareness, then commit that phrase to memory and carry it into my day's consciousness and activity as much as possible. A few months ago, pondering Philippians 1:3–11, the phrase "with the compassion of Christ Jesus" caught my attention. My journal notes on that day observe the following: "How do I live my life in this manner? Not by railing inwardly at the deceit and 'idiocy' of the far Right in their frenzy to discredit Obama. Can I see the reactionary Right as 'sheep without a shepherd'—even though they would not think so?" When I find myself reacting with fierce emotion to political rhetoric—talking aloud at the kitchen table to invisible foes as if the ethers could somehow convey my reasoning and convince them of their ideological errors—I know that I still have much to learn about the Christ life from the Holy Spirit!

Contemplation in the more general sense comes naturally to me; reflecting on my life in light of the divine presence and my faith perspective has been one of my lifelong spiritual practices. Exploring a more specific form of contemplative prayer, one that leads my spirit to the edge of the unknowable and unnamable, has proved to be a more arduous process. I find centering prayer a helpful approach, in part because it encourages me gradually to detach from my addiction to practicality. One journal excerpt after a recent period of centering prayer acknowledged this: "My mind keeps angling for utility. Kyrie eleison—loose me from the need for even this prayer to be 'effective.' All my waking consciousness drives toward usefulness, efficiency, measurable purpose, and outcome. Lord have mercy." More than any other form I have discovered, this prayer invites me over and over simply to rest in God's love, enter nonproductive time (Sabbath), allow my spirit to accept whatever God chooses to do with it, and absorb wordless wonder.

Music has also been both a gift and a practice in my spiritual life from early years. My earliest musical memory, from age three, was of a beautiful organ piece played in my grandmother's church in Aplington, Iowa, while my family was on home leave from Thailand. Many years later I would learn the name of that deeply imprinted music: "Jesu, Joy of Man's Desiring." I learned to play piano, joined choirs, and sang familiar hymns as a form of prayer while driving long distances. Recently, I found myself affirming the perspective on song in worship penned by scholar-musician Don Saliers and his musician daughter Emily: "If the words and the musical forms are adequate to the mystery of being human—to suffering and joy—then the sound itself becomes a medium of formation and transformation."[4] Certain music has the power to express and touch my soul, to elicit prayer that cannot be put into words but carries both emotional resonance and interior commitment of will that are surely intelligible to God. Good music elicits from me a profound conviction

---

4. Don Saliers and Emily Saliers, *A Song to Sing, A Life to Live: Reflections on Music as Spiritual Practice* (San Francisco: Jossey-Bass, 2005), 36–37.

of spiritual reality and a powerful desire to respond with my whole being to the divine love expressed in such exquisite beauty. Returning to the piano after too many years of neglect, the music I make, even with rusty fingers, can carry me to places poignant with delight or sorrow. Such music, by virtue of its beauty, can only belong to the realm of God.

CULTIVATING HOLY HABITS OF HEART

As mentioned, my emphasis has shifted over the years from time-specific practices toward situation- or activity-based practices. Naturally, the years I spent in time-based ways of prayer and scriptural reflection allowed the Spirit to form me in a deeper relationship with God, the foundation of any spiritual life. All relationships require time and space to be nurtured. The growth of love takes time, as the flowering of intimacy takes time. Although the weight of my practice has shifted toward situational response, time-based practice continues to help me bring a more attentive spirit to my daily interactions and circumstances. It is precisely this integration of prayer with the whole of my life that I most desire and hope gradually to embody more fully.

The shape of my spirituality is now directed toward cultivating certain habits of mind and heart as intentionally as I can. By developing the habits of a whole heart, I try to practice the life in Christ already given me by baptism. Practicing the new life is my responsibility, although I can do nothing apart from the Holy Spirit whose grace I seek in prayer by faith. The habits of heart I desire to know in Christ include certain conscious intentions: recognizing my attitudes, assumptions, and ways of perceiving and responding to life; guarding my thoughts, especially pessimism, cynicism, and judgments against others; turning to wonder when I find myself in serious disagreement with someone; encouraging the good rather than carping over the bad; staying my mind on those things that are "honorable, just, pure, pleasing, and commendable" (Phil. 4:8); cultivating gratitude, even in adverse conditions—indeed, expressing thankfulness to God in advance as an expression of trust and faith; and choosing to turn from cursing to blessing, as my colleague Bob Morris taught me many years ago, describing his prayer practice in response to daily frustration.[5]

The cultivation of holy habits calls me above all to listen deeply to others, to creation, to my better angels, and to the astringently holy grace of the Spirit enlivening and recreating all things. When I have listened well, the call

5. See Robert Morris, "The Second Breath: Frustration as a Doorway to Daily Spiritual Practice," *Weavings* 13, no. 2 (March-April 1998), 37-45.

is to responsive obedience. Divine love is demanding beyond my capacity and generous beyond my prayers. My best hope in life and death is to lose my futile battle for security and control, surrendering freely and with deep relief to the love of God until "it is no longer I who live, but it is Christ who lives in me" (Gal. 2:20). That brief phrase of Paul's describes the state of being through which any of the faithful may see and feel and know life as God intends it. Should I be graced to reach such a union of self and source, perhaps I shall truly have something to say about the Christian spiritual life!

8

Behold the Beauty of the Lord

An Aesthetic Spirituality

MICHAEL JINKINS

One thing I asked of the Lord,
that will I seek after: to live in the house of the Lord
all the days of my life,
to behold the beauty of the Lord, and to inquire in his temple.

Psalm 27:4

PORTALS OF TRANSCENDENCE
AND THE TIES THAT BIND

The cotton fields that once lined the roads of East Texas between Lufkin and Dallas looked like row upon row of popcorn bouquets by late September, not long after which defoliating would begin, with crop dusters spraying and leaves dropping to expose the cotton for harvest. I remember vividly the stark beauty of the crops, the thick white tufts set in green foliage against a field of rich black earth.

One particular drive along these fields stands out from the many. My grandfather and I were in his car. I can't recall how old I was, but I couldn't have been much more than eight. We had delivered my grandmother to Dallas to stay a few weeks with her mother (Big Momma), and we were returning home. The little bronze Ford Falcon flew along the two-lane road, windows down. (This was the early 1960s BCA: before conditioned air.) On the front seat between my grandfather and me lay a sheaf of music with a rock on top to keep the pages from flying out the windows. There was music from all our favorite collections: *Stamps Baxter Quartet Specials*, *Happy Haven Radio Songs*,

Golden Steps, Songs by Vep Ellis. My grandfather was the choir director for the Redland Baptist Church (a nonpaid position) and a fine Scots-Irish tenor who never met an instrument he couldn't master in an afternoon.

The indelible imprint of that hot September day is of an old man and a boy singing their hearts out. I remember wind and love and song. I would have stayed in that front seat forever if I could have. I would have built three tabernacles there if I'd known how. It was the house of the Lord on wheels with a standard transmission.

I daresay that one reason the highly technical theological doctrine of divine *perichoresis*—which we inherited from fourth-century patristic Trinitarians like Athanasius, Basil of Caesarea, and Gregory of Nyssa—made perfect sense to me immediately, intuitively, when I confronted it as a seminary student dates from that memory. The singers, the grandfather and the child, and the music they sang bore a striking similarity (though the dissimilarities were striking too, of course) to the divine Giver, and the Gift, and the eternal act of Giving; the divine Lover, and the Beloved, and the Eternal Love; the Father, the Son, and the Holy Spirit.[1] Even Hans Urs von Balthasar's soaring tribute to the mystery of the triune God, which I would not learn about for another forty years, was fully prefigured for me on the front seat of that old Ford: "that what is absolutely primal is no statically self-contained and comprehensible reality, but one that exists solely in dispensing itself: a flowing wellspring with no holding trough beneath it . . . the pure act of self-pouring-forth."[2]

The church's doctrinal attempts to point toward the divine reality never seemed like theoretical abstractions to me but were lived approximations of the God in whom I had participated (though imperfectly and after a creaturely fashion, "through a mirror in a riddle") as a child.[3] After all, I had sung with my grandfather. I had known deep in the marrow of my bones something of

---

1. The nature of this *perichoretic* life of God is expressed beautifully in James Torrance's essay on the theology of John Duns Scotus in which he writes: "In the eternal Trinity, God loves himself and enjoys communion in himself. But he freely wills to share this life of love and communion, and so freely decides to create 'co-lovers' of his infinitely lovable nature (*condiligentes Deo*). It is this love which is revealed in Jesus Christ who is the Father's co-lover and who comes to draw us as co-lovers into that life of love. Perfect love longs for the beloved to be loved by others. The Father's love for the Son and the Son's love for the Father long for us to share in that love, and that love is shed abroad in our hearts by the Holy Spirit." James B. Torrance and Roland C. Walls, *John Duns Scotus in a Nutshell* (Edinburgh: Handsel Press, 1992), 8–9.
2. Hans Urs von Balthasar, *Credo: Meditations on the Apostles' Creed* (New York: Crossroad, 1990), 30.
3. The passage quoted is from 1 Corinthians 13, though the rendering of the text is from an English translation of Barth's take on it in *Church Dogmatics*, II/2, *The Doctrine of God*, ed. G. W. Bromiley and T. F. Torrance, trans. G. W. Bromiley et al. (Edinburgh: T. & T. Clark, 1957), 608.

the truth of that life and love and music that is the Spirit shared by the Father and the Son caught up in adoration, joy, and mutual love.[4]

Years later, when I performed in jazz, blues, and rock groups in high school and college, I discovered the deep magic of improvisation. Playing with small bands of musicians who created something among ourselves at once practiced, disciplined, and utterly new and unexpected every time we performed, it was as though I was again tapping into this reality at the heart of creation—this otherness, beauty, and holiness, this something beyond things woven into life by a prodigiously talented God who enjoys sharing with us the music essential to creation's nature. My musical tastes expanded considerably beyond Vep Ellis and the Stamps Quartets to Miles Davis, Henry Purcell, Wolfgang Amadeus Mozart, Duke Ellington, Carl Orff, and Igor Stravinsky, but the love, life, and spirit remained essentially the same. In many ways I have always been a child trying from time to time to tap into the perichoretic wonder that I experienced while singing harmony with my grandfather. Recently it occurred to me that my lifelong spiritual pilgrimage is also an aesthetic journey. Rooted in various places and in many relationships, always it has remained, whether acknowledged at the time or not, a quest to behold the beauty of the Lord.

My grandfather, Bonnie Corley Fenley, died suddenly when I was twelve and he was sixty-three. Abruptly, I fell away from church and remained infrequent in attendance until I was halfway through high school, when a fellow musician in our school's jazz ensemble approached me with a proposition. We had just finished a stage band rehearsal for an upcoming performance, and I had just "taken a couple of rides" (code for improvised solos) on the trombone. George was our drummer. He was an extraordinary talent who went on to become an accomplished professional studio and touring musician. He was also a devout Christian. George told me he liked the way I played and asked if I would be willing to join the backup band for his church's huge youth choir. I told him that I might, but I didn't have any interest in coming to church. He said that I would only have to come to church when they were performing; otherwise, I could just attend rehearsals.

Every time I tell this story I am reminded of George Herbert's poem in which he describes God's "Fine nets and stratagems to catch us in / Bibles laid open, millions of surprises / Blessings beforehand, tyes of gratefulnesse / The sound of glorie ringing in our eares."[5] Of course, I didn't just attend rehearsals. I made friends, came to worship, and was ensnared by webs of grace.

---

4. Those who wish to explore more fully the relationship of theology to the arts will find the following studies by Jeremy Begbie instructive: *Voicing Creation's Praise* (Edinburgh: T. & T. Clark, 1991); and *Theology, Music, and Time* (Cambridge: Cambridge University Press, 2000).

5. George Herbert, "Sinne," in *A Choice of George Herbert's Verse*, ed. R. S. Thomas (London: Faber & Faber, 1967), 25.

Music brought me back to church. Friendships sealed the deal. And within a year of returning to church I began to sense a call to ordained ministry. This call changed my life's direction. Or perhaps it only returned my life to the direction God intended from the time when my grandfather and I drove past those fields of cotton singing the gospel hymn "What a Wonderful Exchange."

I did not know then (and I don't know if the author of that gospel anthem knew at all) of the resonance of that term "wonderful exchange" (Lat. *mirifica commutatio*). Its roots trace to Irenaeus, who taught that the Son of God became the Son of Man so that we children of humanity might become fully and forever children of God. All I knew was that my grandfather with whom I sang loved me and I loved him, and we were caught up in singing like there was no tomorrow. And the song we sang together was somehow greater and sweeter than anything we could have sung alone. The act of singing together felt so right, so real, as though a cord ran through our hearts connecting us to the love at the heart of being itself.

Sometimes my memories skip like a stone over the past, and I remember an evening when our youth choir played and sang for church campers on the banks of the Frio River in the Texas Hill Country. I recall the exultation, pure and sublime, that I experienced when playing piano for them. I recall the afternoon on a visit home from college, sitting in a darkened room playing blues guitar with my friend Ben, just before he joined the Navy, and trading the melody back and forth in a musical conversation, and I realize that there is no way under heaven to express the deep rightness I sensed in that music. It was as though we were tapping into something, some rhythm, some harmony or melodic line at the core of creation, something perfect and real and good. The stone skips across a surface of something deeper than I can imagine, and it is the weight of the depth below that makes the stone stay airborne before it takes its final plunge and disappears.

Perhaps it is because my spiritual journey began in music that reverence and awe for God's holiness has been its touchstone. Music is a doorway to transcendence; the mystery of music remains shrouded to me to this day. I do not know where the music comes from. Certainly when I play a piano it does not seem to come from within me; it seems to be waiting for me in the keyboard of the piano itself or in the air between me and another musician. Music was the first art to capture my imagination, to transport me beyond myself, to confront me with the intractability of transcendence, the otherness that remains tenaciously and stubbornly beyond us. Other portals to transcendence opened in time, especially through the visual arts, through photography and painting, through writing and reading, but music remained for me the original means of grace.

When I became an adult, the aesthetic realm took on these additional dimensions, and gradually I realized that the transcendence we experience aesthetically is but a gesture toward that unutterable transcendence of a holy God beyond all we know. There is, I believe, resonance, but also discontinuity; analogy, but never simply correspondence.

We can sense the shuffle of hushed tones, hear footsteps tapping on stone floors, see motes drifting in the silted air through light refracted by ancient glass. We can almost feel the whispers of tongues half-silenced conveyed in the deep, muted tones and shadows of J. M. W. Turner's paintings of Durham Cathedral. But as lively and inspiring as Turner's paintings are, his art falls short and provides only a gesture toward the divine reality of the God who breathes through that holy place where saints lie buried but remain alive in the presence of Christ and where God still speaks to those who still listen. Even when the organ shakes the beams of that cathedral and one is tempted to compare the way the music rends the air to the presence of God, one knows in one's soul that the comparison is pale and weak and as thin as water. The soaring arches and soaring music utter some small words about that which defies speech and demands silence.

THE CRYPT BENEATH THE CATHEDRAL

My wife, Deborah, and I had promised ourselves many years ago that we would return to the Argyll coast of western Scotland and the Valley of Kilmartin someday. We promised ourselves that when we returned we would walk the length of the valley from end to end. Thus, we found ourselves making our way up the valley one day last summer. Something more than curiosity, something deeper than intellectual interest, drew us there. We are not alone in being drawn to this valley. It is one of Almighty God's grandest artistic accomplishments. People have been drawn there over the course of thousands of years to live, to worship, and to be in the presence of a breathtaking spiritual landscape embellishing God's works in nature.

Imagine, if you will, standing on the hill beside the modern village church. Taller hills rise up on every side, forming an extravagantly lush glen several miles long. The present church was built in 1836. It replaced previous churches dating from 1798 and 1601. But the site was used for Christian worship long before these latter-day structures were built. The Christian burial ground surrounding the church dates from the medieval period. At the entrance to the cemetery stands a Celtic cross, carved in the ninth or tenth century, marking the place where Christian Celtic priests preached even earlier. Hidden in the hills above the valley are beehive cells of native stone

where these Celtic priests and monks and their predecessors had dwelt since
St. Brendan, St. Columba, and their followers brought Christianity from Ire-
land to Scotland in the sixth century. But even these artifacts, dating back at
least a thousand years, are Johnny-latecomers by comparison to what lies in
the valley at your feet.

Stretching for miles along the valley floor are sacred sites, the origins of
which stretch back into prehistory. Burial cairns, monumental stones, and
earthworks—some, incredibly, older than the pyramids of Egypt, older even
than Stonehenge—bear eloquent and enduring testimony to the faith of persons who worshiped in this place for some eight thousand years and through
at least three discrete religions. You can walk the entire length of this valley,
make your way among the cairns and henges older than remembered time,
listen to the wind playing upon the grassy fields recovered long ago from
bogs, hear the dark, peaty waters sizzling over rocks and the bees stirring
about their fertile work, and wonder what it means to worship God in a village church surrounded by these ancient witnesses of stone.

If one ever wonders what in God's name Rudolf Otto was trying to say
when he spoke of the "numinous" and of the "*mysterium tremendum*," when
he stuttered and sputtered and poked at that feeling of awe and reverence
"sweeping like a gentle tide, pervading the mind with tranquil mood of deepest worship," or that "attitude of the soul" which is "thrillingly vibrant and
resonant," or of those eruptions from deep in the spirit "in the presence of
that which is a mystery inexpressible," then all one needs to do is to walk
among these stones of Kilmartin as the darkness gathers about and unremem-
bered generations bear eloquent though mute testimony to the limitations
of our little world in the name of the God who resists all names and beside
whom even our most ancient cairns are trifling innovations.[6]

The holy places we stand in today were consecrated long ago by people
who do not share our ways of faith. This historical fact serves as a parable of
the spirit, as I was recently reminded by a book I had not read in a decade
or more.

When I was a young minister, I came across C. G. Jung's lectures on
analytical psychology. I have always felt that Jung was more interesting if he
was considered a philosopher of religion rather than a psychologist. Perhaps
he was a better spiritual pilgrim than either a philosopher or a psychologist.
He certainly was not a scientist in the strictest sense. One particular lecture
confirmed this judgment for me and has contributed to my own lifelong
spiritual quest.

6. Rudolf Otto, *The Idea of the Holy*, trans. John W. Harvey (New York: Oxford University Press, 1923), 12–13.

In the course of interpreting a dream, Jung observes that the great cathedrals of Europe express "the Christian philosophy or *Weltanschauung* of the Middle Ages" and that they do so in a surprising manner. Beneath every great European cathedral, Jung says, lies a crypt. In many cases, these crypts originated as pagan worship sites centuries before they were claimed for Christian usage. He writes: "The crypt at Chartres was previously an old sanctuary with a well, where the worship of a virgin was celebrated—not of the Virgin Mary, as is done now— but of a Celtic goddess. Under every Christian church of the Middle Ages there is a secret place where in old times the mysteries were celebrated."[7]

This passage may also confirm the judgment that Jung was not much of a historian. I don't think many church historians would agree with that last sentence. On a spiritual level, however, he is right. Beneath every Christian church there is a secret place, a cryptic place, full of pagan mysteries—a place where we encounter the God who is infinitely larger than our creeds, the God who speaks not only through prophets and apostles and saints but also through artists, like the ones who crafted the sacred landscape of Kilmartin and beautifully embellished their stones. This fact does not detract from the legitimacy of the Christian identity of the church, but it does wonderfully complicate this identity.

As a Christian theologian of the Reformed tradition, I am both aware of and appreciative of Karl Barth's understanding of religion as a human endeavor, particularly bearing in mind his historical context and the perils he faced. Barth famously described religion as "unbelief," calling it "the one great concern of godless [humanity]."[8] Inasmuch as religion is understood as a system of rituals and beliefs used by humanity to justify themselves with reference to God, I would agree with Barth.

Religion has always been a human endeavor, just as surely as theology and the sciences and art. All that we make and do and think and feel are human endeavors. Religion has been plagued by the human inclination to create gods in our own image, and idolatry (including idolatry that emerges among Christians) must be resisted in the name of the God who is not reducible to our own convenience or manipulation or utility. However, if I take seriously the witness of prophets, apostles, saints, *and* artists, and if I believe with them that God is actively engaged in a creation that owes its origin and continued existence to God's present grace and power, and that God created us in God's image to participate in God's creative activity, then I cannot categorically dismiss the human sense of awe in the presence of the holy that pervades these

7. C. G. Jung, *Analytical Psychology: Its Theory and Practice: The Tavistock Lectures* (New York: Vintage/Random House, 1968), 128–29.

8. Karl Barth, *Church Dogmatics*, I/2, *The Doctrine of the Word of God*, ed. G. W. Bromiley and T. F. Torrance (Edinburgh: T. & T. Clark, 1956), 299–300.

places where we worship—in the shadow of others whose worship of God
predates our own—and where we are invited to enjoy and invest in God's
artistry through aesthetic means.[9]

Walking in the vale of Kilmartin, one is humbled by the monumental
handiwork of ancient others testifying to their engagements with the holy, the
same holy whom we believe dwelt among us in Jesus Christ, to whom we bear
testimony in the village church on the hill. Descending steep, dark steps into
a crypt beneath a cathedral, stepping down into a place of mystery shared over
time by worshipers pagan and Christian, one need not necessarily fall onto
the rocks of a lowest-common-denominator relativism, but, on the contrary,
one may fall into the grasp of the holy who has awed and given comfort to
humanity for millennia. By the same token, emerging from a crypt, stepping
up into the startling light flooding through stained- or clear-glass windows,
into the blinding glare of the beauty produced by the human artistry that
confronts us as a sign and seal of God's glory, we are invited aesthetically
to surrender ourselves to the holy who, in darkness and in light, takes our
breath away, stirs our souls, and turns our hearts to ice. There is harmony and
dissonance at play all around us, drawing us deep into relationship with the
God who is the Ground of Being, whose inner life as Trinity gives rise to all
creation, to all we are and all we make.[10]

CHRIST-HAUNTED PLACES

G. K. Chesterton once observed that the genius of Christianity lies in part in
its peculiar brand of syncretism. Christianity has the ability to bring together
the faith of Israel and the paganism of the ancient classical world. Christianity's faith is syncretistic in order to be fully catholic. Chesterton's appreciation for the mystery of faith and the sanity of reverence comes through when
he writes: "Mysticism keeps men sane. As long as you have mystery you have
health; when you destroy mystery you create morbidity. The ordinary man
has always been sane because the ordinary man has always been a mystic. He
has permitted the twilight. He has always had one foot in earth and the other
in fairyland. He has always left himself free to doubt his gods; but (unlike the
agnostic of today) free also to believe in them."[11]

9. Paul Woodruff, *Reverence* (New York: Oxford University Press, 2001), 11.
10. See Bernard McGinn, *The Mystical Thought of Meister Eckhart: The Man from Whom God Hid Nothing* (New York: Herder & Herder, 2001). McGinn's discussion of the way in which Meister Eckhart made use of the term *grunt*, and the relationship of this German term to the Latin *principium*, is especially illuminating in this context (42–43).
11. G. K. Chesterton, *Orthodoxy* (London: John Lane, The Bodley Head, 1908), 46–47.

Chesterton has been on my mind recently, especially as I have read anew the writings of his latter-day fellow Roman Catholic, Flannery O'Connor, in light of a new biography about her.[12] Perhaps it seems a long way from Chesterton's fairyland to O'Connor's gothic and Christ-haunted American South. But these regions lie next to one another on the aesthetic map of the Spirit.

O'Connor's art was a direct extension of her faith. Her exaggerated and grotesque characters, like Hazel Motes of *Wise Blood*, a mad atheistic evangelist driven to preach against Christ, were necessary, O'Connor believed, to shock her contemporaries into seeing themselves as in need of redemption (not mere refurbishment or renewal) and thus into hearing the gospel of Jesus Christ.[13] O'Connor's artistry liberates her from what William Blake described as "the dull round," the abrogation of transcendence that afflicts conventional perception and restrains many people from ever inquiring beneath the surface of life.[14] Brad Gooch traces the development of O'Connor's understanding of her theological mission as a novelist, observing that in a talk she gave at Eastern High School in Lansing, Michigan, she said that "modern writers must often tell 'perverse' stories to 'shock' a morally blind world." Gooch quotes her conclusion: "It requires considerable courage not to turn away from the story-teller."[15]

O'Connor escorts us into the realm of holiness via the portal of profound weirdness, strangeness, delinquency, perversion, cruelty, and violence, through situations that make us wince and our skin crawl, as though to confirm the Augustinian message of faithful *agnosis*: *If you think you've conceived of*

12. Brad Gooch, *Flannery: A Life of Flannery O'Connor* (New York: Little, Brown and Company, 2009).

13. Flannery O'Connor, *Mystery and Manners: Occasional Prose*, ed. Sally and Robert Fitzgerald (New York: Farrar, Straus & Giroux, 1969), 36-50, 154-68. Hazel Motes, the central character of O'Connor's novel *Wise Blood*, in one sermon says, "Well, I preach the Church Without Christ. I'm member and preacher to that church where the blind don't see and the lame don't walk and what's dead stays that way. Ask me about that church and I'll tell you it's the church that the blood of Jesus don't foul with redemption." Flannery O'Connor, *Wise Blood*, 2nd ed. (New York: Farrar, Straus & Giroux, 1962), 105. Motes's own road to redemption follows the ascetic path of a medieval mystic, a course of action soundly criticized by his landlady who, after observing the barbed wire the self-blinded Motes has wrapped around him, asks, "What do you do these things for? It's not natural. . . . It's not normal. It's like one of them gory stories, it's something people have quit doing—like boiling in oil or being a saint or walling up cats" (224).

14. Indeed, O'Connor's artistic project is reminiscent of Blake's "prophetic" writings in which the poet tried to teach people how to perceive the divine vision in their midst. William Blake, *Milton*, ed. Kay Parkhurst Easson and Roger R. Easson (New York: Random House, 1978), 170. A contemporary poet who took these lessons to heart but found a way to express them in a much more accessible form is Jane Kenyon. She uses a passage from William Maxwell as the epigraph for her volume of poems *Let Evening Come*: "So strange, life is. Why people do not go around in a continual state of surprise is beyond me." Kenyon, it should be noted, seems (like Blake and O'Connor) to go around not merely in a state of surprise but of awe. Jane Kenyon, *Let Evening Come* (St. Paul: Graywolf Press, 1990), 1.

15. Brad Gooch, *Flannery: A Life of Flannery O'Connor* (New York: Little, Brown & Co., 2009), 274–75.

God, think again! You're not even in the suburbs of the outskirts of the City of God in your highest and holiest thoughts. God lies on the other side of all that you can humanly conceive.

Reading a Flannery O'Connor novel or short story and discerning in the cruel gaps an aching emptiness, a void that cries out for a corresponding grace, a yearning for divine redemption larger even than the original sin, is not unlike finding yourself flat-footed in the presence of Jasper Johns's monumental gray crosshatch painting *Between the Clock and the Bed* (1982–1983) and realizing with a shock of amazement that these abstracted lines gesture beyond themselves to Edvard Munch's dark, melancholic deathbed scene of the same title (1940–1942) and through and beyond Munch's painting to a human longing for tenderness, a consciousness of grief and sorrow, that is itself a witness-bearing to love.[16]

Art in its fullness often reveals humanity in its emptiness. But this is potentially redemptive, because truth telling, even when the truth is painful, serves God's ends. Art can serve as a refiner's fire, to draw upon a biblical image. Whether we are speaking of Mark Rothko's expanse of black upon black that illuminates the Rothko chapel and dares the viewer to contemplate the inconceivable abyss yawning at the boundaries of human existence, or of the haunting second movement, "Lento E Largo—Tranquillisimo," of Górecki's Symphony no. 3, the text for which was drawn from a prayer scratched on the wall of a cell in the basement of the Gestapo headquarters in Zakopane, Poland, art has the power to usher us into experiences of self-transcendence often by removing from us every false prop that keeps reality at bay. As poet Mark Jarman writes in the opening and closing lines of his stark and beautiful poem "Epistle," "We want the operation because we want the cure. . . . / Thus God performs his surgery, closing and opening simultaneously, always with new reasons to go in."[17]

ARETHA FRANKLIN AND AN OLD PAGAN PRIEST

A few years ago, my daughter Jessica and I were making our own way across another swath of Texas. We were traveling from Austin to East Texas to sit at my grandmother's bedside as she lay dying. As we rode along, more than thirty years after my grandfather's death, my thoughts naturally returned

---

16. See James Rondeau and Douglas Druick, *Jasper Johns: Gray* (New Haven, CT: Yale University Press, 2007), 59–61. This book served as the catalog for the "Jasper Johns Gray" exhibition at the Metropolitan Museum of Art in New York, February 5–May 4, 2008.

17. Mark Jarman, "Epistle," in *The Best American Poetry, 2000,* ed. Rita Dove (New York: Scribner Poetry, 2000), 93–94.

to that other road, traveled long ago between Dallas and Lufkin, and to my grandfather and me singing our songs of Zion. So much was similar, yet so much had changed.

Jessica and I laughed and told each other stories, some of them irreverent, and we sang our hearts out too. We did not sing Stamps Baxter gospel music, but Aretha Franklin. Yet the resonance with those earlier songs was unmistakable. Decades passed in the blink of an eye. And as we sang "You Make Me Feel (Like a Natural Woman)," the love that held us together was as genuinely perichoretic as the love my grandfather and I knew singing of Christ's "Wonderful Exchange."

The thing that made those moments with my grandfather "holy" was not the religious content of the songs we sang, but the spirit of love in which we sang them. And that was the same spirit suffusing the songs that Jessica and I sang. Karl Barth's critique of "religion" serves as a reminder that faith is not concerned with the defense of a cult, but the exploration of a reality. And so we are liberated to hear the Word of God who speaks in every time, in every place, in every tongue, by all appropriate means. As von Balthasar has written in the first volume of his magisterial work *The Glory of the Lord: A Theological Aesthetics*, "God's truth is, indeed, great enough to allow an infinity of approaches and entryways. And it is also free enough subsequently to expand the horizons of one who has chosen too narrow a starting point and to help him to his feet."[18] The beauty of the Lord comes to us in many forms, often surprising us with the awareness of the holy.[19]

The old pagan priest in C. S. Lewis's novel *Till We Have Faces* has been my teacher in this matter for at least twenty years. The old priest says that if we want to understand "holy things" we must abandon the rationalism of a philosophy that imagines "the gods" can be apprehended "clearly," as though they are "no more than letters written in a book." Speaking to his sovereign, the old priest continues: "I, King, have dealt with the gods for three generations of men, and I know that they dazzle our eyes and flow in and out of one another like eddies on a river, and nothing that is said clearly can be said truly about them. Holy places are dark places. It is life and strength, not knowledge and words, that we get in them. Holy wisdom is not clear and thin like water, but thick and dark like blood."[20]

18. Hans Urs von Balthasar, *The Glory of the Lord: A Theological Aesthetics*, vol. 1, *Seeing the Form*, ed. Joseph Fessio and John Riches, trans. Erasmo Leiva-Merikakis (San Francisco: Ignatius Press, 1982), 17.

19. Perhaps no one has explored this theological idea more profoundly than Rowan Williams, "Trinity and Pluralism," in *On Christian Theology* (Oxford: Blackwell Publishers, 2000), 167–80; and Kathryn Tanner, *Theories of Culture: A New Agenda for Theology* (Minneapolis: Fortress Press, 1997), 120–75.

20. C. S. Lewis, *Till We Have Faces: A Myth Retold* (Glasgow: Collins, 1956), 58.

In a time when so many Christians seem to equate faithfulness with certainty and are only too eager to tell everyone, including God, exactly what God is like, what God cares about, and what God wants—in a time when some even assume that their spiritual experiences and religious understandings equate to God[21]—it is refreshing to remember the warning of the old pagan priest about the thick, dark, bloody character of holiness. The priest reminds us of St. Augustine who prays to God, "So too let him rejoice and delight in finding you who are beyond discovery rather than fail to find you by supposing you to be discoverable."[22]

The intimations of transcendence that haunt our memories echo to this day, pointing beyond all that we can know, all that we can yearn and hope for, beyond even the most sublime beauty we have ever beheld to the beauty of the Lord, the beauty of God's holiness, the holiness that renders us human and humble and whole.

---

21. Paul Woodruff equates this attitude with hubris, which represents the very opposite of reverence. He observes that it is possible for people, in the name of "faith" to act "against reverence": "They are human beings, and yet they suppose they know the mind of God. . . . Reverence requires us to maintain a modest sense of the difference between human and divine." Woodruff, *Reverence*, 18–19.

22. St. Augustine, *Confessions*, trans. Henry Chadwick (Oxford: Oxford University Press, 1991), 8.

9

The Spiritual Life with the Help of Favorite Poets

ELIZABETH LIEBERT, SNJM

When I was a child, I was frequently surprised by Holy Mystery, as I suspect many children are. Sometimes as I would steal into the twilight of my cavernous parish church and see the tabernacle light flickering way up in front, I would know with absolute certainty that I was in the presence of Mystery. The liturgy, with its ever changing readings, colors, and moods, would sometimes crack open, and I would be face-to-face with the mystery that God was present in this ancient ritual. The soft quietness of the host on my tongue convinced me that God was closer to me than I was to myself. But try as I might, I could not find adequate words to express the Mystery. I still cannot. Everything I say to describe these encounters is flat and lifeless compared to the encounter itself. Yet I too experience Emily Dickinson's reality. She speaks of God as a mystery as deep as the sea, for whom the more she searches the more she finds, and the more she finds the more she is driven to search.[1]

After entering the religious congregation to which I belong, receiving my first professional education as a teacher, and surviving a baptism of fire teaching junior high science and math, I was offered the opportunity to further my education. I headed off, I realize now, to probe the Holy Mystery and the words we use to describe our encounters with it. In the midst of my doctoral studies, I found myself still seeking the Mystery and still unable to express the reality in my poor words, now more complicated and complex and abstract and accompanied by even more words as a result of all the study. The words of poet Rainer Maria Rilke addressed to "neighbor God" accompanied me during those years:

---

1. See Emily Dickinson, *Dialogues*, chapter 167, cited in Joan M. McCarthy, CSJ, ed., *Poetry to Accompany the Spiritual Exercises of St. Ignatius*, privately printed, November 2009.

77

Always I hearken. Give but a small sign.
I am quite near.

Between us there is but a narrow wall,
and by sheer chance; for it would take
merely a call from your lips or from mine
to break it down,
and that without a sound.

The wall is builded of your images.

They stand before you hiding you like names.[2]

Though I've focused my ministry as a spiritual director around attending to how people speak about God and helping them to bring these encounters to speech, I still find that my own attempts at speaking leave dust in my mouth. So every year when I head off for my own retreat, I find tucked into my bag alongside my Bible and journal a book of poetry. Hopkins, Levertov, Oliver, Herbert, Dickinson, Rilke, Neruda, and my all-time favorite, the Psalms—they've all had turns at helping me see the Mystery permeating my life and bringing it into speech.

It so happened that the time I had set aside to write on the spiritual life immediately followed my latest poetry-infused retreat. The poets who had been helping me express my own spiritual life simply kept speaking, offering me words and images to describe that elusive reality. The spiritual life is, after all, about responding to Holy Mystery, isn't it?

WHAT IS SPIRITUALITY AND THE SPIRITUAL LIFE?

A Supreme Court justice is reputed to have said about pornography, "I may not be able to define it, but I sure know it when I see it." Concerning spirituality and the spiritual life, I have learned that we neither know how to define it nor always know it when we see it.

Consider the following vignettes, all describing a person of similar gender, age, and circumstances. Which of them exhibits a spiritual life? Any of them? All of them? How does one make such an assessment anyhow?

---

2. Rainer Maria Rilke, "You, Neighbor God," in *Poems from the Book of Hours*, trans. Babette Deutsch (New York: New Directions, 1941), cited in Peter Coughlan, Ronald C. D. Jasper, and Theresa Rodrigues, OSB, eds., *A Christian's Prayer Book: Psalms, Poems, and Prayers for the Church's Year* (Chicago: Franciscan Herald Press, n.d.), 174.

- A young woman, barely eighteen, puts aside her stylish clothes for a long black dress and veil, says good-bye to her parents, and walks through the cloister door. (This could have been me, except my clothes were never stylish!)
- A young woman, barely eighteen, leaves the convent for the world, taking off her long black postulant dress and slipping into a skirt and blouse and flats. She walks out through the cloister doors into the rest of her life.
- A young woman, barely eighteen, says goodbye to her high school friends and activities, leaves home for college, and jumps headlong into sorority rush, excited to finally be on her own.
- A young woman, barely eighteen, shops for a dress for her August wedding to her junior high sweetheart.
- A young woman, barely eighteen, hugs her parents at the gate and boards a plane for Guatemala, where she plans to spend a year volunteering at an orphanage and seeing what life is like in another part of the world.

Do we know the spiritual life when we see it?

For a Christian, the first clue to the meaning of the term "spirituality" is found in Paul's First Letter to the Corinthians:

> For what human being knows what is truly human except the human spirit that is within? So also no one comprehends what is truly God's except the Spirit of God. Now we have received not the spirit of the world, but the Spirit that is from God, so that we may understand the gifts bestowed on us by God. And we speak of these things in words not taught by human wisdom but taught by the Spirit, interpreting spiritual things to those who are spiritual. (1 Cor. 2:11–13)

Here Paul uses the adjective "spiritual" to describe the things of the Spirit of God. Whatever else it has come to mean, "spiritual" at least means, "life lived in the power of the Holy Spirit."

Yet it is clear that the Holy Spirit works differently in different parts of creation, enabling each part to fulfill its proper place. Stars, so tiny from our vantage point, are constantly being born, burning, and becoming extinct in the vast reaches of the universe. Rocks come in various types and densities and properties. Fish, in their astonishing variety, inhabit every corner of the oceans and the smallest mountain freshets. Human beings, too, are embedded deeply in creation. They—we—bring to the universe an ability to reflect, undetected (as yet, anyhow) in any other being in the universe. What of human beings?

> I see your handiwork in the heavens:
> the moon and the stars you set in place.
> What is humankind that you remember them,
> the human race that you care for them?

You treat them like gods, dressing them in glory and splendor.
You give them charge of the earth, laying all at their feet.
                                        (Ps. 8:4–7 ICEL)

Listen to another voice, the nineteenth-century Jesuit Gerard Manley
Hopkins:

> The sun and the stars shining glorify God. They stand where he placed
> them, they move where he bid them. "The heavens tell the glory of
> God." They glorify God, *but they do not know it.* The birds sing to him,
> the thunder speaks of his terror, the lion is like his strength, the sea
> is like his greatness, the honey like his sweetness; they are something
> like him, they make him known, they tell of him, they give him glory,
> but they do not know they do, they do not know him, they never can,
> they are brute things that only think of food or think of nothing. This
> then is poor praise, faint reverence, slight service, dull glory. Never-
> theless, what they can *they always do.*[3]

We could say, especially if we want to give more luster to creation's praise
than Hopkins does in this particular lecture,[4] that though there is a spirituality of each part of creation, it is humans who can "have a spiritual life."
    Without turning ourselves into knots, it is a straightforward move from
"spirituality" to "spiritual life," understanding the latter, as Paul suggests, as
a life lived in the power of the Spirit. Humans alone may use their reflexivity
and their free will to choose a life in harmony with or in divergence from the
Holy Spirit. Hopkins continues: "But man can know God, *can mean to give
him glory.* This, then, was why he was made, to give God glory and to mean to
give it; to praise God freely, willingly to reverence him, gladly to serve him.
Man was made to give, and was meant to give, God glory."[5]
    Here, then, is my working definition of the spiritual life: *a life intention-
ally lived in harmony with the inspiration of the Spirit of God.* However, things
get complicated very quickly! Could each of those eighteen-year-old women
intentionally be following the lead of the Holy Spirit? How would we know?
Who is the Holy Spirit? How do we recognize the inspirations of this Holy
Spirit? What of children, who cannot (yet) exercise intentionality? Do they
not have a spiritual life? Spirituality has to quickly enter the realm of theology
to answer such questions. But let's stay with the poet:

---

3. "Principle or Foundation," in *Gerard Manley Hopkins*, ed. Catherine Phillips (Oxford:
Oxford University Press, 1986), 291.
    4. Hopkins, in fact, has a high view of God's presence in creation—for example, "there lives the
dearest freshness deep down things" from "God's Grandeur." See *Gerard Manley Hopkins*, 128.
    5. "Principle or Foundation," 291.

Each mortal thing does one thing and the same;
Deals out that being indoors each one dwells;
Selves—goes itself; myself it speaks and spells,
Crying *What I do is me: for that I came.*

I say more: the just man justices;
Keeps grace: that keeps all his goings graces;
Acts in Gods' eye what in God's eye he is—
    Christ. . . .[6]

This section of another famous Hopkins poem suggests that we serve God by being what we are most deeply created to be, and that we live out God's creative impulse as we become more and more bound to the image of Christ—and that this process is the work of God's Holy Spirit. The spiritual life, to the degree that it is intentional, becomes so first by the creative impulse of the Spirit of God. The spiritual life, then, is *responsive intentionality* to do and be as deeply as possible who God has created us to be.

The Celtic tradition developed this intentionality to a high degree. Every common activity became the occasion for encounter with God and a moment for prayer. The *Carmina Gadelica*, a compilation of oral interviews conducted by Alexander Campbell in northern Scotland in the last half of the nineteenth century, reveals the intention to be intimately connected to God in every smallest action. Among the hundreds of examples of prayers and blessings, we can find not only morning and night prayers but also farming prayers (prayers for sowing, reaping, milking, shearing, driving cows to and from pasture), household prayers (prayers for kindling and "shmooring" or putting the fire to sleep, letting down milk, milking, churning, spinning, warping the loom, and grace before and thanks after meals), prayers for journeys, especially dangerous sea voyages, prayers for birth and death, prayers for healing and protection against every sort of evil. Prayers are often for loved ones as well and blessings abound.[7]

We still have those eighteen-year-old women, and for that matter, eighteen-month-old toddlers, to consider. Do they have a spiritual life? Pondering this question suggests another characteristic of the spiritual life: that it is developmental in nature.

The eighteen-month-old cannot be intentional in the sense of the eighteen-year-old, nor can either of them be intentional in the same sense that

---

6. "As Kingfishers Catch Fire," in *Gerard Manley Hopkins*, 129.
7. *Carmina Gadelica: Hymns and Incantations with Illustrative Notes on Words, Rites and Customs, Dying and Obsolete*, comp. and trans. Alexander Carmichael (Edinburgh: Floris Books, 1994). See also *The Celtic Vision: Prayers, Blessings, Songs and Invocations from the Gaelic Tradition* (Liguori, MO: Liguori/Triumph, 2001) for selections from the *Carmina Gadelica* collected by headings and introduced by Esther deWaal.

someone such as Dietrich Bonhoeffer, Dorothy Day, or Simone Weil were. Bonhoeffer carefully weighed the risks and imperatives of his choices to become involved in a plot to assassinate Hitler and became convinced that it was his duty.[8] Dorothy Day methodically took steps to enter the Catholic Church once she became convinced God was calling her to do so. Simone Weil resolutely refused to enter the same church, convinced God was calling her to remain on its edges. Clearly humans develop biologically and psychologically, and express their spiritual lives within the constraints of their human developmental potential and the constraints and opportunities that life deals them. Rilke, writing at the turn of the twentieth century, mused:

> First, childhood, no limits, no renunciations,
> no goals. Such unthinking joy.
> Then abruptly terror, schoolrooms, boundaries, captivity,
> and a plunge into temptations and deep loss.[9]

Catechists and parents of developmentally impaired children and adults know that the spiritual life of these human beings is no less real or valuable than the spiritual lives of others without such developmental challenges and that, in fact, the spiritual lives of such persons may be more vivid and intense. Ordinarily, however, the spiritual life changes in tandem with psychological development, with each developmental phase of life bringing a new set of spiritual challenges. As we grow as persons, our spiritual lives have the potential to become correspondingly more expansive. But the spiritual life is developmental in another sense as well. There is a developmental trajectory in the way God reveals God's self to individuals, a progression in the relationship that marks the spiritual life intentionally pursued. The history of Christian spirituality is replete with metaphors and descriptions for how the relationship with God might progress: Teresa of Ávila's interior castle, John of the Cross's dark nights of the soul, Ignatius of Loyola's three degrees of humility, Francis de Sales's devout life, and John Bunyan's description of Christian's journey, to name but a few. The spiritual life is developmental in both of these senses.

---

8. Bonhoeffer did not see his participation in the plot to assassinate Hitler as "God's call" but as his duty, for which he would cast himself on God's mercy. Bonhoeffer wrote of his decision: "The man who acts out of free responsibility is justified before others by dire necessity; before himself he is acquitted by his conscience, but before God he hopes only for grace." Dietrich Bonhoeffer, *Ethics*, ed. Clifford Green, trans. Reinhard Krauss et al. (Minneapolis: Fortress Press, 2005), 283.

9. "Imaginary Biography," in *Selected Poems of Rainer Maria Rilke: A Translation from the German and Commentary by Robert Bly* (New York: Harper & Row, 1981), 171.

Not only is the Christian spiritual life developmental, but it is also *communal*. Contrary to a postmodern tendency to value autonomy and independence as the highest of virtues, Christian spiritual life is learned and deepened in community and is marked by interdependence. This reality holds even when the community presents as many obstacles and challenges as supports. Note, however, that "communal" should not be too quickly collapsed into "church" or "congregation." The stories and examples of families, peers, friends, as well as liturgy, sacraments, catechesis, and the community that is the fruit of a rich congregational life are foundational. I shall return to this element shortly.

One last descriptive adjective bears mentioning: the spiritual life is *transformational*. Bit by bit, a life in the Spirit leads to our becoming new people. We can outgrow crabbed, egocentric selves as we are invited—indeed pulled—beyond the self with which we have grown comfortable. Rilke often writes of this mysterious transformation, which sometimes occurs when we least expect it:

> You have not grown old, and it is not too late
> To dive into your increasing depths
> Where life calmly gives out its own secret.[10]

And again:

> My eyes already touch the sunny hill,
> going far ahead of the road I have begun.
> So we are grasped by what we cannot grasp;
> it has its inner light, even from a distance—
>
> And changes us, even if we do not reach it,
> into something else, which, hardly sensing it, we already are.[11]

In sum, the spiritual life, in a Christian understanding, is an intentional and developmental response to the life of the Holy Spirit that transforms us more and more into the image of Christ, individually and collectively.

CHALLENGES AND ALLIES TO THE SPIRITUAL LIFE

My encounters with Holy Mystery as a child notwithstanding, the spiritual life rarely deepens spontaneously; it must be initiated, nourished, and sustained under sometimes difficult conditions, both internal and external. The

---

10. "You see I want a lot," in *Selected Poems of Rainer Maria Rilke*, 27.
11. "A Walk," in *Selected Poems of Rainer Maria Rilke*, 177.

internal climate for the spiritual life includes the givens of an individual personality, the habits and choices with which the individual gradually constructs a life from among the possibilities available, and the effects of sin and the mysterious workings of grace in the individual soul. Each of us is unique; no two persons share the same configuration of these qualities. Another fragment from Rilke, which addresses God, points to this uniqueness:

> You create yourself in ever-changing shapes
> that rise from the stuff of our days—
> unsung, unmourned, undescribed,
> Like a forest we knew.
>
> You are the deep innerness of all things,
> the last word that can never be spoken.
> To each of us you reveal yourself differently;
> to the ship as a coastline, to the shore as a ship.[12]

As this poem suggests, the spiritual life is also uniquely expressed, though there are patterns that have proven helpful and that can guide us in our spiritual journeys. Primary among these patterns and guides, for Christians, are the biblical narratives, which give us the authoritative story of God's creative and indwelling and redeeming presence with God's creation. Mentors are also helpful. These may include parents, teachers, spouses, friends, members of the faith community past and present, pastors, spiritual directors, and poets who make concrete a variety of ways of living the spiritual life. Fortunate, indeed, is the person who can draw from a mentor both encouragement and modeling for a richer spiritual life.

Grace and sin are ubiquitous; we all experience both. Sin, the Christian name for our human alienation from God, dogs our relationships with God, self, other humans—indeed, all creation. As the apostle Paul reminds us, we do not do the good we want, but we do the evil we do not want (Rom. 7:15). Our own history of sin, then, as well as our participation in sinful patterns of other persons and of the larger societies in which we live, becomes a given in our spiritual lives, not only as something to be overcome as we progress but, more fundamentally, as a vulnerability that constantly reminds us of our inability to save ourselves. In the context of this vulnerability, however, the grace of God abounds more (2 Cor. 9:8).

As finite creatures, we are born and we live and die within certain determined structures: family, culture, race, gender, socioeconomic status, religion, and education, to name the more obvious ones. These structures offer certain

---

12. "You Are the Future," in *Rilke's Book of the Hours: Love Poems to God*, trans. Anita Barrows and Joanna Macy (New York: Riverhead Books, 1996), 119.

possibilities but just as decisively either foreclose or limit other possibilities. We cannot become just anything we fancy, but we must work out our spiritual lives within the givens of our concrete lives. Indeed, one of the challenges of spiritual growth is to accept responsibility for becoming oneself, limited and finite, particular and actual. Unless we accept this responsibility, we remain the spiritual equivalent of a child.

Examining exterior challenges to the spiritual life brings us, willy-nilly, into the present day. Today, those of us who live in industrialized societies must deal with affluence, isolation and alienation, progressive atheism, and the siren call of "things that glitter." Each of these realities presents particular challenges to the spiritual life. Affluence tempts us to believe that we are not contingent beings, reliant on God for the next breath. Isolation breeds alienation. Ironically, alienation becomes more rampant as affluence increases; we no longer need each other to survive, and others—any others—too often seem to be an impediment. Face-to-face communities wither, yielding to the virtual communities of Facebook and MySpace. Privatization of the spiritual life deprives us of community support. Atheism appears to be a viable spiritual option, now more endorsed in the culture than the spiritual life as this life has been traditionally understood. Those things that glitter, such as money, cars, drugs, sex, power, and success, entrap us into living on the surface of life, snuffing out or blunting the radical possibilities of the spiritual life radically embraced. Madeline DeFrees, my first poetry teacher, writes in "Skid Row":

> Out of the depths I have cried, O Lord,
> Where the lean heart preys on the hardened crust,
> Where short wicks falter on candle-hopes
> And winter whips at a patchwork trust.
>
> . . . .
>
> Out of the depths have I cried in vain
> And the still streets echo my lonely calls;
> All the long night in the moaning wind
> The bruised reed breaks and the sparrow falls.[13]

Antidotes to these contemporary challenges can be found by grace: seeking out spiritual mentors and guides; intentionally connecting with and committing oneself to building a vigorous Christian community of diverse individuals across generations, genders, races, and cultures (were it as easy to do as to say!); seeking out personal and communal spiritual practices that address and

---

13. From *Blue Dusk: New and Selected Poems, 1951–2001* (Port Townsend, WA: Copper Canyon Press, 2001), 51.

redress the particular challenges of our time; and searching for and honoring and strengthening the good, true, and beautiful wherever they may be found in one's life.

The way forward is to follow spiritual practices that enhance the good, the true, and the beautiful; to follow spiritual practices that result in deepened fruit of the Spirit (Gal. 5:22); to follow spiritual practices that bring balance to life—to redress both the cultural imbalances mentioned above and the personal imbalances caused by the determinisms in which each one lives and by one's own particular pattern of sin; to follow spiritual practices that bring us out of our individualism and plunge us into vibrant communities of faith. The particulars will vary with each person and within each person's own developing spiritual life, as well as with each faith community and cultural setting. There are no hard and fast rules: The spirit of the Lord is freedom (2 Cor. 3:17).

CONCLUSION

I think back again to the five eighteen-year-old women with whom I began this meditation and conclude our pondering about their spiritual lives with one last poem, again from Rilke:

> God speaks to each of us as he makes us,
> then walks with us silently out of the night.
>
> These are the words we dimly hear:
>
> You, sent out beyond your recall,
> go to the limits of your longing.
> Embody me.
>
> Flare up like flame
> and make big shadows I can move in.
>
> Let everything happen to you: beauty and terror.
> Just keep going. No feeling is final.
> Don't let yourself lose me.
>
> Nearby is the country they call life.
> You will know it by its seriousness.
>
> Give me your hand.[14]

Amen.

14. "God Speaks to Each of Us," in *Rilke's Book of the Hours*, 88.

PART II

Prophets

10

A Spiritual Person*

In 1904 Professor James Bissett Pratt of Williams College circulated a questionnaire containing ten questions about religion. In the introductory paragraph, he noted, "It is being realized as never before that religion, as one of the most important things in the life both of the community and of the individual, deserves close and extended study." He added that such study "can be of value only if based upon the personal experiences of many individuals," and addressed the recipient of the questionnaire: "If you are in sympathy with such study and are willing to assist in it, will you kindly write out the answers to the following questions and return them with this questionnaire, as soon as you conveniently can." He asked respondents to answer the questions "at length and in detail" and not to give "philosophical generalization, but your own personal experience." He sent a questionnaire to William James, professor of philosophy and psychology at Harvard University, and James responded by answering the questions.[1]

The questions that have particular interest for me here are the ones that ask the respondents what they mean by "spirituality" and to "describe a typical spiritual person." To the former question, James wrote, "Susceptibility to ideals, but with a certain freedom to indulge in imagination about them. A

*Although commissioned for this book, this essay was published first in the *Journal of Religion and Health* and is used here with kind permission from Springer Science + Business Media: *Journal of Religion and Health*, "A Spiritual Person," January 1, 2010, Donald Capps.
    1. James's answers are published in *William James: Writings 1902–1910*, ed. Bruce Kuklick (New York: Library of America, 1987), 1183–85. Pratt's writings include *Psychology and Religious Belief* (1907), *The Religious Consciousness: A Psychological Study* (1920), and *Matter and Spirit: A Study of Mind and Body in Their Relation to the Spiritual Life* (1926).

certain amount of 'other-worldly' fancy. Otherwise, you have mere morality, or 'taste.'" To the request for a description of a typical spiritual person, James wrote "Phillips Brooks." This, of course, was hardly a description of a typical spiritual person, but it was consistent with James's tendency, evident in *The Varieties of Religious Experience*, to draw attention to individual exemplars of various features and manifestations of the religious life.[2]

In this chapter, I will expand on James's insight that Phillips Brooks was a spiritual person by asking what it was about Brooks that made him so. In a sense, James provides his own answer to this question by first indicating what he means by spirituality: a "susceptibility to ideals, but within a certain freedom to indulge in imagination about them" and "a certain amount of 'other-worldly' fancy." I believe, however, that we can gain a more nuanced understanding of what made Brooks a "typical spiritual person" by focusing on several of his sermons and on the poem "O Little Town of Bethlehem," and then conclude with a few brief reflections on his physical presence. First, though, is a brief summary of his life.

THE LIFE OF PHILLIPS BROOKS

Phillips Brooks was born in Boston in 1835 and died there in 1893.[3] He was the second of six sons. The family religious tradition was Congregationalism, but his mother and aunt were confirmed in the Episcopal Church when he was five years old. His father was confirmed seven years later. The rector at St. Paul's Church, Dr. A. H. Vinton, was Phillips's lifelong mentor. Brooks attended Boston Latin School and then entered Harvard College in 1851 at the age of sixteen.

After graduating from Harvard in 1855, he taught at Boston Latin School but resigned before the year was out. Following several months of indecision, he enrolled at Virginia Theological Seminary in the fall of 1856. He completed his seminary education three years later and considered three viable options: to become the assistant to Dr. Vinton, who had recently become rector of Holy Trinity Church in Philadelphia; to remain

---

2. In his *What Pragmatism Means* (New York: Macmillan, 1909), Pratt points out that for James, the distinguishing feature of pragmatism among the philosophical schools was not that it was concerned with the practical (for other schools of thought could make this claim), but that it was concerned with the concrete and the particular as opposed to the abstract and the general. Thus, James's response to Pratt's requests for a description of a spiritual person is a clear reflection of his pragmatism (85–86).

3. My source for this brief summary of Brooks's life is Raymond W. Albright, *Focus on Infinity: A Life of Phillips Brooks* (New York: Macmillan, 1961).

at Virginia Theological Seminary as head of its preparatory school and chapel assistant; or to become rector of the Church of the Advent in Philadelphia. He chose the latter. He remained at the Church of the Advent for two and a half years and then became rector of Holy Trinity Church when Dr. Vinton moved to New York City. He stayed at Holy Trinity for seven years (1862–1869). In 1865, at the age of twenty-nine, he traveled to Europe, engaged in some brief theological study in Germany—enough to convince him that he lacked the necessary background and technical skills to be a scholar—then went to the Holy Land. There he wrote the words to "O Little Town of Bethlehem," which were set to music by the church organist, Lewis H. Redner.

In 1869 he accepted a call to Trinity Church in Boston. During his tenure at Trinity, a new church edifice was built, he became well-known for his preaching, and he was heavily involved in ecumenical activities in Boston. In 1877, he was invited to give the Beecher Lectures at Yale University, which afforded the opportunity to reflect on his preaching principles, and Harvard University awarded him the doctor of divinity degree. In 1881, he was offered the position of preacher to Harvard University and a professorship in Christian morals but, after much reflection, turned down the offer. In 1882, he asked the wardens and vestrymen of Trinity Church to grant him an extended vacation in order that he might regain his perspective on life.

On his return he remained at Trinity Church for eight more years and then was appointed bishop of the Massachusetts Diocese. This appointment was controversial because he was considered too liberal by many. In fact, several of his actions as rector of Trinity Church, such as presiding over the marriage of a couple even though the groom was a nonmember, had been censured by the previous bishop. Brooks died two years later (at age fifty-eight) of diphtheria, contracted when he visited a church one evening in his official role as bishop and was exposed to this highly contagious disease.

Brooks never married, so his only survivors were several brothers and their families. His death, however, was a major event in the history of Boston. Harvard students carried his body on their shoulders, and persons of all faiths felt the loss of his spiritual presence among them. Trinity Church stands in Copley Square, and on one side of this imposing edifice is a statue of Brooks by Augustus Saint-Gaudens. It portrays a large man (he was six feet four inches tall) with one hand upraised in a gesture of benediction and triumph. Jesus, a full head taller but considerably slimmer, and clothed in a full-length robe and hood, is standing immediately behind him. A cross looms behind them both. There is a pulpit to the left of Brooks and in front of Jesus, suggesting that Brooks's reputation was built on his preaching.

THE SERMONS: RESOURCES AND IDEALS

I would now like to turn to a brief discussion of Brooks's sermons. Given the vast number of sermons that he preached and the fact that many were published during his own lifetime, this discussion will necessarily be selective. However, if one sits down to read his sermons, one can hardly escape the impression that a central—perhaps *the* central—theme in his sermons is that our problems and difficulties in life would seem more manageable if we would recognize our vast store of personal and spiritual resources. In failing to recognize that we already possess these resources, we allow our problems to immobilize us. Thus, in "Visions and Tasks," he discusses the role that vision plays in inspiring persons to carry out difficult tasks.[4] Individuals who reach middle adulthood tend to lose their enthusiasm for the tasks they are responsible for performing:

> A man we see sometimes who, as he comes to middle-life, finds his immediate enthusiastic sight of ideal things grown dull; that is the almost necessary condition of his ripening life. He does not spring as quickly as he once did to seize each newly offered hope for man. A thousand disenchantments have made him serious and sober. He looks back, and the glow and sparkle which he once saw in life he sees no longer. He wonders at his recollection of himself, and asks how it is possible that life ever should have seemed to him as he remembers that it did seem.[5]

What can such a person do? What resources do persons in midlife already possess to bring them out of their dullness and disenchantment? In Brooks's view, the simple fact that they once had visions and dreams they now suspect to be illusions is the very resource that they may now draw upon in order to remain constant in their tasks. The very fact that life once seemed bright and filled with possibility is now their "most valued certainty." A person should therefore not part with that assurance for anything. All the hard work that he does now is done in the strength and light of that remembered enthusiasm. Every day the dreams of his boyhood, which seem dead, are really the live inspirations of his life.[6]

In effect, persons who are discouraged in middle life have the necessary resources to overcome this discouragement if they can only recognize that this is so. The preacher's task is to direct their attention to these resources.

---

4. My source for sermons discussed here is William Scarlett, ed., *Phillips Brooks: Selected Sermons* (New York: E. P. Dutton).

5. Ibid., 141.

6. Ibid.

In "The Egyptians Dead upon the Seashore," Brooks addresses the criticism that his continual emphasis on the resources available to persons to cope with the problems of temptation and sin is "the mere dream of an optimistic sermon." In response, he appeals to his listeners to consult their own experience and ask whether "God has not sometimes given you the right to such a hope."[7] In looking back over the past, have there not been some real victories in your life? For example:

> Are there not at least some temptations to which you yielded then to which you know you can never yield again? Are there not some meannesses which you once thought glorious which now you know are mean? Are there no places where you once stumbled where now you know you can walk firm?[8]

He goes on to say, however, that he is not appealing merely to experience but to the Christian truth about humanity. When Christ takes hold of the natural person, no longer can that nature think itself doomed to evil: "Intensely sensitive to feel the presence of evil as he never felt it before, the Christian man instantly and intensely knows that evil is a stranger and an intruder in his life. The wonder is not that it should one day be cast out; the wonder is that it should ever have come in."[9]

Thus, Brooks contends that his appeal to the resources that an individual has for dealing with any problem is not mere optimism but is rooted in the conviction that the Christian faith has real, practical power. If the outcome were already assured, one would have no need of hope. But hope is grounded in the assurance that Christ is a living resource and that through him there is victory over temptation and sin.

In short, Brooks affirms over and over again that we have not adequately understood the problems that beset us until we have taken account of the resources available to us for dealing with them. While we are inclined to recognize only the strength and tenacity of the problem or difficulty that we face, he bids us to pay attention to the greater strength we possess for overcoming it. As long as we look only at our limitations, our self-knowledge and our understanding of God are seriously distorted: "How can he know what lurking power lies packed away within the near-opened folds of this inactive life? Has he ever dared to call himself the child of God, and for one moment felt what that involves?"[10] Brooks concludes: "There is nothing on earth more

---

7. Ibid., 110.
8. Ibid., 111.
9. Ibid.
10. Ibid., 114.

seemingly insignificant than men's judgment of their own moral and spiritual limitations."[11]

Other sermons could be cited in support of the claim that the central theme in Brooks's sermons is that we already have resources available to us that we fail to recognize. These two, however, make the point that some of these resources derive from who we are or the persons we have been, while others derive from the fact that we are the beneficiaries of the living Christ and are therefore not alone in the struggles of life. Thus, some resources are personal, others are spiritual, but the very fact that we embrace—internalize—the latter makes it relatively pointless to try to differentiate the two.

William James cites a sermon of Phillips Brooks in "What Makes a Life Significant," one of three lectures that he delivered to students at women's colleges.[12] It occurs in the middle of a discussion of ideals, which as we saw earlier are for James an essential element in his understanding of spirituality. He asks what makes "morally exceptional individuals" different from the rest: "It can only have been this—that their souls worked and endured in obedience to some inner *ideal*." He acknowledges that "these ideals of other lives are among those secrets that we can almost never penetrate," although something about the person "may often tell us when they are there."[13]

To illustrate such an ideal, he cites examples of persons who have embraced the ideal of voluntary poverty and notes that this is an ideal of which Phillips Brooks has "spoken so penetratingly." An extended quotation from Brooks's sermon "How to Be Abased" follows, a few sentences of which provide a general sense of what Brooks has to say about this ideal:

> No life like poverty could so get one to the heart of things and make men know their meaning, could so let us feel life and the world with all the soft cushions stripped off and thrown away. . . . Poverty makes men come very near each other, and recognize each other's human hearts; and poverty, highest and best of all, demands and cries out for faith in God. . . . I know how superficial and unfeeling, how like mere mockery, words in praise of poverty may seem. . . . But I am sure that the poor man's dignity and freedom, his self-respect and energy, depend upon his cordial knowledge that his poverty is a true region and kind of life with its own chances of character, its own springs of happiness, and revelations of God.[14]

11. Ibid.
12. William James, "What Makes a Life Significant," in *William James: Writings 1878–1899*, ed. Gerald E. Myers (New York: Library of America, 1992), 861–80. James's source is Phillips Brooks, *The Light of the World and Other Sermons* (New York: E. P. Dutton, 1891), 159–76.
13. James, "What Makes a Life Significant," 873.
14. Ibid., 874–75.

Following this citation from Brooks's sermon on the ideal of poverty, James goes on to clarify what he means by an ideal. He suggests that it "must be something intellectually conceived, something of which we are not unconscious, if we have it; and it must carry with it that sort of outlook, uplift, and brightness that go with all intellectual facts." In addition, "there must be *novelty* in an ideal—novelty at least for him whom the ideal grasps." In other words, it cannot be the expression of mere "sodden routine," although "what is sodden routine for one person may be ideal novelty for another," and this very fact indicates that "there is nothing absolutely ideal," for "ideals are relative to the lives that entertain them."[15]

In the paragraphs of his lecture that follow these reflections on the nature of ideals, James emphasizes that ideals alone are not enough to make life significant, for ideals need to be coupled with an active will that seeks to unite ideals with the real world so that progress occurs, for without a sense of progress, life has little significance. Education is a means of multiplying our ideals and bringing new ones into view, but having a "stock of ideals" is not enough. In fact, in the abstract, "mere ideals are the cheapest things in life," and "everybody has them in some shape or other, personal or general, sound or mistaken, low or high," and some of the "most worthless sentimentalists and dreamers" possibly have them "on the most copious scale."[16] There must, therefore, be a fusion of ideals and "effort, courage, or endurance," for ideals are insufficient in themselves.[17]

IDEALS AND THE ACTIVE IMAGINATION

If the fusion of ideals and active will is essential to the sense that our lives have significance, do we possess an agency that inspires us to bring about this fusion of ideals and active effort? I suggest that James provides an affirmative answer to this question when he describes spirituality as "a susceptibility to ideals, *but with a certain freedom to indulge in imagination about them.*" Imagination is the agency that we all possess, though in differing degrees, which inspires us to make an ideal a living reality.

If this is so, what made Phillips Brooks a spiritual person was that he used his imagination, especially as a preacher, to envision the realization of ideals in the real world in which his listeners lived their lives. In contrast to Don Quixote, whose imagination energized ideals that were realizable in an unreal

15. Ibid., 875.
16. Ibid., 877.
17. Ibid., 875.

world, Phillips Brooks used his imagination to envision the realization of his listeners' ideals in the world of everyday life.[18]

In a sense, there is nothing especially novel or noteworthy in the claim that Brooks's spirituality was reflected in his use of his imagination. After all, the use of the imagination is central to the spiritual exercises of Ignatius Loyola. As Louis Martz points out in *The Poetry of Meditation*, in the method of meditation that Ignatius developed, the first step is to "compose the place" on which the meditation will center, and this requires the use of one's imagination. Thus, in meditating on the birth of Christ, one imagines an open place without shelter, and a child wrapped in swaddling cloths and lying in a manger, and then one may imagine oneself present in the very spot where the birth occurred, or imagine the birth occurring in the very place where the meditation is being carried out, or imagine that the birth is happening within one's own heart. From this composition of place the meditation proceeds to the three stages of meditation proper: *memory* involves recollection of God in relation to the event that is the subject of meditation; *understanding* involves forming a true, proper, and thorough concept of the event that is being meditated upon; and *will* involves acting on the understanding that has been attained.[19]

In *The Poem of the Mind*, Martz points out that this meditation structure underwent considerable refinement in the years following the initial impact of *Spiritual Exercises*. For example, Francis de Sales, in his *Introduction to the Devout Life*, recognized the difficulty the average person has in attempting to "compose the place." The usual tendency was to accomplish this task by means of similitude, or developing images of various elements of the scene based on one's experience of similar objects in one's own environment. De Sales contended that the making of such images can be burdensome to the mind, especially when one's experience is limited. He advocated therefore that one begin with a simple proposal of the *theme* of the event or scene being meditated upon. Thus, the theme of meditation on the birth of Christ might be humility or adoration. The three stages of the meditation process remain, but they are now guided by a clear conception of the theme to which the meditation is directed.[20]

18. However, one can make a case for the value of Don Quixote's approach if we recognize that the unreal world that he creates is actually a world that existed two centuries earlier. See my "Don Quixote as Moral Narcissist: Implications for Mid-Career Male Ministers," in Philip L. Culbertson, *The Spirituality of Men: Sixteen Christians Write about Their Faith* (Minneapolis: Fortress Press, 2002), 66–92.

19. Louis Martz, *The Poetry of Meditation*, rev. ed. (New Haven, CT: Yale University Press, 1961), 25–39.

20. Louis Martz, *The Poem of the Mind* (Oxford: Oxford University Press, 1966), 37–38.

Martz concludes that "the enormous popularity of methodical meditation in this era may be attributed to the fact that it satisfied and developed a natural, fundamental tendency of the human mind—a tendency to work from a particular situation, through analysis of that situation, and finally to some sort of resolution of the problems which the situation has presented."[21] He also points out that the meditation process developed by Ignatius was adapted by the Puritans to focus on the individual's personal experience. The scene might be an event in the life of Christ or a saint, but it could also be an event in one's own life, especially one that called for self-examination.[22]

Brooks's poem "O Little Town of Bethlehem" provides an excellent illustration of his own adoption of this meditation model, and especially of his use of imagination to activate one's ideals. As noted, the writing of this poem was stimulated by his visit to the Holy Land in 1865. However, the Bethlehem that he imagines in his poem is not the city that he visited in 1865 but the little town of Bethlehem at the time of Jesus' birth. This is a town that is in a deep and dreamless sleep above which the silent stars go by. An everlasting Light shines in its dark streets, and the hopes and fears of all the years are met in this little town because this very night Christ has been born of Mary. As mortals sleep tonight the angels keep their watch of wondering love, and as dawn begins to break, the morning stars proclaim the holy birth and sing praises to God the King and proclaim peace on earth.

Reflecting on this quiet scene, Brooks observes how silently the wondrous gift of God has been given and has imparted to human hearts the blessings of heaven. This very silence tells us that no ear may hear the coming of God, but wherever in this world of sin meek souls receive him, the dear Christ enters therein. Brooks prays that the holy child of Bethlehem will descend on us, cast out our sin, and enter in, and be born in us this very day. If we listen, we hear the angels proclaiming the great glad tidings, and we pray that our Lord Immanuel will come to us and abide with us.

What stands out in this poem is the sense of the stillness of the town and the silence of the gift that God has given. This gift does not appear with noisy fanfare but comes ever so silently. Also noteworthy is that all that we have hoped and all that we have feared converge on this quiet stable scene where a

---

21. Martz, *Poetry of Meditation*, 39.

22. Ibid.,121–22. An interesting example of this adaptation of the meditation process occurs in an entry in *The Diary of Cotton Mather*, vol. 1 (New York: Frederick Ungar, 1911): "I was once emptying the *Cistern of Nature*, and making *Water* at the Wall. At the same time, there was a dog, who did so too, before me. Thought I: 'What mean, and vile Things are the Children of Men, in this mortal State! How much do our *natural Necessities* abase us, and place us in some regard, on the same level with the very *Dogs*!'" Then, however, his thoughts continued, and he declared: "Yet I will be a more noble Creature; and at the very Time, when my *natural Necessities* debase me into the Condition of the *Beast*, my *Spirit* shall (I say, *at that very Time*!) rise and soar, and fly up, towards the employment of the *Angel*" (357).

mother gives birth to a seemingly helpless child. Most importantly, the poem is a prayer—a prayer that this child who was born in Bethlehem will be born in us today, and having been born in us, will continue to abide with us.

Thus, Brooks imagines that the birth that occurred long ago in a little town in the Holy Land may occur again in our own hearts. As the holy Child of Bethlehem entered this world of sin, so the dear Christ enters into our hearts today and casts out the sin that impedes the realization of our inner ideals.

BROOKS'S PHYSICAL PRESENCE

Aside from his poem "O Little Town of Bethlehem," Brooks was best known for his sermons. At the same time, those who heard him preach frequently commented on the fact that they were not so much inspired by the words that he spoke but by the fact that he was the one who spoke them. Three months after his death on January 23, 1893, the *Harvard Graduates Magazine* stated that "men listened, for the most part, not to the sermon, but to him," and added that he aimed "directly at the heart of his hearers," giving them not theology but "the presence of a strong, loving, aspiring, and believing soul."[23]

An infrequent listener to his sermons had this to say shortly after his death:

> I recall the curious feeling of physical exhaustion that came upon me as I left the church. It was like nothing so much as relaxation following a severe but victorious struggle in some athletic contest. And I remember wondering even then, "If this so affects me, what must it be to him, and how can he bear it all?" It must have been this which finally wore him out, rather than the pressure of what most of us call work. When he was preaching he was pouring out strength as no other man could, as well as putting the power of his listeners to the utmost strain.[24]

By exuding great physical strength, Brooks embodied his conviction that all individuals possess greater inner resources than they realize. As a minister, he saw his task to be that of encouraging his parishioners, by word and example, to recognize and utilize the vast store of personal and spiritual resources available to them. The statue of Brooks that stands outside Trinity Church today portrays the presence of a strong, loving, aspiring, believing soul, a man

---

23. Cited in Kim Townsend, *Manhood at Harvard: William James and Others* (New York: W. W. Norton, 1996), 133.

24. Cited in Albright, *Focus on Infinity*, 392.

whose right arm is raised in a gesture of victory over the fears that reduce our ideals to empty words and phrases. But his imposing presence would not be that of a spiritual person were it not for the fact that another figure is standing behind him, and that this silent figure, who towers over him, is gazing out into the distance—where human hopes cancel human fears.

11

A Rebranded Life

Spirituality and Chronic Illness

ELIZABETH DAMEWOOD GAUCHER

The bumper sticker on the car ahead of me made a claim that held my attention: "We are spiritual beings having a physical experience."

This was a sticker for thinkers, no space wasted on neon shapes or quirky characters. I felt a slow smile warm my face and wondered why that message wasn't in front of me twelve years ago. Then, upon second thought, I remembered. In 1998 the universe ran out of patience waiting for me to "get it." An intervention of the highest order was around the corner, and I had already let the claims of too many bumper stickers and philosophies du jour waste my time.

Solid reasons for not disclosing our most vulnerable moments abound. One of the most compelling reasons is that disclosure might change others' impressions of a carefully crafted "personal brand." Worship at the altar of one's own marketing machine is becoming a ritual today, and while I confess that I am attracted to the control and management the branding appears to offer, I am equally repulsed by language commoditizing human beings. Long-term, by ignoring the complexity of human nature, such language seems destined for failure. People are not products, but we occasionally try to manage ourselves as if we are. We know that allowing others a glimpse behind our branding curtain, especially one that betrays our public trademark, risks potentially serious consequences. Those who have invested in our "brand" may become disoriented or even feel betrayed. If someone has yet to know us, he or she may decide that there is something there not worthy of engagement, now or ever. One's flaws may even be considered contagious.

As human beings we are drawn powerfully to the idea that we are to manage, control, decide, and dominate. Much of this attitude comes from fear.

101

We are afraid to be wrong, afraid to be surprised, afraid to be open to something we don't direct. We are all hungry to believe that our reliance on physical workouts and reading the latest books and blogs will connect our bodies and minds to the capacity to control our own destinies. Living exclusively on the intoxication of our own power, however, is also an effective way to lose touch with one's spirit. It makes reconnection to one's spirit more difficult when physical and psychological elements grow giddy with their own influence, and they become increasingly resistant to being quieted when their voices grow too loud.

Some integration of mind, body, and spirit clearly is indicated for a balanced and healthy life. The simplicity of this idea on paper, however, often masks the complex relationship of the elements that make us human. This integration cannot be reduced to some kind of mathematical equation—for example, one that helps us determine that we are spending too much time in our heads so now we should go for a run. Nor is integration as simple as noting an absence of prayer time and devoting extra hours to the process until we recalibrate. Challenges related to the integration of mind, body, and spirit rest in the need for a twofold starting premise: that our minds and bodies both serve and take direction from our spirit, and that our spirit is *ours*, although it is on loan as a piece of God. When our bodies and our minds are gone, our spirit will return to God.

It took a long time, but I have turned the corner on my concerns about losing my original personal brand. What remains for me is to find a more complete peace by telling my story in the one-sided yet public way that writing provides. Answers do slip through,[1] though I believe they cannot be forced, nor found by sheer human effort or will. I believe the answers to the most important questions in life can only be delivered and received through the act of purposeful, focused physical and psychological surrender. This surrender requires a willingness to relinquish the idea of ultimate authority over one's life through personal effort. I believe that until one has experienced an answer received in such a state of submission and release, there will be an ongoing struggle between the body and the mind that limits spiritual power.

My intention is not to preach, but to witness. I am a Presbyterian. We are rather mild-mannered people, eternally hopeful that intellect will help us work through the complexities of the words of Jesus Christ. We hope that all will come to the rational, well-considered conclusion that the blood of the Lamb was shed for human salvation—oh, and also, that you really should get your act together.

---

1. I take this idea from Gail Godwin's essay in this book, "Musings on the Spiritual Life."

What happens when your act *is* together? You've played by all the rules, and you appear to be winning. Why change the game? Twelve years and a few days ago I was a thirty-year-old woman living a charmed life, and exactly twelve years ago I came within an angel's breath of leaping out of a moving car in a desperate attempt to quiet my raging mind. *That* is a game changer. It is also the consequence of allowing the mind and the body to hijack the spirit, with devastating results.

In retrospect I had been getting sick for a long time, though my infirmity broadened in form. A therapist originally diagnosed me with depression in my mid-twenties and then with panic disorder a few years later. Talk therapy, dietary changes, antidepressant pharmaceuticals, and stress management helped me—some. It's difficult to maintain the charade of calm, however, when one is walking through the largest gourmet kitchen and grocery store in North Carolina and suddenly is gripped with the urge to collapse on the floor for no apparent reason, or when one is driving a truck on I-40 and feels an arm go cold and tingly while trying to maintain control.

A cause of my "disorder" would become clearer. One morning in the shower I noticed I could feel the razor blades on my skin on one leg but only pressure on the other. "That's odd," I thought. "Maybe I really did something terrible to my back trying to dig that hole in the yard last week." I chalked it up to a pinched nerve and assumed I needed an X-ray.

But the morning I woke up with retching heaves of vomit brought on simply by tilting my head one degree the wrong way eliminated all doubt that this was exclusively a psychological issue or simply a pinched nerve. This was very physical. It was also very dangerous. I knew I was in trouble. I took a deep breath and dragged myself off the bed, onto the floor, and across the hall to the bathroom, throwing up the whole time. If I can just get to the tile floor, I thought, it will all be okay.

My husband found me lying on the floor with my face pressed against the toilet's cool porcelain. As any sane and caring person would do, he urged me to let him help me up, but I cried and begged him to let me stay on the floor. I had found comfort. The world was no longer hurling me in deep loops from east to west by my brain stem, and I literally saw no past and no future, only that moment. God help the person who tried to take me out of that moment!

My husband did the only thing he could think of, and it turned out to be the right thing. He called my mother states away and asked for her help. As I recall, the telephone was held up to my ear as I lay on the floor, and Mom calmly but insistently told me that I had to get up, that I had to get in the car, and that I was going to the doctor. There is something about your mother's voice that cuts through everything sometimes. Hearing her speak, I knew I had to get up.

I think I threw up a few more times en route to the doctor's office. I remember trying to lie motionless in the moving car, which was not successful. I remember being lifted into a wheel chair when the door to the building was only steps away. After that, I don't remember much, only some medication to get the vomit under control and a follow-up appointment scheduled.

At the follow-up appointment, I felt much better. No more throwing up, no more world spinning maniacally, no more patches of sensation loss. I felt better than I had in a long time. "What a relief," I told my doctor. "That sure was crazy, wasn't it? So glad *that's* over." When one is invested in a certain outcome, the mind truly can work miracles of denial.

I assume that these are the moments they try to prepare students for in medical school. A doctor has to tell the perky blonde girl standing on the verge of everything she ever dreamed of that he is referring her for an MRI over at Duke University, *just to rule out MS*. God bless Dr. Crummett. I know now he had to be sure what was going on, and that he didn't want to scare me.

I had the MRI, and I was diagnosed with relapsing-remitting multiple sclerosis when I was thirty years old. This had to be a mistake. *This was not part of my personal brand.*

Anyone who has been diagnosed with a serious disease or suffered a painful loss understands the extended period of processing the event. Denial, anger, bargaining, and depression tend to hallmark the early stages of grief, though these phases do not occur sequentially or even necessarily in proximity to one another.[2] The phases do all have a singular focus, however, in the human attempt to reach ultimate acceptance of a new reality. Without such acceptance, life can never move forward.

I initially experienced the phases of grief as my body and mind warred over which would control my destiny in the new light of multiple sclerosis. It was as if psychological and physical effort were the front line of the old guard trying to defend my perceived personal brand of "hard-working, goal-oriented, results-getting gal." I could feel myself stubbornly headed down a dead-end road. It was only through eventual and complete submission of both body and mind and a corresponding openness to spiritual influence that I began to reform my understanding of what defines my life.

Multiple sclerosis is a progressive disease with no known cause and no known cure. The body is misfiring, identifying the fatty insulation of nerve fibers called myelin as a foreign and enemy presence. When there is an invasive presence, what the body does is a wonderful thing. The immune system establishes laser focus on the enemy and rallies all of its resources to rid the body of the intruder. The trouble with MS is that the body turns against

2. See Elisabeth Kübler-Ross, *On Death and Dying* (New York : Macmillan, 1991).

itself—and no one wants to lose her nerve-fiber protection, ever, under any circumstances. If you've seen an appliance or computer with wiring shorts, you have a picture of the path a human being is headed down when the myelin starts to go. The machine still starts up. It can still do pretty much what you want it to do. But it begins to get a little scary when it "shorts out" with more frequency and pop. You start to wonder if the machine should even be on. When you begin to feel like a ghost in the machine, it's more than a little scary. It is terrifying.

Only one week after diagnosis, it was a hot summer day on the drive down to the family beach house, and I was vacillating between complete denial and sheer panic. I was still trying to be in the proverbial driver's seat. No chronic disease was going to stop me from doing everything I had planned to do. I had just been admitted to law school at UNC-Chapel Hill. Capable, intelligent people did that. I had a vacation planned with friends. These were especially cool friends, so I must be smart and fun. This diagnosis was a blip on the radar, complete bullshit, really, and life was going on as usual.

In retrospect, this was an amazing and bitterly comic haze of hubris.

Rolling down beach highway 17, I suddenly made a physical and mental connection with what doctors call the "demyelination process." I could feel the coating in my nervous system being attacked. My face went numb. My legs turned ice cold. My arms felt like bags of wet sand, and a strange pattern of tiny lightning bugs faded in and out across my field of vision.

I realized in that second that I had always assumed I wouldn't really experience this impending loss, not in real time. Somehow I had convinced myself that people with a progressive chronic disease slowly but surely lose certain capacities, but that life is generally the same on a day-to-day basis. Perhaps they wake up five or six years after diagnosis and reflect on how things have changed, I thought. It can't really be that it happens right in the middle of one's daily life! I clung to this misperception like a creed. It was the right attitude, one that was going to carry me through. After all, it reflected the consistency of my personal brand: complete reliance on me and my perceptions of reality, exclusively—and my perceptions were rarely wrong.

This was the most frightening moment of my life. I saw how much I had convinced myself that I was responsible for my reality, and also that my interpretation of this reality was utterly flawed. Worse still, I didn't have a plan B. Due to my complete devotion to my own idea of personal power, there wasn't anything to fall back on. I could see nothing of the end and no way to make the nightmare stop. I put my hand on the door of the car and watched the oncoming traffic with a bizarre sense of gratitude and anticipation. This could all be over. All I had to do was use my personal power to open the door and fling myself out. I knew I was in a very bad place as I imagined the relief and the freedom of my body making impact with two thousand pounds of steel at seventy miles an hour.

I believe that in that crazy moment God said, "Do you see how you are doing this *to yourself?* I love you. It's time to stop trying to control everything in your life and come to me."

Mercifully, it seems that if we are paying even a little bit of attention, God won't let us be wrong forever. God extends a relationship of love to all people, and also endless opportunities to open ourselves to that love and to accept its redeeming power. I believe, too, that God led me along a specific journey so that I could find the truth using a process that I understood. I really do think too much—the Presbyterian that I am—yet God offered the necessary patience to hold my hand down a long and twisted road, knowing it would take coming to the edge of giving up on my own thoughts to open my spirit to its proper role in my recovery. In that moment I was in the presence of a deeper awareness. It's difficult to describe what I felt. A force of love like none I have known wrapped itself around me with an assurance of answers. I didn't literally hear anything, but it was as if I heard a whisper of caring and direction on the way forward.

I let go of the car door and became quiet and still.

That night I knew that I had to take the next step. I was afraid. I had never prayed before. I had said memorized words, and I had asked for things or tried to focus on certain outcomes when addressing God. But I had never prayed in a state of complete surrender, letting go of my wants and even needs and with no concern for specific results. It could be that this kind of surrender requires a severe personal crisis. I was in the midst of mine, and I knew that to keep going I must relinquish control—over my illness *and* my life.

Both the idea and practice of relinquishing control are easily misunderstood. It is crucial to be an active participant in our own lives, but we must be conscious of a pattern of relying on *only* ourselves—"ourselves" defined as our minds and our bodies—to solve our deepest and most challenging problems. These core elements of our humanity long to be united with our spirit, but the spirit will only take them up and share power when they agree to be led. When one has relied on the mind and the body as stand-ins for the spirit, the concept of real prayer is overwhelming. I did not know what I was doing, but I knew enough not to reinvent the wheel. Though I did not know exactly how it worked, I knew there had to be very good reasons why the Twenty-third Psalm is read on the battlefield.

I lay on my personal battlefield and began recite silently, "The Lord is my shepherd. I shall not want."

Unexpectedly, I melted rapidly from recitation into connection. I felt myself calling God, not so much directly as inevitably. The world of my room grew fainter. Other people were in the house, but I might as well have been alone on the moon. I was still lying on the bed in the dark, but the physical surroundings were like the outline of a dream. "He maketh me to lie down in green pastures. He leads me beside the still waters. He restoreth my soul." I continued through the entire psalm, stopping to repeat lines that increased the feeling of connection, moving forward and back through the verses without rules. Each pass through the words loosened the human grip on my thinking and on my state of mind. I stopped trying to manage my thoughts and was drawn rhythmically into rounded waves of comfort, peace, and strength.

I cannot say how many hours this continued. I know I never deviated from the words of the psalm, and I know it had to be less than eight hours because the sun had not yet risen when my calling on God was interrupted. It seems to be most common for people who have connected intimately with higher spiritual power to say they "heard" the words of God or that God "spoke" to them. While I understand this expression, I want to avoid it. My experience was closer to words appearing in my mind, as if a hand were writing on my brain like a flame on the wall. There was an immediate consciousness of a single thought.

It is already done.

Instantly I was out of my prayer state and into the room. It was as though a house that had been swirling in a tornado dropped instantly yet harmlessly to earth. My eyes scanned every corner, looking for a physical sign of my messenger, but there was none. I knew I had the answer. I also knew I was overwhelmed with a blessing in hand, and it was time to release myself to the world of sleep and to engage my gift in the light of day.

I believe the four words presented to me were a revelation of a mystery that is painfully difficult to articulate but ever worthy of efforts to understand. The words "It is already done" serve to connect me more deeply than I ever dreamed possible to God's suffering in the human form of Jesus Christ. Those words also became a bridge between the idea of Christ's sacrifice for humanity and the reality of that redemption. In that light the next day, and for every day for more than a decade since, I have welcomed the beauty, intensity, peace, and challenge of my gift.

In every moment I have that threatens to spiral into extreme fear, I hear those words. *It is already done.* Always, I am drawn away from worry and toward an assurance that any challenge I face in life has already been met and conquered. It is never as simple as believing there is nothing for me to struggle through or overcome, yet it is now as simple as knowing I never do it alone, and as simple as knowing that what is at the end is peace.

Life changed dramatically when I entered the world of chronic disease, and most of those changes have been surprisingly positive. I have clarity around what is and is not important in my life. I make purposeful decisions each day about my priorities, my relationships, and my goals. Many battles I was willing to fight in the past simply do not even get a passing glance now, and I am a healthier person overall for it. Rather than always looking to the future for satisfaction and achievement, every day is ripe with accomplishment and gratitude.

When I changed this much, it meant that some of my relationships changed as well. My first marriage ended, for a long list of reasons but most succinctly because I became a different person. My husband was very supportive in every way he knew how to be; he just had the misfortune of marrying someone who changed more than either of us had bargained for. One constructive change affecting all of my relationships was that my ability to tolerate loud and aggressive people dissipated into thin air, and therefore my willingness to engage certain associates, personally and professionally, went along with it. I dabbled in politics for a few years but have since permanently retired that interest. Sometimes I think some people believe I've stopped caring, but really it's the opposite. I care too much to spend time and energy struggling with things that will not change. I am completely focused on how I need to be different.

The most difficult but influential overall change is connected closely to the personal rebranding process. My sister spent many of our early years visualizing me as holding "the flaming sword of righteousness" aloft with one straight arm. Rarely would I discuss topics I hadn't thoroughly researched, and when I did discuss them I was never without an ironclad opinion. These opinions were usually connected to someone being wrong, and I could explain in great detail why. To call it judgmental would be an understatement.

I'd be dishonest if I claimed I don't still try to find the side of right. But I've lost my interest in having a reputation for being right and gained a strong desire to build a reputation for other qualities. Recently when my alma mater initiated a search for a new president, it advertised for someone with "the qualities of warmth, compassion, fairness, humility, accessibility, and collegiality . . . energy, passion, fearlessness, and enthusiasm." You'll notice they didn't advertise for someone who is right. In sum, I think it's fair to say they advertised for someone who knows the importance of leading with a mind guided by one's spirit.

By surrendering my mind and body to my spirit, I inherited a completely reordered life. I no longer want to be right. I want to be compassionate and fair and all of those things, but above all, I want to be *fearless*. I avoided disclosing my story for the past twelve years for a range of reasons. I don't want you to see me as a disease or condition. I don't want you to make decisions about me that are probably based on ignorance. I don't want you to think I'm out of my mind that I truly believe God made a direct and transformational connection with me. And I have grown very comfortable with my guard more than a little bit up, and when I tell you my story it will be down, permanently. But honestly, the more I reflect on that, the better I feel. So if I may, today is the official launch of my new personal brand. After all, only one kind of person lives with her guard permanently down—fearless.

Because it's already done.

12

On Spirituality

ISMAEL GARCÍA

Discussions of spirituality and spiritual formation, given the plurality of interpretations concerning their substance and practices and the differences of opinion on how to best to learn and teach them, are both challenging and frustrating. Different religious traditions argue for different visions of the spiritual life and for the unique practices that such a life involves. Even within a particular religious tradition, such as Christianity, one finds that the theological convictions that give each denomination and religious group its unique identity also sustain different views and practices of spirituality.

INCARNATIONAL SPIRITUALITY

My own understanding of spirituality has been shaped by personal and social experiences, particularly as I have reflected on them from the perspective of my Christian faith and identity. At the most basic level, I understand spirituality to consist in our growing desire to look, interpret, and respond to the world from a theological point of view. It is the disposition and longing to bring the presence of God to bear on every dimension of our life, and to respond to the multiple challenges we confront in full awareness of the presence of the holy, that sustains all spheres of our existence. Spirituality is, in short, a way for the community of believers to consciously and intentionally express their lives in ways that fit their identity as Christians.

The language of spirituality has been an integral part of my life journey. As a young man living in Puerto Rico, I was raised in and was an active member of the church. In fact, my initial vocational instinct, which was recorded in

111

my high school yearbook, was to pursue ordained ministry. This was, to a great extent, the result of a nurturing church experience and of having the good fortune of being exposed to excellent pastoral models. Some of the pastors who nurtured my faith modeled a strong commitment to service. Others exemplified excellent community-building skills. Still others modeled the kind of oratory that was both inspirational and challenging. In short, the church provided a safe and supportive environment for the cultivation of what I understood at that time to be a healthy spiritual life, a life lived in openness to God's will and purpose.

Ever since, I have believed that spirituality must be a constant concern and a permanent legacy of the community of faith. Spirituality is, in the fullest and most literal sense of the word, a tradition of the church, an indispensable dimension of what it means to be a Christian. I have come to believe equally that spirituality and spiritual formation are intertwined with what it means to be human. The human condition, among other things, includes our being spiritual creatures.

A turning point in my spiritual journey occurred during my college years. I began to realize that the safe and supportive environment the church provided could be problematic, as could the vision of spirituality that was part of it. As a college student at the University of Puerto Rico, I became engaged in the student movement. I joined many others in opposing what I firmly believed was an unjust war, the colonial war against Vietnam, into which an inordinate number of Puerto Ricans were drafted even though we had no say in electing the persons who made such political decisions. The unjust nature of the war became tied to the injustice of the island's colonial status. This status follows from Puerto Rico's being a commonwealth of the United States. While Islanders are American citizens and have the power to elect their own governor and local representatives and control matters of local taxation, they have a representative in Washington who has a voice but no vote in Congress. The federal government controls all matters relating to citizenship, international commerce and trade, migration, military obligation, and communication. The federal government also has the power to decide the political status of the island, which can and does disregard the will of Islanders. Those who support Puerto Rico's becoming the next American state do so because present federal control results in the humiliation and domination of its people. In these supporters' views, which they tend to share with the political left, the commonwealth sustains a colonial status that keeps the Islander a second-class citizen.

These were critical times for most Islanders. During these years the island experienced a rapidly deteriorating economy. The agricultural base of our economy was devastated to the point that we were importing foods that we had traditionally produced. The industrial sector was not growing and could not absorb the displaced agricultural labor force. Unemployment and underemployment were increasing at a rapid pace, and so was the poverty rate. Many persons and families became dependent on public welfare, and our traditionally strong work ethic was seriously undermined. A drug culture emerged, another consequence of the Vietnam War, destroying the family structure and the basic fabric of society. Crime reached unprecedented high levels. Major cultural institutions were politicized, including the university, in ways that undermined their cultural missions. Political corruption became rampant, and the use of politics to obtain immediate economic gain took the place of spirited public service. Political strife affected every dimension of life. People used to say that one needed to choose one's barber in light of his political beliefs. Social life became conflict-ridden, and the space for civil dialogue was seriously undermined.

In the midst of this rapidly deteriorating context, the church, with very few exceptions, remained silent and marginal. The church's colonial status became obvious. It promoted the expression of exuberant religious feelings and speech that took the place of deep analysis and realism regarding what was going on within the world the church was called to serve. The churches became focused on cultivating the private beliefs and practices of their members—on "inner spirituality" essentially divorced from social and political realities. Churches placed little-to-no energy on determining what would be a realistic public response to the challenges within society. It was particularly frustrating to see the church express more concern about matters such as women's dress codes than any of the crucial issues confronted by most Islanders. There was an extended debate at the time concerning the acceptability of women wearing pants to school and to work. There was a parallel debate regarding the length of hair that was proper for males. Hardly any debate pertained to deteriorating life on the island.

I began to realize that the predominant view of spirituality within most churches was limited to practices that nurtured one's inner life and personal relationship with God. Prayer, Bible study, church attendance, and religious rituals sought to nurture personal growth in one's relationship with God, with the main concern being one's personal salvation. It was assumed that such spiritual formation need not and should not be concerned with, and much less mediated by, the struggles carried out in the larger social context. A socially and politically mediated spirituality was not only suspect, but in fact was denounced as a negation of a life lived in the spirit of Jesus. It was perceived as a distraction of what really matters to God. It was important that people confess that God was in Christ, but they need not inquire what God was doing. If they did so inquire the answer was, "Seeking my personal salvation, not justice."

If there was to be any type of social engagement, any response to the multiple crises experienced by Islanders, it was done within the context of charity
or social service. The purpose of social services was evangelistic in nature,
meaning not so much allowing people to hear about Christ, but to enhance
congregational growth. Those pastors who departed from this point of view
and wanted to become politically and socially involved were ostracized or
suspended from their ministerial roles.

This ahistorical and apolitical understanding of spirituality did not feel
genuine to me. It depicted a God who is supposed to be loving while at the
same time remaining insensitive and unconcerned with the social and political
sufferings people were experiencing. At a time when the church could proclaim the good news of the gospel in a liberating mode, I witnessed the church
encouraging social alienation and passivity in the name of God.

This vision of spirituality had a strong, negative impact on me. It forced
me to consider alternatives to the ordained ministry. But more significantly
for our present purpose, it made me suspect of the language of spirituality.
Even today when someone argues for the importance of spiritual development, I hear it as code for promoting and supporting social conservatism,
private virtue, and personal self-righteousness and piety. I always wonder if it
is just another attempt to use theological and religious claims to justify social,
political, and moral indifference and irresponsibility.

As a graduate student and later as professor of ethics at two theological
seminaries, I have heard the debate over spirituality and spiritual formation
continue with more or less intensity. The content of the debate has been quite
similar to what I experienced before. My views, however, have become more
nuanced and optimistic.

During the last ten years, seminary students, laypersons, pastors, church
leaders, even academic accrediting bodies have clamored for courses in and
programs for spiritual formation. Laypersons want their pastors to be, among
other things, professionally capable of helping them see how they can respond
to God's presence in their performance of their secular vocation and their
day-to-day lives. Laypersons seek to become more theologically sophisti-
cated and want pastors who are challenging and well prepared in the areas
of spiritual growth and the care of souls. Pastors recognize that they need a
strong spiritual grounding in order to perform the ever growing and more
complex pastoral tasks entrusted to them. They recognize that a strong spiritual grounding is an indispensable part of the support system that sustains
them in their efforts to form and give direction to their faith communities.
Seminary students expect their course of study to nurture their vocational
identity, nurture that includes honoring their commitment and longing to see
more clearly how their academic studies are part and parcel of their Christian

journey. Accrediting agencies want to promote both sound academic standards fitting the practice of ministry while preserving both the professional mission and the religious identity of Christian institutions as distinct from other centers of academic learning. Church leaders believe that the spiritual formation of pastors and laypersons will enhance the health and wholeness of the institutional church and of congregational life.

All seem to agree that spirituality, spiritual growth, and spiritual formation do not just happen. They believe spiritual growth must be an intentional task of the church, a task that needs the guidance of those within a faith community who have an understanding of the community's spiritual traditions and practices. Some argue that there is need for spiritual specialists, people trained and practiced and who have an in-depth understanding of the dynamics of spiritual development that fosters spiritual maturity.

I have come to believe that these voices cannot be ignored and should not be dismissed as a religious fad. As I mentioned above, I now see spiritual formation as an essential concern and a traditional legacy of the community of faith. It is a necessary and indispensable dimension of what it means to be a Christian and is intrinsically intertwined with what it means to be human. Just as we are social and political beings, we are spiritual beings. I strongly believe that one cannot be a Christian without seeking to live a life in the spirit in which Jesus lived or in imitation of Christ. The imitation of Christ, of course, does not mean that we are called to do what exactly Jesus did. Such a claim would be a denial of the unique political, social, cultural, and historical dimensions of our own incarnations. The imitation of Christ consists in living in the same spirit that Jesus lived, a life of faithfulness to God and of service to those, in particular "the least of these" (Matt. 25:40, 45), with whom we have been called to share our lives.

However, it is quite difficult for me to give a precise definition of spirituality. Moreover, I do not expect that my understanding of spirituality will be readily accepted by all faithful and reasonable people. Spiritual talk is and probably should remain ambiguous, conflict-ridden, and subject to many interpretations. To better understand what I mean by spirituality, I will follow Aristotle's advice regarding moral understanding and practice—that the best way to learn about the virtues and morality in general is to follow the virtuous and morally good person. My view of spirituality is based on the modeling of those whom I identify as spiritual saints and spiritual mentors. The former reveal to me the ideal of spirituality, and the latter reveal what is possible and required.

My sense of spirituality thus is founded upon some of the basic traits of those I consider spiritual giants and people who have been formative in allowing me to understand my own experiences and my faith commitments. Among the

giants whom I identify as spiritually grounded people, I would include Martin
Luther King Jr., Mahatma Gandhi, Mother Teresa, Cesar Chavez, Desmond
Tutu, Oscar Romero, and Dom Helder Camara, just to name a few of the most
well-known. There are many lesser-known but equally important people who
have also modeled for me what an authentic spiritual life looks like, such as
the Maryknoll sisters Maura Clark and Ita Ford, the Ursuline sister Dorothy
Kazel, and lay missionary Jean Donovan, who were assassinated in San Salva-
dor for their work with refugees and the poor. Closer to me historically are
those brothers and sisters in Christ who have paid the ultimate price for their
struggle for human rights to serve refugees, the economically oppressed, the
politically dominated, and those made culturally and religiously marginal and
silent. These saints have occupied pews next to or near me and have made an
indelible mark on me regarding what it means to be a disciple of Christ.

I have found three elements to be characteristic of these saints. First, they
all assume a theocentric point of view. They respond to the many challenges
of life, both to those unique crisis situations such as natural disasters, untimely
death, economic devastation, political chaos, violence, and persecutions, as
well as to the more day-to-day challenges such as birth, aging, and other life
changes, in light of their understanding of God's nature and purpose. Second,
their theological commitments provide them with a strong moral dimension.
A faithful life is one lived in the pursuit of a good life, a life lived by committing to projects and causes greater than one's narrow self-interests. Finally,
they recognize the need to engage in serious social analysis and cultural interpretation in order to live a faithful life that is effective in responding to God's
presence in our midst.

Let me attempt to unravel some of the implications of these three dimensions for my understanding of the spiritual life.

A THEOCENTRIC POINT OF VIEW

A theocentric perspective entails a holistic interpretation of God's presence
and purposes. God is not limited to the religious, the private, or the intimate
spheres of life. Rather, God is sovereign within *all* spheres or realms of life:
the private and the public, the intimate and the relational, the church and the
political realm. This understanding was an essential element of my experience in the movements of political resistance and within the various organizations committed to the empowerment of Latino-Americans. In these
contexts, I experienced how the transcendent is related to and inclusive of
the historical. I believe that spirituality is most genuine when it is mediated
historically and that contrary to removing us from history, politics, and social

existence, an authentic spirituality gives history, politics, and social existence their true meaning.

In my experience with Central American base communities, I discovered how the traditional practice of the spiritual disciplines, including prayer, contemplation, Bible study, meditation, and many others, must be accompanied by the concrete historical practices of justice, love, charity, and other forms of service. The intentional and disciplined cultivation of piety that is essential for spirituality must go hand in hand with the public-spiritedness that motivates one to a concern for public life and to be inclined to serve and enhance the common good. As the study of the Scriptures gives light to the historical events in which we are engaged, concrete engagement allows us to read Scripture in a different way. The classical spiritual practices and the sociohistorical practices of service to others nurture and give more depth to each other, thereby assisting in the process of discerning God's presence and discerning how best to respond.

A covenant interpretation of the Sabbath command, for example, uplifts its communal and nurturing dimension rather than limiting it to one's own self-interest and needs. The command demands more than ensuring a day of rest. More than a command or right to respite, it is fundamentally a mandate from God to the community to be sure that it provides all its members with work. Not to do so would mean that the community itself becomes an obstacle for some to abide by the command, since those who do not work cannot rest. The focus is on creating an inclusive and caring community and on providing work for those who need it, so all may be full members and participate in all matters that define the community.

In this context, the claims of King, Chavez, Romero, and Gandhi—namely, that the cosmos is inclined toward justice and peace—come alive. Our present historical moment is one in which the economic, social, cultural, and political dimensions of our existence call for close attention and action. A spirit-full life has to respond to suffering people in one or more of these dimensions. It becomes self-evident that the integrity and authenticity of spirituality remain tied to historical praxis or transforming action. As spirituality fosters contemplation, it does so for the sake of a more faithful active presence in the world; as it fosters creative introspection, it does so for the sake of service to others. Integrity also demands that there exists a consistency between the word proclaimed and the action taken. Furthermore, when speaking of service we must not limit it to charity and social well-being, important as these are, but we must also include political empowerment, cultural authenticity, and economic emancipation.

I have been fortunate to share my life with friends who witness how spirituality becomes a historical force, whose lives demonstrate a dimension of what it means to be a historically efficient person. They have revealed to me, and I have tried to respond in kind, that one must commit and contribute to a historical project. There are many such projects that seek to humanize the world and bring our sociohistorical reality closer to our understandings of God's reign. Spirituality is an effort of incarnation, of allowing the Spirit to become flesh. I have come to believe that the greater danger for the spiritual life is not to be too immanent in its focus, but for history to leave us behind or for us to opt to leave history behind.

THE MORAL OR COVENANT DIMENSION
OF SPIRITUALITY

I teach ethics in part because I have a moral interpretation of the religious. I have come to believe that spiritual formation must engage one in the pursuit of moral goals, both personal and communal, that are worthy of one's life energy. My commitment to Hispanic theological education is one of those goals. A covenant notion of spirituality seems the most fitting, since it uplifts the thoroughly social and relational understanding of human existence and highlights the moral imperative of regard for others as essential to morality and human existence. We must care about the quality of our relationships and commit to society's betterment not only because these commitments may provide us with the things we need to achieve our purposes, but mainly because they express and are formative for our humanity. Life in community, therefore, is good in itself and not just instrumentally good. The covenant nature of spirituality also emphasizes that community is not a human creation or a social contract, but rather a gift. We are born and nurtured in community, and communities exist before we join them and remain after we depart.

Our relational nature reveals our dependence. We are dependent on God our creator, redeemer, and sustainer, and we are dependent on one another. We could not survive, much less flourish, were it not for the many tender mercies that we receive from those with whom we share life. Human autonomy, while an important value, particularly in North American culture, is a secondary one.

A key element in the wisdom of Hispanic cultures is that we recognize that our capacity to give ourselves goals and life plans is very much an outcome of our relationships, both personal and structural. Hispanics' sense of community is quite strong. We believe the claim that "it takes a village to care for a child" is literally true. If it were not for the provision, protection, and nurture we receive from others, we would not survive, much less flourish.

In this perspective, the talents and skills we have naturally, and the ones we develop through hard work and discipline, are seen ultimately as gifts. Given the gift of life, we are called in all we do to take into consideration how this gift affects not just our well-being, interests, and desires, but also how it affects those with whom we share life. The moral point of view does not demand that we only be self-sacrificial. It is legitimate to seek after one's self-interests. What is demanded from the moral point of view, and from my sense of spirituality, is that in the pursuit of our self-interests we must also remain deliberately aware of how our self-interests may account for the needs and the well-being of others. In choosing one's vocation, for example, a covenant of spirituality calls us to consider how it serves others and not just ourselves. In choosing which skills and talents to develop, we should not opt for the easiest ones but for the ones that serve others and contribute to their life possibilities. This is what is meant by a spirituality of public-spiritedness.

A covenant spirituality recognizes that life in community is difficult to achieve and maintain. One of the things I learned early in my commitment with solidarity groups is that they are not communities of saints. In my experience, to sustain and enjoy community, we all need to practice what I consider to be Jesus' main political teaching: forgiveness, patience, and sacrifice. It is impossible for me to think of any lasting relationship in which I have not practiced forgiveness, patience, and sacrifice and in which others have not practiced these toward me. There is no possibility of community without these practices. Forgiveness, patience, and sacrifice allow us to begin again and mend the breaches that we cause to our relationships due to our failures. Forgiveness and sacrifice are essential to community, since it is the nature of human activity, particularly in one's collective actions, that there are unintended consequences, unforeseen and unwelcome accidents, and unexpected surprises. These practices free us to continue to venture into an uncertain future. Patience, forgiveness, and sacrifice enable us to reconcile with one another and give us the capacity to be steadfast, so our relationships endure. Few genuine relationships, personal or political, are "tit for tat"; there is always at least one party that gives more than it receives. In all the movements in which I have participated, sacrifice and learning how to carry each others' burdens, which are never equally distributed, have been necessary for these movements to continue and flourish.

Covenant spirituality affirms the claim that to know God is to do justice, understood as the struggle to emancipate the poor and marginal. Justice is one of the indispensable conditions for the creation of what Martin Luther King Jr. called a multicultural, beloved community. Such a community recognizes that if it is true that all must have in order to be, it is still the case that the purpose of being is not simply having or consuming. Justice seeks not only basic provision for all its members, but to create spaces and occasions for all to be active participants in those matters that affect their lives in significant ways and to be recognized as full and viable members. Hispanics debate whether the struggle for emancipation is primarily one of cultural affirmation or of political empowerment. We all recognize, however, that attention to both dimensions of life is essential to the liberation of our people.

Covenant justice is contextualized spirituality. For many of us, spirituality is a historical force that both denounces the sin or evil that exists within our present structures and announces the possibility of a new order as an integral part of the good news of the gospel. The centrality of justice in our sense of spirituality also leads us to underscore a belief in the preferential option of the poor, which includes God's preference and our own. We give the poor preferential treatment not because of their superior moral character or because they are uniquely deserving. They are preferred because God so wills it. Humanly and politically speaking, the poor reveal the direction that the community must take in order to overcome the unique forms of suffering that afflict it and to forward social justice.

Opting for a life of commitment to the emancipation of the socially and culturally marginal, the racially and sexually victimized, the economically oppressed and the politically dominated is itself an expression of the presence of the Spirit's loving, just, and reconciling intentions. It is humbling to hear the *testimonios* (witness) of simple folk confessing how the Spirit not only calls them to such a life commitment but, more importantly, gives them the strength and courage to remain steadfast.

It is somewhat paradoxical that we are called to reject the unjust suffering that curtails the life possibilities of the poor while at the same time being called to endure the suffering brought upon us because of our refusal to conform to an unjust state of affairs. Those who struggle for justice know quite well that the struggle entails sacrifices. It is by the power of the Spirit that we can endure and resist. By the power of the Spirit we can bracket our self-interest and give generously of ourselves to struggle side-by-side with the poor. And as our saints reveal to us, in our self-giving we must remain humble and not expect praise and recognition. In fact, it helps us contain the temptation to fall into self-righteousness and nurture attitudes of superiority to recognize that we are the ones who must show gratitude to those we serve. We need to be grateful, since it is in solidarity with "the least of these" that we find a way of life full of meaning and fulfillment and discover a unique way of being human. We also experience how the struggle for social justice, economic equality, and political inclusiveness is integral to our personal relationship with God.

The struggles for the emancipation of the poor are complex, difficult, and frustrating. There are many needs and challenges. None of us can respond to them all. But all of us can choose at least one struggle toward which to contribute whatever we can. Structural changes are difficult to visualize and even harder to bring about. The resistance that one encounters from the powerful who feel that their interests are adversely affected, and the resistance one encounters from the poor themselves, who fear the retaliation of the powerful and who doubt whether they will benefit from the sacrifices asked from them, generate many pitfalls and frustrating moments. It is amid such frustrations that one experiences how the Spirit frees us from the temptation of cynicism, resignation, and despair, which feed our apathy, and from being careless and wasteful in the use of our vitality and energy. All struggles of emancipation need spirituality stronger than fear and terror. Only through the Spirit may we respond creatively to meet the exigencies or demands of the struggle while remaining open to new historical possibilities.

People committed to struggles of emancipation of the poor experience the core of hope that is part of all genuine spirituality. To act in hope is to proclaim that the ultimate mystery of reality is one of goodness and is worthy of our commitment. Hope is a call to action, to bring about the best possibilities hidden within reality. In spite of the limitations and distortions that all processes of emancipation go through, those who struggle with the poor discover hope within hopeless situations. The hope of the poor is grounded not in political success but in a primordial act of confidence in God. This hope is grounded in a conviction that, in spite of all, good (and God) is real and mightier and more basic than evil. In hope one affirms that ultimately the depth of reality embodies justice and kindness. Hope affirms that the acts that fit the goodness of creation will endure throughout history. In this sense, hope is more judicious than hopelessness.

SOCIOCULTURAL INTERPRETATION

Spirit-full people strive for truthfulness. They approach reality not only in its hope and possibilities but also in all its sinfulness. As the saying goes, spirit-full people must "speak truth to the power and principalities" that sustain dominance of some over others. Spirit-full people denounce gaps in wealth, power, and cultural recognition, and they affirm the capacity to fulfill one's potential for sin. We are sinful when we violate God's primordial harmony by keeping humans separate from and in conflict with each other. Sin is not only personal but also structural. It manifests in the human capacity to dominate not only through personal selfishness but also in the ways that social, national, and global arrangements sustain the life possibilities of some at the expense of others.

Spirituality calls for the kind of truth telling that is also truth making. Spirituality refuses to accept oppression and domination as natural and inevitable, and it rejects the philosophical and theological justification of dehumanizing poverty and powerlessness—namely, that "the poor will always be with you." Spirituality makes it clear that the presence of the poor is a sign of the absence of God's love and care, and it faithfully unveils poverty and powerlessness as historical realities that can and must be changed. Truth, therefore, comes part and parcel with the struggle for justice and the practice of love.

To be effective in this task, it is indispensable that we make use of the various social sciences available to us today. They are indispensable conversation partners in the struggle to emancipate the powerless and marginal. Knowledge provided by the social sciences helps us see the dynamics, including contradictions, present in every social organization, which provides an opportunity to unveil redeeming possibilities within them. The social sciences are essential for assisting us in changing the current balance of power in the pursuit of more inclusive and humane social circumstances. This suggests that those seeking to live a spiritual life do well to learn from social-scientific research and practice and to incorporate these insights into the ways they live.

These three elements of a spirit-full life—a theocentric point of view, moral and covenantal commitments, and sociocultural interpretations—as modeled by the saints I mentioned above, have been instrumental in sustaining my commitment to the various organizations that have sought to improve the conditions of Latino-Americans. These elements have helped sustain my belief that what is real is governed by love, harmony, and justice as elements of the nature and purpose of God. These elements have also nurtured my conviction that humanizing the world is a task that is self-justifying. Moreover, these elements of a spirit-full life have made me recognize that people of goodwill, believers and nonbelievers alike, can be in solidarity. We are called to be agents committed to creating a new state of affairs more inclusive and life sustaining for all of us. In the end, goodness will endure, and even though the struggle for justice seems never ending, it is meaningful in itself, so that our achievements will last.

13

Keeping an Open Heart
in Troubled Times

Self-Empathy as a Christian Spiritual Practice

DEBORAH VAN DEUSEN HUNSINGER

How do you keep your heart open when you see person after person afflicted with trauma? I used to think that 95 percent of the female population in this country had been sexually abused as children. Were the statistics of sexual abuse vastly underreported, I wondered, or was my perception skewed because of my work as a pastoral counselor? When you listen to stories of pain day after day, how do you keep your own spirit alive? The root meaning of the word *compassion* is "to suffer with." What do you do when you reach the limit of your capacity for compassion?

We are contextual beings whose many contexts exist not simply outside us but also within us. As one member of a particular family, each of us internalizes every member in it, along with the family culture as a whole with its unique dynamics, both for good and for ill. Similarly, as cultural beings we dwell within a particular culture, but that culture also dwells in us.[1] We internalize the context in which we live, a context so complex that it would take hours adequately to describe it.

The overarching context that each of us has internalized—that affects us daily, body and soul—includes the tragic events of September 11, 2001, the wars in Iraq and Afghanistan, and the daily terror and anguish of those in the Middle East. Depending on which issues live in our hearts, we may also bear the pain of those who suffer from HIV-AIDS, political oppression, torture, or any number of tragic features of today's world. As members of a common humanity, each of us participates in the world's distress. A challenge for those in ministry is that we internalize certain levels of pain by virtue of

1. A. J. van den Blink, "Empathy amid Diversity: Problems and Possibilities," *Journal of Pastoral Theology*, Summer 1993, 8.

our commitment to be fully present with the handful of persons we serve on a daily basis. The cumulative effect of being in the presence of so much pain puts us in danger of compassion fatigue, in which we simply reach our limits.[2] We stop caring, not because we want to but because we no longer have the capacity to take in anything more.

Philip Hallie, author of the book *Lest Innocent Blood Be Shed*, describes the danger of having a vocation that continually confronts one with suffering and evil. On the Nazi era, he writes:

> For years, I had been studying the slow crushing and grinding of a human being by other human beings. . . . Across all these studies, the pattern of the strong crushing the weak kept repeating itself and repeating itself, so that when I was not bitterly angry, I was bored at the repetition of the patterns of persecution.
>
> When I was not desiring to be cruel with the cruel, I was a monster—like, perhaps, many others around me—who could look upon torture and death without a shudder.[3]

Being exposed to evil in this secondhand way had taken a heavy toll on Hallie's spirit, even without his knowing it. Harry Wilmer, a Jungian analyst who studied the repetitive nightmares of Vietnam veterans ten years after the war had ended, acknowledges something of the personal cost: "It goes almost without saying that my work with these men was often painful to me. Many times I asked myself why I had taken it on, or more correctly, why it had taken me on. At times I experienced war nightmares and dreams of combat. Then I knew that the suffering of the men was getting to me."[4]

Although Hallie apparently defended against the pain for a while, he came to see that he had done so at the cost of his own humanity. Wilmer, by contrast, allowed the veterans' suffering to affect him intimately. Years after the war ended, he himself awoke at night in a sweat of terror. The war lived on, as he says, "in the nightmares of combat veterans and in the collective unconscious of us all."[5]

In January 2006 my husband, George Hunsinger, organized a national conference for religious and military leaders, human rights activists, and lawyers to launch the National Religious Campaign Against Torture, an organization of "national, regional, and local religious and secular organizations committed to ensuring that the United States does not engage in torture or

---

2. See Beth Hudnall Stamm, *Professional Quality of Life: Compassion Satisfaction, Compassion Fatigue, and Secondary Traumatic Stress*, http://www.proqol.org.

3. Philip Hallie, *Lest Innocent Blood Be Shed* (New York: Harper & Row, 1979), 2.

4. Harry A. Wilmer, "The Healing Nightmare: A Study of the War Dreams of Vietnam Combat Veterans," *Quadrant* 19, no. 1 (spring 1986): 57.

5. Ibid., 47.

cruel, inhuman and degrading treatment of anyone, without exceptions."[6] My husband spends hours each day reading volumes of material on the Internet about our current world crisis. Books on torture are piled on the breakfast table, in the living room, and on the floor beside the bed. Stories of torture fill his heart, fueling his commitment to do what he can to bring these horrifying practices to an end.

One evening some months ago, as I went to him to say goodnight, he began to tell me about what he was reading. Worried about the next day's responsibilities, I interrupted him, stating emphatically that I couldn't bear to hear stories about torture right before going to bed. I was anxious about lying awake for hours seeing these images over and over in my mind's eye. No longer able to keep my heart open, I told my husband with considerable energy that *I just could not bear* to hear one more story of trauma.

As I have reflected on that moment, I have come to see something of the cost of telling myself that "I cannot bear it." First, I cut myself off from the solace of shared suffering, in this case my husband's and my own. In subsequent weeks, my husband acknowledged that he was now consciously keeping such stories from me. Second, I found that I was shielding myself from any news that might upset my peace of mind or interfere with my ability to concentrate. Third, I felt regret over constricting my awareness in this way, limiting my freedom to learn and to act. The victims of torture were actually suffering torture while I could not even bear to hear about it. Wanting to *expand* my capacities for compassion rather than shrink away from such stories in self-protection, I found myself at odds with my core values.

This, then, is the dilemma: How do I keep an open heart toward those who need my compassion, whether it is my husband with whom I share my life; myself, as I face my very real limits; or the victims of torture living in prisons or dungeons whose very lives may depend upon the willingness of others to feel their plight and act on their behalf?

NONVIOLENT COMMUNICATION: SELF-EMPATHY

In his book *Nonviolent Communication: A Language of Life*, Marshall Rosenberg teaches a mode of consciousness and a set of skills that enable us not only to practice empathic reception of others but also to learn how to respond empathically to ourselves.[7] While empathy is considered an essential skill for pastoral care, I do not believe that it can flourish apart from self-empathy.

6. The quotation is from the organization's Web site: http://www.nrcat.org.
7. Marshall Rosenberg, *Nonviolent Communication: A Language of Life* (Encinitas, CA: Puddle-Dancer Press, 2003); see, for example, chap. 9.

In order to hear another with compassion, we need first to hear ourselves with compassion. If our anxiety is triggered (as mine was when my husband wished to share something with me), we are unable to hear little beyond our own internal static. As I have written elsewhere, "Much of the self-discipline required in listening to others without interjecting one's own reactions develops as one learns to pay attention to one's anxiety. In order to focus on another, one must know, paradoxically, how to pay attention to oneself."[8]

Through nonviolent communication (NVC), Rosenberg teaches us how to pay attention not only to our feelings but also to the underlying needs or values that are causing the feelings. Needs are understood to be universal qualities that enhance life. They are life-giving by definition. Thus, all human beings have physical needs, such as food, rest, water, warmth, and shelter. But just as essential to human thriving are our interpersonal needs for love, acceptance, understanding, community, and mutuality, among others. In addition, we might identify spiritual needs for forgiveness, hope, courage, trust, faith, and integrity. These brief lists are meant to be suggestive, not definitive. What is pertinent here is that needs are evidence of our basic humanity. Though they transcend culture, each culture has its own particular way of understanding and expressing them. For Rosenberg, human needs are the underlying motivation for all our choices, whether we are conscious of them or not.[9] When our needs are met, we typically feel satisfied, delighted, or joyful. When our needs are unmet, we might feel frustrated, angry, sorrowful, or perplexed.

When we have chronically unmet needs, we experience emotional pain and need healing. When we attune ourselves inwardly with an attitude of caring attentiveness toward ourselves, seeking to understand our own feelings and needs, we are practicing self-empathy. I believe that we cannot remain openhearted toward others unless we know how to metabolize our own pain. In the example I have given, I was unable to connect with my husband's pain because I was not fully present to my own. I needed more understanding of my reaction to his request to share what he was reading. Why, I wondered, did I interrupt him with such intensity?

I have come to regard moments like these, when I am triggered into uncharacteristic reactivity, as significant nodal points of potential healing and growth. I believe that any time I react, rather than respond, it is because forces outside my awareness are at work. This is the "psychopathology of everyday life" that Freud describes so lucidly. Slips of the tongue, moments of lightning rage, or an irritability over which I have no apparent control

---

8. Deborah van Deusen Hunsinger, *Pray without Ceasing: Revitalizing Pastoral Care* (Grand Rapids: Wm. B. Eerdmans, 2006), 85.
    9. Rosenberg, *Nonviolent Communication*, esp. chap. 5.

are opportunities to become aware of unknown forces at work within me. In NVC terms, these are opportunities to practice self-empathy in order to connect with unmet needs.

The life-giving human needs at work in me were as yet impossible for me to grasp. On the surface, my need for rest seemed paramount. Yet the intensity of my reaction signaled that something deeper was possibly at stake. In the days and weeks that followed, I found myself repeating the words "I cannot bear it." I would say to myself, "I cannot bear to hear the stories of abused and tortured human beings; I simply cannot bear it." Though I understood this kind of self-talk to be life-alienating, something that disconnected me from myself and others, I did not know how to change it.

PRACTICING SELF-EMPATHY

Self-empathy gives us the opportunity to listen to our own hearts with the same quality of compassionate attention that we would offer another in our best moments. However, simply *finding words* that accurately describe our feelings and needs is not the same as actually *connecting with them*. The process of connecting with an activated need in any particular situation requires us first to notice what is happening in the body. We ask ourselves gently what it is that we are seeking: "What is the longing of your heart?" As we listen for the answer, we focus on what goes on in our body, not on words in our mind.

As we attend to the body, we are seeking to name the unmet need that activated the feeling of frustration or pain. NVC teaches a kind of exquisite awareness of the range and variety of human needs. When several needs are tied up together in a gnarled ball, it takes some time, care, and patience to identify each one. When we discover and accurately connect with the activated need or needs, we experience an internal shift in the body. By internal shift, I mean something similar to what we experience when we finally remember a person's name that has been on "the tip of our tongue." When we discover the name, our body relaxes; we might give a deep sigh and say, "I am so *relieved* to have remembered her name." In NVC, a similar feeling of shift and relaxation comes when we find the need that matches our feeling.[10]

For example, when I am upset by dirty dishes piled high in the kitchen, I want to identify my underlying need. Is it a need for order? Am I upset because I value a sense of order and beauty in my surroundings? Or is my underlying

10. Readers familiar with Eugene Gendlin's method of *focusing*, will see close parallels with the practices he teaches. Both Rosenberg and Gendlin were students of Carl Rogers. See Eugene Gendlin, *Focusing* (New York: Bantam, 1982).

need one for trust and reliability? Perhaps I had a conversation with a family member who promised to clean the kitchen before going off with friends but did not follow through on that promise. Or is it really support that I need most of all? Are guests coming in thirty minutes, and am I desperately in need of support to make everything ready? The need, in other words, is always nested in a set of particular circumstances. I alone can identify my true need by attuning myself to how my body responds. What need, if met, would bring about palpable relaxation in my body?

The feelings I identify then become the thread that takes me deeper into my underlying longings. The feelings are usually more on the surface, whereas the needs are the buried treasure. We can feel the same feelings for weeks, months, even decades; they remain inert, a simple story that we tell again and again unless we connect with the unfulfilled desires that are causing the feelings. In NVC it is not necessary to understand the problem intellectually to bring about clarity or release. In fact, intellectual understanding can actually delay or block the desired liberating shift.

In order fully to connect with my need (rather than merely identifying *the word* that describes my need), I might imagine a situation where that need is fully met. For example, I *connect emotionally* with the joy I feel whenever I see this quality (e.g., a desire for order, trust, reliability, or support, to return to the example above) in myself or anyone else. In other words, truly to connect with the need means that I imagine it as something fulfilled and present rather than as something lacking.

Truly to connect with the need is to experience its life-giving power. When I check how it feels in my body not to have the need met, I notice a heavy, tight, or constricted feeling. In order to connect with its *life-giving value*, by contrast, I shift to imagine its being fully met. How do I actually feel *in my body* when I have order and beauty surrounding me, for example, or when I trust that those I live with will follow through on their promises? When I identify the actual need at work in the specific circumstances, I will experience a shift *in my body* when I ask myself this question. As I look inwardly with self-empathy, I am looking for an inner sense of release or relaxation, an "aha" feeling: "*This* is the quality of being that I want in my life. I want my surroundings to be orderly and beautiful because it gives me peace and joy." I don't focus, in other words, on the dirty dishes or messy kitchen, but rather on the feeling in my body when the need is met.

Connecting with the need means to connect with its beauty, as one NVC trainer has put it.[11] Connecting means that we live in a consciousness of this

---

11. I first learned of the "beauty of human needs" from Robert Gonzales at an NVC International Intensive Training session in Rochester, New York, in July 2004.

need or quality as an enduring value in our life. When we dwell in the need, we celebrate its presence and mourn its absence. When we feel the pain associated with its absence, we shift our attention to the joy of its intrinsic beauty or preciousness. Connected inwardly to its life-giving goodness, we may consent to living vulnerably with our unfulfilled longings.

SELF-EMPATHY AS OPENING THE HEART

In an NVC workshop on self-empathy, NVC trainer Robert Gonzales gave participants instructions on how to identify some sentence in our minds that seemed to disconnect us from ourselves or others. I knew that the sentence "I cannot bear it" truly disconnected me from others because I had seen how it disconnected me from my husband. I was also aware that it alienated me from myself.

With Robert's guidance, I began to repeat, "I cannot bear it." Because we were working on "old" material (as opposed to a current trigger), Robert encouraged me to repeat the phrase several times until I could become fully connected to the emotions associated with it. After several repetitions, the underlying pain searing my soul emerged. What was it *in particular* that I was telling myself I could not bear? What was the *specific observation* that I was reacting to?[12] In this case, the observation was not something my husband had actually said but was something that I had remembered from an earlier conversation. What in particular I could not bear was the torture technique of waterboarding, in which human beings are brought to the very brink of drowning, and the hypothermia techniques that put naked prisoners into cold prison cells. Shivering and miserable, they are denied the most basic human need for warmth. As I lay snug in my bed at night with my down comforter wrapped around me, I would meditate on their plight until I thought I would go mad with the terror, the rage, and the sorrow of it.

As I began to tell Robert the specific images that haunted my imagination, my tears began to flow to the point that my words were swallowed up by sobs. Robert did not simply hear my agony; he listened *for my needs*. He heard and reflected back each need with care: "You long for compassion for these prisoners. You want respect *for all people*, no matter what their sins or crimes. You

---

12. In nonviolent communication, it is necessary to specify the exact thing one is reacting to so that there is clarity about the triggering issue. One aims to describe the specific observation (the precise words or events that were seen, heard, or remembered) in any communication with oneself or others. The NVC "template" for complete communication is OFNR: observation, feeling, need, request.

want the truth to be spoken. You want it known what our country is doing to human beings in our name."

It required intense concentration as I struggled to give words to every facet of the pain. Then suddenly, unexpectedly, *when every need had been fully heard and named*, I became calm. I said quietly, "I can bear it because I just did. I can bear it because you were willing to hear it."[13]

As I processed what had just occurred, I was astonished to realize that in shielding myself from the pain I felt, I had been perpetuating the very thing that I abhorred. In a strange way, I was unwilling to acknowledge what we were doing to other human beings because I continually told myself that I could not bear to do so. I was unwilling to speak the truth as I understood it because I feared plunging others into the same nightmare of raw pain, fear, and grief that I was avoiding in myself. I myself thus kept the very complicity of silence that would enable these practices to continue. Were there others, I wondered, who also told themselves that they could not bear to acknowledge the truth? Did I now understand something of the horror and shame, the sickening feeling that might have swept the hearts of our German brothers and sisters during the Nazi era when they heard whispers of what was being done in their name?

SELF-EMPATHY AS A CHRISTIAN SPIRITUAL PRACTICE

NVC is a form of consciousness and set of skills that has an implicit spirituality all its own. Depending upon the theological assumptions of any particular teacher, different aspects will be emphasized. I have been instructed and edified over the years as I have learned from serious practitioners of other religious paths how NVC has contributed to their ability to live out their deepest convictions. This ongoing interreligious dialogue is a fascinating subject that, unfortunately, lies outside the scope of this essay. From the beginning of my own study of NVC, however, my interest has been in how it can be used practically in living out the gospel. My specific focus here is how I understand self-empathy as a Christian spiritual practice.

As a Christian, I am aware that my needs and core values are deeply shaped by the gospel. Whenever I seek to respond empathically to others, I am assuming that they, like all human beings, have, in the words of John Webster, "a

---

13. One of the reasons I felt so fully heard and received was the expression of anguish on Robert's face as he listened. I was moved by his willingness to enter into my suffering with such compassion. The example also shows the interconnection between empathy and self-empathy. I was unable to have empathy for myself until I had received empathy from another.

given teleology. . . . They are not simply discrete units of personal need, but are what they are as they belong to an order of reality with certain ends."[14] I understand the order of reality to which they belong as the kingdom of God. In other words, I understand all human need in the light of the prayer that Jesus taught, that God's kingdom come on earth as it is in heaven (Matt. 6:10).

In my personal anguish over the plight of the tortured, I recognized my own urgent need for the balm of human compassion. What I could not bear to imagine was the apparent lack of compassion for the suffering of human beings who were denied access to the most fundamental human need for breath and warmth. How could human beings so harden their hearts toward other human beings who, like them, were made in the image of God?

It is a curious fact that in the New Testament the verb for our word *compassion* is used only of Jesus or of the God-figure in Jesus' parables.[15] I have come to see that my understanding of compassion has an inevitable christological shape. My faith has been decisively shaped by the stories of Jesus' compassion for the blind, the deaf, the lame, the ill, and the grief-stricken. I am moved by the stories in which Jesus has compassion on the crowds, in which he feeds the thousands who hunger for bread and for the smallest morsel of hope. I am astounded by his words of compassion toward those who brought about his death. In all these ways and more, I understand Jesus' compassion to be "a window of access into the nature of . . . God's vulnerability and willingness to suffer with us."[16] "Compassion," writes Andrew Purves, "reveals the inner nature of God."[17] I believe that Robert's willingness to open his heart with compassion toward me had its source in God's grace, enabling him to "participate in God's compassion for the world."[18] Compassion, in my understanding, does not arise out of our own limited human capacities, but is grounded instead in *God's* love for the world.

Whenever I practice self-empathy, I am in search of what I most deeply need in any given situation. Though I can sometimes be badly mistaken in assessing my true need, in Christian worship, song, and prayer I confess my need of God and of God's grace in its rich multiplicity of forms. When discouraged, I need patience or courage. If I am disappointed in myself, I may identify my need as a sturdy sense of integrity or a more complete honesty. When afraid, I may recognize that I am lacking trust. If I only had more

---

14. John Webster, "Response [to Caroline Simon]," in *For the Sake of the World: Karl Barth and the Future of Ecclesial Theology*, ed. George Hunsinger (Grand Rapids: Wm. B. Eerdmans, 2004), 163.

15. Andrew Purves, *The Search for Compassion* (Louisville, KY: Westminster/John Knox Press, 1989), 16.

16. Ibid.

17. Ibid., 12.

18. Ibid.

faith, I could act with more freedom. If I am in despair, I recognize my need for hope. Our human needs, in other words, are all ultimately rooted and grounded in God. They are not finally qualities that we can develop on our own but rather come as gifts from above.

It follows, therefore, that self-empathy as a Christian spiritual practice leads directly to prayer: to asking God for what I need. When I turn to God in prayer, I don't simply rattle off requests as if I were making a grocery list. Instead, I meditate on the true nature of my need and offer it up to God, trusting him as the author of every good and perfect gift. I cling to the promise that God will hear my requests and meet my needs (or else give me the strength to live in the midst of unmet need): "Rejoice in the Lord always. . . . The Lord is near. Do not worry about anything, but in everything by prayer and supplication with thanksgiving let your requests be made known to God. . . . And my God will fully satisfy every need of yours according to his riches in glory in Christ Jesus" (Phil. 4:4–6, 19).

Prayer connects us to God and to all the needs that are fulfilled in him.[19] Through its stories and images of our core human needs fulfilled in the person of Jesus Christ, the gospel actually shapes the awareness of our needs. Jesus Christ is presented as the light of the world, fulfilling our human longings for illumination, for wisdom, for understanding. As the bread of life, he is seen to fulfill our daily need for basic sustenance, in both body and soul; as the water of life, he is understood to assuage the thirst of every soul that aches for justice and peace. There is no longer any separation between *your* need and *my* need; there is simply *human* need, which God alone can fulfill. Praying fervently about our needs deepens our sense of longing for God's kingdom to come on earth as in heaven. Indeed, it magnifies our longing until we join the groaning of creation for the new world to come (Rom. 8:22–23).

The gospel also underscores our fundamental need of one another. In the body of Christ, the church, we recognize our profound need for community, for mutual care, forgiveness, and love: "The eye cannot say to the hand, 'I have no need of you,' nor again the head to the feet, 'I have no need of you'" (1 Cor. 12:21). Our attempts to be self-sufficient are revealed as signs of our fallenness and sin. Karl Barth writes, "My humanity depends upon the fact that I am always aware, and my action is determined by the awareness, that I need the assistance of others as a fish needs water."[20] Barth later goes on to say that my humanity *also* depends upon the fact "that I need to *give my assistance*

---

19. See Deborah van Deusen Hunsinger, "Practicing *Koinonia*," *Theology Today* 66, no. 3 (October 2009): 346–67.

20. Karl Barth, *Church Dogmatics*, III/2, *The Doctrine of Creation*, trans. G. W. Bromiley, ed. G. W. Bromiley, T. F. Torrance. (Edinburgh: T. & T. Clark, 2004), 263.

to others as a fish needs water."[21] Thus, Barth underscores Rosenberg's basic conviction that mutual and reciprocal care lies at the very heart of what it means to be human.

I believe that God's love is the wellspring from which we draw when we need compassion for ourselves or others. Not only Robert's caring presence toward me, but my own ability to accept my human limitations, were finally sustained by a transcendent source of caring: the unfathomable abyss of God's love. Though my meditation began in deep grief, it led *through* the anguish for the tortured to compassion for myself and for every human being who consents to bear a portion of the world's suffering. I was filled with gratitude for Robert and for all those willing to keep their hearts open in longing and vulnerability in order to share in the suffering of our frail and fallen humanity.[22]

I believe that it is finally our connection to this transcendent source of compassion that enables us to keep our hearts open in troubled times. When I am exhausted or confused or lost in a wilderness of sorrow, worry, or despair, I believe that there is one to whom I can turn for strength. In worship, in the great hymns and creeds of the church, in the comfort that comes from the simple compassion of another human being, I am comforted by the comfort of the gospel. The New Testament presents Jesus Christ as taking the suffering of the entire world into his own heart. He does not leave us to suffer the anguish of our mortal condition, nor the consequences of our sin, alone. He actively intercedes for us. Though I cannot fathom the depth of such a love, nor comprehend the mystery of his atoning sacrifice, nevertheless, I am able to anchor myself in a transcendent ground for hope, a vision of the redemption of the entire world. Like the saints who have gone before us, I too long for the kingdom of God to come on earth as it is in heaven, where all human needs matter and every human need is fulfilled, where at a great banquet the human family feasts in mutual joy.

CONCLUDING REMARKS

I have sought to introduce a spiritual practice that has given me hope in a time when I desperately needed to be anchored in hope. The events following 9/11 have compelled me to dig more deeply in an attempt to be equal to the times. How do we keep our own spirits alive and not plunge into a sea of despair?

---

21. Ibid., 264.
22. While empathy and self-empathy are interlocking technical skills, compassion, in terms of one's willingness to suffer with others, says Purves, "is only possible for us in and through our relationship with God." Purves, *Search for Compassion*, 12.

My ability to speak out followed my willingness to enter a cauldron of grief and rage. Until I was able to have compassion for my own suffering, I was paralyzed by the frozen grief in my soul.

The prophetic witness and action to which we are called as Christians cannot endure without a willingness to suffer with those who suffer. Yet we cannot do this work with a glad heart unless we know how to drink regularly from the wellspring of God's compassion for all people. Those of us who work as ministers, counselors, or human helpers know that mourning is itself the work of healing. Active, fully engaged mourning and crying out in lament to God is precisely what enables us to keep our hearts open in troubled times, because we thereby open ourselves to the immeasurable compassion of God for each vulnerable, human heart.

14

Nursing, Eucharist, Psychosis, Metaphor*

KERRY EGAN

Because there was no shade on the window, winter moonlight poured onto the rocking chair and onto the baby and me. It was below zero, as it often is at four in the morning in December in Iowa, and cold seeped through the glass. The baby didn't seem to mind. In the blue light his mouth looked like a tiny morning glory flower planted on my nipple, and his hands held and stroked my breast, as six month-olds do when they nurse. Every now and then he stopped and opened his eyes. When he saw me he would smile for just a second and resume suckling at twice his former speed.

In a few minutes he fell asleep again. As his mouth went slack and his face fell away from me, a trickle of milk flowed from his mouth down his cheek.

Even after he was done nursing, I stayed in the chair, my feet up on an ottoman and a blanket thrown over both of us. Not entirely awake but certainly not asleep. For months, this hour that was not quite morning but no longer really night was the only peaceful time of the day. It was the only time my brain would slow down, the only time that memories of my son's birth did not dominate my thoughts, crashing through and leaving me shaking, crying, in a state of confusion, unable to function, terrified and terrorized.

On this night a thought seeped through. By the time I noticed it, I had been repeating a phrase over and over again: "Take this and eat it. This is my body."

I looked down at Jimmy as he clung to me. "Oh," I said aloud. He stirred, lifted his half-closed eyes to me, and then rooted around until he found the nipple again and settled back into my armpit.

*This essay was published previously in *From the Pews in the Back: Young Women and Catholicism*, ed. Kate Dugan and Jennifer Owens (Collegeville, MN: Liturgical Press, 2009).

"So that's what that means," I whispered.

After thirty-one years as a cradle Catholic, the Eucharist finally made sense.

When Jimmy was born by emergency c-section, the anesthesia failed mid-surgery. When my legs began thrashing on the operating table, the anesthesiologist gave me 200 milligrams of ketamine, a powerful hallucinogenic drug that knocked me into a psychotic break so severe that it functioned as a sort of dissociative anesthesia. Basically, I no longer felt any pain because my mind had been chemically severed from my body.

On ketamine, I had no body but was immersed in a small pink tunnel that swirled around me. The tunnel was some sort of an entity, also bodiless but somehow all encompassing and alive. I was suspended in this being, and I was asking this thing questions. Very patiently, and with a bit of sadness, the entity answered me.

"This can't be all there is," I said, over and over again.

"Yes, this is it. This is the only thing that's real."

"But what about the world?"

"No, that's not real."

"But it is real. I've been there. It was real."

"No, that all comes from your imagination. This is what's real. The rest is just what you want to be real. You made all that up."

"And so there's no meaning to it at all? It all means nothing?"

"That's right. There is no meaning. None of it's real. All the things in the world—you people just made that up to make yourselves feel better."

"This just can't be. This can't be all that is real."

"No, this is it."

And so on, over and over for what I thought was eternity. The entity, either unable or unwilling to comfort me, just kept repeating that it was the only thing that was real.

Nothing mattered; nothing was real. All of existence was a misperception. If nothing else was real, if nothing else mattered, then what was the point of my life? What was the point of life at all?

I had built my adult life around questions of meaning. I was a hospital chaplain. Day in and day out I sat with people as they struggled with questions of suffering and purpose—of their lives, of their illnesses, of their deaths—and it was my job to help them construct meaning out of painful realities. Just a few days before the birth, I'd sent in to the publisher the final revisions of a book I had written about grief and prayer. This was the work I had wanted to devote my life to: to give meaning to loss and suffering. My faith had meant everything to me, and now I was terrified that what this entity said was true. I was terrified of God. I was terrified of life. I lived in a perpetual state of fear and confusion, unable to trust even my own experiences. I didn't know what was real anymore. My waking life felt like sleep, and the desolation of the tunnel was reality.

"Psychosis" literally means "soul sickness," and the infection that caused the disease was this: the idea that all of life meant nothing, that reality was just a dream, and that God did not care one bit what suffering this might cause. The infection seeped into every thought, every feeling, every moment I was awake.

The half-life of ketamine is about twelve hours, but for months after it was physically out of my system, its effects remained. Drug-induced psychosis turned into untreated post-partum psychosis. For most of the day, I was disconnected from my body and seemed to be floating around it. I was often unable to understand what other people said to me. I could read individual words but couldn't comprehend sentences. Sometimes I couldn't muster the energy or desire to move. Images of the pink tunnel burst into consciousness a dozen times an hour. I could drive these images away by shaking my head violently back and forth, but whenever my mind wandered towards prayer or even thoughts of God, my heart would pound and every cell of my body burned with terror and I would have to run away from the thought, either out the front door and into the street, or into the bathroom where I could cover my head with a towel.

But nursing Jimmy in the darkness, half-asleep in the glider, I was in my body and terror never intruded. Sometimes I even felt something akin to happiness.

I remember as a child and even into my teenage years craning my neck during Mass at the time of the transubstantiation, waiting to see or feel something when the little bells rang. "Take this and eat it. This is my body, given up for you." As far as I could see, nothing happened. Certainly no alchemical change from bread to body. In theology classes at my Catholic high school, the more the teachers insisted that the bread and wine literally turned into flesh and blood, the less meaningful the whole ritual became for me. Any person could see that it was a piece of wafer and bad wine.

In college religion and theology classes, the Protestant ideas that God is with and around the bread and wine, or that it was a ritual of remembrance, seemed to make much more sense. And the criticism that the Eucharist was cannibalistic seemed uncomfortably accurate. I became embarrassed of the Catholic insistence on transubstantiation.

As I grew older I did find some meaning in symbolic understandings of what Communion meant. But the literalism at the heart of the Roman Catholic assertion that bread and wine become the substance of God, and that substance is flesh—is the body of Jesus—was not just creepy but unfathomable.

When a woman holds her breast to a baby's mouth and patiently strokes the nipple across a newborn's lips, she is telling the baby to take this and eat it. That it is her body and she wants her baby to have it. There is joy and solace and peace in offering your child your body for her sustenance, for her comfort, for her strength.

I nursed Jimmy for the first time in the neonatal intensive care unit, where he was taken at birth because of meconium aspiration syndrome and two collapsed lungs. He was five days old and I was topless. One nurse held Jimmy, wrangled the various tubes and wires connected to him, and checked to make sure his oxygen saturation didn't dip too low. Another nurse adjusted pillows and me, showing me how to position the baby so that no monitors were set off. A lactation specialist dripped sugar water on my breast and tried to coax Jimmy's mouth open with her other hand. Suddenly, and almost roughly, she shoved the baby onto my breast and he clamped down. He sucked for perhaps a minute and then fell asleep. It didn't seem as though anything had happened, and yet when the nurse took him from me, there was the thin, white liquid drooling from his mouth and drops on my skin.

As strange as it was to think that my body had created this new person, it was even stranger to have milk dripping from me. It seemed miraculous and magical and even a little bit frightening that my body—any mother's body—could be food for someone else. But by the time a mother and baby hit the two-month mark, nursing is pedestrian and routine, even as it remains intimate and cozy. There is nothing creepy or cannibalistic about it at all. It is both mundane and sacred.

It was the literal understanding of the Eucharist that was salvific for me in the months of untreated psychosis. The Roman Catholic insistence that this is not symbolic, this is not just an idea, this is not a metaphor for the love of God—that this is literally the substance of God you ingest, that becomes a part of your flesh—was something that made sense in my body when my mind was broken.

As I sensed it that night, if Christ wants to nurture me with his body, and I want to nurture my baby with my body, than God must feel for me something like I feel for my child. In those hours God was no longer terrifying, no longer cold and uncaring. If I felt this way about nursing my baby, how must God feel about me?

At a time when I was struggling with delusions, many of them religious in nature, and at a time when I dealt with depersonalization, derealization, and dissociation, a corporeal understanding of God was something I clung to for months and years as I clawed my way out of postpartum psychosis. I was nursed that night by God just as surely as I nursed my child.

Cloistered monks and nuns pray throughout the day and night. They rise every three hours, believing that their prayers are transforming the world they cannot see. Mothers of newborns are also up every three hours, day and night. I've come to think of those four-in-the-morning nursings as prayer at a time when I could not pray as I once did.

Jesus said that we must be like little children to enter the kingdom of God. Perhaps like suckling infants.

This idea was new to me, but it wasn't a new idea. The importance of nursing as a metaphor for the love of God is found throughout the history of Christianity, in medieval and Renaissance painting, in the poems and theological reflections of mystics, in the Bible.

The psalmist tells us, "But I have calmed and quieted my soul, like a child quieted at its mother's breast; like a child that is quieted is my soul" (Psalms 131:2 [RSV]). And the prophet Isaiah, speaking of Zion: "Rejoice with her Jerusalem, and be glad for her, all you who love her; rejoice with her in joy, all you who mourn over her; that you may suck and be satisfied with her consoling breasts; that you may drink deeply with delight from the abundance of her glory" (Isaiah 66:10–11 [RSV]).

In Catholic theology, the Church has long been described as a mother nursing her children, the faithful. Nursing has also been an important trope in the cult of the Virgin Mary. The classic Renaissance image of the Madonna and Child shows Mary bare-breasted, encouraging her baby to nurse. A fat, naked baby boy stands or sits in his mother's lap, one exposed breast, round and pale, at the center of the image. The image of Mary nursing Jesus was present, though rarely used, in Christian art since the second century. In the early fourteenth century, however, a veritable deluge of paintings of the *Madonna lactans* burst into Tuscany. The pictures were something of a visual revolution in theology at the time. Previously, Mary was usually depicted as the Queen of Heaven, with crown, splendid robes, and retinue of angels. When she was depicted with her baby, both were usually formally posed, staring stiffly at the viewer. The Christ child usually looked more like a miniature king with regal bearing, standing tall on his mother's lap, than a hungry baby.

At this time, wealthy Italian women did not nurse their own babies. If the family could afford it, a wet nurse moved into the parents' house to breastfeed the child for up to four years. In most cases, the infant was sent to the home of a nurse and her family out in the countryside. The image of Mary nursing her child told the viewer that she was a common woman who could not afford a nurse. The image of Christ as a baby hungrily nursing told the viewer that Jesus was a vulnerable infant like any other human. The popularity and importance of these images of *Madonna lactans* is hard to overstate.

During the Council of Trent, part of what is known as the Catholic Reformation or Counter Reformation, a decree was issued about the portrayal of sacred figures in art that restricted nudity. And so the *Madonna lactans* faded in iconographic importance in the Catholic imagination. The mother and child were increasingly painted all covered up.

Medieval mystics embraced the breastfeeding metaphor. Catherine of Siena and Teresa of Avila wrote about God's nourishing breasts. It was Julian of Norwich, a fourteenth-century English anchoress, however, who wrote more than any other person of a maternal God. An important part of her theology was Jesus as a nursing mother. In her thought, Jesus nurses us not with milk but with the blood of his wounds: "The mother may lay her child tenderly to her breast, but our tender mother Jesus, he may only lead us into his blessed breast by his sweet open side."

Girls and young women entering the convent were sometimes given toy cradles and dolls of the infant Jesus that they could take care of, pretending to nurse and swaddle and rock the baby as a spiritual devotion. A crib and doll given to a German nun named Margaretha Ebner in 1344 led to a series of mystical dreams in which she was awakened by the Christ Child in his crib and breastfed him back to sleep.

But there is, sometimes, something not quite right in these images and ideas of breastfeeding. They are beautiful, surely, but they can be sentimental, idealized, romanticized into a picture of nursing that many women might not recognize as anything resembling their experiences trying to breastfeed their child. We never see Mary's cracked nipples, the psalmist never complains about plugged ducts or mastitis, and Julian never addresses the issue of what it would mean if the milk never came in, or supply was too low and the baby began losing weight.

When my daughter was born a little more than two years after Jimmy, I looked forward to nursing. I stood in the shower one day at the end of the pregnancy, rubbing my nipples to try to bring on labor, and had a sudden physical memory of nursing and a rush of joy and anticipation. But it was different with Mary Frances. Almost from the beginning, we had trouble.

On November afternoons, when it was dark by four, we sat on the couch in our low-ceilinged living room, trying to nurse. A stream of *Sesame Street*, *Blue's Clues*, and *Booh Bah* blared from the television every day.

"Me play Mommy," Jimmy said, at first plaintively and then angrily. "No nurse baby," he yelled as he pulled on my shirt and pants. "Please Mommy Mommy Mommy."

"Okay Jimmy, just watch TV, sweetheart, please," I begged as Jimmy cried and Mary screamed and twisted and arched her back till she almost fell out of my arms. Nursing was not warm and cozy for either of us. Mary would nurse for a few minutes, and then pull away to scream and arch, then come back to the nipple to nurse for a little while longer, crying while she drank, tears smearing across my breasts. She clawed my skin, drawing blood, and mashed my nipples between her gums. She often spit up while trying to suckle, and choked herself on her own vomit. We have very few pictures of her first months of life, and in those that we do, her eyes are always swollen half shut, her face is a mottled red, and she is grimacing. She sometimes stopped in a moment of calm and looked at me. I thought I saw reproach and devastation in her bloodshot eyes.

The three of us drove around in the car when we couldn't take being trapped in the house anymore. Mary screamed. Jimmy threw crackers at her, tried to pull her car seat over, and shouted, "Stop it baby!" I turned up the stereo as loud as it would go and clutched the steering wheel with arms straight out in front of me and elbows locked, pressing my body hard into the seat. I curled my fingers around the wheel till the nails left deep purple crescents in my palms. My pediatrician suggested getting a coffee for me and munchkins for Jimmy at the Dunkin' Donuts drive-through, and then parking the car and standing outside of it for fifteen minutes. This way I could still see the baby, but her screams would be muffled. Anything to not shake the baby.

"I'll stop nursing, if that would be better. I'll do anything."

"Don't stop nursing. If you think it's bad now, it'll be far worse on formula. Just keep trying," the doctor said when I brought the baby in every week, convinced she was dying.

I stopped eating onions, I stopped drinking milk, I stopped drinking caffeine. I nursed her on only one side at a time, I pumped for five minutes before nursing her, I spooned watery oatmeal down her gullet. I propped her up into a sitting position to nurse, I wore her hanging upright on my chest until I could no longer raise my arms from the pain in my back and shoulders. Nothing changed. We tried Zantac, then more Zantac, then Pepcid, then Prevacid, and then more Pepcid.

After months of screaming in pain, things finally started to change. Mary still vomited at least half of what she drank, sometimes spraying it out five feet across the floor and couch and dogs, and she still sometimes cried inconsolably, but only for twenty minutes at a time, instead of hours. At four months, she began to smile.

But the damage seemed to be done. She hated to nurse. She began losing weight, ushering in blood tests and weekly weigh-ins. I started supplementing with a bottle, popping it into her mouth every chance I had, when she was distracted by toys or Jimmy and wouldn't notice that it was a bottle and not a pacifier in her mouth, just to get a few more milliliters into her.

She nursed less and less, and I produced less and less milk. She turned her face away from me and would not latch on, much preferring her bottle filled with a thick, nasty-smelling cereal-soy formula combo. Finally, when she was ten months old, there was no milk left. I didn't cry like I did the first time I weaned a child. I was relieved, and I imagine maybe she was too.

I felt like the life had been sucked out of me when Mary finally stopped screaming at eight months. I felt like I had failed her. And I am ashamed to admit it, but I resented the nursing battle, and sometimes I even resented my baby. I resented how needy she was, how she fought me with all her might when I was trying to help her, how she alternately demanded and rejected me.

The eighteenth-century English novelist William Makepeace Thackeray wrote, "Mother is the name for God in the lips and hearts of little children." That's a heavy burden to any mother, especially the mother who cannot comfort her child, who comes to resent needing to comfort her child.

Does God ever feel this way about me? I wondered. I hoped not. The question that was comforting the first time I breastfed a baby was now dispiriting. The more I thought about this nursing and Eucharist analogy—the more I tried to make it fit into a logical framework—the less sense it made. And so my metaphor falls apart at some point, as all talk about God eventually does.

Metaphor is a product of the mind that can extract a concrete image from an ineffable experience, the mind that can extrapolate from symbol to symbolized, and discern idea from reality, hope or fear from delusion. Metaphor inhabits the realm of reason—the place that becomes sick with psychosis. Flashes of grace—a wash of peace or forgiveness or even clarity that comes from outside, that descends upon you at times unsuspecting, that jolts like a shock of static electricity—these flashes of grace bypass that place. They can speak to a part of the soul and brain that does not depend on healthy, abstract, or rational thought—the part that can be comforted in mental illness.

The metaphor falls apart, but the experience—the clarity, the comfort—remains crystallized in my mind.

I cannot offer any systematic, theological explanation of what the Eucharist means. I cannot even explain what it means in my own spiritual life, three years after psychosis. I'm no closer today to being able to explain what I learned that winter night in Iowa when I was so sick, than I was the day after it happened. I have no clarity to offer on the mysteries of the Transcendent or the mind. I spend my days in an endless cycle of cooking, feeding, playing, cleaning, and washing. I watch my children grow up. How they can change so much every morning from the night before is enough mystery to fill my head.

The other day, Mary sat in her high chair in the kitchen in our house in Massachusetts eating lunch. She picked up her last glob of smushed lasagna, reached out, and offered it to George the dog. George, of course, gobbled it right out of her hand. When she realized that she had no more food on her tray and that George was not going to give the lasagna back, she began to cry. Jimmy approached her and patted her hand, murmuring, "It's okay. It's all okay." It's what I used to sing-song over and over, as much to myself as to Mary when she sobbed while nursing. I didn't know Jimmy had been listening to me all those months until I heard my son mimic me in comforting his sister. It reminded me of Julian's most famous words, growing out of her maternal God imagery: "All shall be well, and all shall be well, and all manner of thing shall be well."

The promise of the Eucharist—the words a woman unthinkingly murmurs to soothe her child—a morsel of hope in the pain and terror of psychosis—that it will all be okay.

15

Fantasy Literature
and the Spiritual Life

RICHARD R. OSMER

I have read and loved fantasy literature since I was a child. As an adult, I waited eagerly for each new book of the *Harry Potter* series, and even forced myself to read the *Twilight* saga to see what all the fuss was about. I find fantasy literature for adults, like Mary Russell's *The Sparrow* and Ursula Le Guin's *The Left Hand of Darkness*, fertile ground for theological reflection. I have come to believe that C. S. Lewis was right when he pointed out that fantasy literature for young people is not worthwhile unless it also can be read and appreciated by adults.[1] I can hardly imagine getting into bed at night or spending an entire weekend without opening a book that takes me long ago or far away.

What started as personal passion and delight has become a part of my academic career as a professor in a school of theology. Over the past decade I have taught two courses several times that tap into my love of fantasy literature: (1) Children's Fantasy Literature and Moral Formation and (2) Science Fiction, Social Criticism, and Eschatological Thinking: Imagining Alternate Worlds. In this essay, I share some of what I have learned from teaching these courses, giving special attention to the relationship between fantasy literature and the spiritual life.

These courses are much loved by students. The most recent offering of Children's Fantasy Literature had almost one-third of the student body enrolled in the course, with spouses and high school students auditing the course as well. While I would love to believe course design and pedagogy had something to do with this interest, I truly believe it had more to do with the

---

1. C. S. Lewis, *Of Other Worlds*, ed. Walter Hooper (New York: Harcourt Brace Jovanovich, 1975), 24.

subject matter than anything else. It is analogous to the incredible response of children and youth to J. K. Rowling's and Stephenie Meyer's writings. A deep chord has been struck, and it is worth asking why this is the case. Why are children, youth, and emerging adults responding so passionately to fantasy literature precisely at a time when so many young people are leaving the church? Why are they so eager to read books when research tells us that, more than ever, young people are participants in a visual and interactive cyberculture stretching across many platforms?

FANTASY LITERATURE
AND THE MYTHIC IMAGINATION

My answer to these questions emerges over the course of this chapter. The simple answer is that fantasy literature appeals to the mythic imagination, using what J. R. R. Tolkien and C. S. Lewis call "mythopoeia," and others "imaginative" or "speculative" confabulation. Fantasy literature fills a void in the scientific, technological culture of global capitalism, a culture that attempts to seduce us into believing our world is reducible to scientific explanations, technological innovations, and the endless trivial novelties of a consumer culture. Fantasy literature also invites us to imagine our world differently by taking us into alternate worlds filled with the mythic power of heroic journeys and off-world travel, of encounters with aliens, magical creatures, and horrific monsters, as well as wise mentors, hospitable hosts, and fellow travelers. It invites us to follow protagonists through journeys of self-discovery and transformation in which they learn the value of friendship, courage, love, and passion, along with the seductive power of evil within and without. When readers return to their everyday lives, fantasy literature grants them the possibility of imagining them differently, as more quest and journey than a following of conventional scripts and roles.

I realize that this is a highly idealized view of fantasy literature. This literature, like all of the arts today, is subject to the long reach of the culture industry, which seems to have an unlimited capacity to snare any expression of cultural creativity and harness it to the purposes of a consumer culture. Much fantasy literature is little more than entertainment. Often it offers simplistic, formulaic scripts of good guys and bad guys and appeals to the human desire for sensationalism, sexual titillation, and violence. There is good fantasy literature and bad. In *The Company We Keep*, Wayne Booth uses the metaphor of friendship to describe our relationship to the books we read.[2] Just as peers

2. Wayne Booth, *The Company We Keep: An Ethics of Fiction* (Berkeley: University of California Press, 1988), chaps. 6–7.

can lead us down paths of darkness or light, so too can fantasy dull or enrich our imaginations. We will do well to pay attention to our literary friends, as well as to the fantasy literature read by those we love.

Good fantasy literature has a great deal to offer the Christian spiritual life. By nurturing the mythic imagination, it cultivates what Richard Bauckham and Trevor Hart call a fundamental human "desire for otherness, for transformation, for transcendence, a desire rooted in a perception of absence or lack in the real."[3] In ways explored more fully below, the stories of this literature may prepare the way for the gospel. They also may encourage Christians to embark on the next stage of their spiritual journeys, helping them imagine the genuinely new and alien, the terrors and lacks of the present, and the ways their lives and world might be different. There is much at stake, therefore, in discerning good fantasy literature from bad, as well as ways that popular but mediocre literature might be engaged.

FANTASY AS A FORM OF LITERATURE

My parents did not read fantasy literature to me when I was growing up. Indeed, I do not remember them reading any sort of bedtime stories to my sisters and me during our childhood. This is unfortunate, for good stories encountered during childhood are probably the best way to gain an initial sense of the difference between good literature and bad. During my elementary school years, I gravitated to the action-adventure stories my friends were reading. My older sister read Nancy Drew; I read the *Chip Hilton* and *Tom Corbett: Space Cadet* series.

Tom Corbett is an eight-book series based on Robert Heinlein's youth novel, *Space Cadet*, which spawned a virtual cottage industry of science fiction comics and TV shows during the 1950s and 1960s. By any measure, the writing was not great. The plots were simple, the characters lacked depth, and the good guys were easy to spot and always won. It was not until high school and my encounter with C. S. Lewis's *Chronicles of Narnia* and *Space Trilogy* that I read good fantasy literature for the first time. How might we discern the difference between good and bad fantasy literature?

Rebecca Lukens provides a simple but useful way of distinguishing good literature from bad.[4] Good literature offers *both* pleasure and understanding. Books read widely and more than once bring pleasure to their readers.

3. Richard Bauckham and Trevor Hart, *Hope against Hope: Christian Eschatology at the Turn of the Millennium* (Grand Rapids: Wm. B. Eerdmans, 1999), 94.
4. Rebecca Lukens, *A Critical Handbook of Children's Literature*, 5th ed. (New York: Harper-Collins, 1995), 1–7.

We read literature because we enjoy it, though the pleasure it brings differs greatly from one person to the next. At the same time, good literature also offers understanding. As Lukens puts it, "This understanding comes from the exploration of the 'human condition,' the revelation of human nature, the discovery of humankind. . . . It is the province of literature to observe and to comment, to open individuals and their society for our observation and our understanding."[5]

As an elementary school student, I enjoyed the *Tom Corbett* series enormously.[6] The quick-moving, suspenseful plots of its stories kept me turning the pages. Occasionally, they even offered a bit of understanding, like the importance of friends in time of crisis. But the quality of writing and depth of understanding of this series pale in comparison to Lewis's *Narnia* chronicles, which are read by many elementary age children as well. Though both induce pleasure, the understanding offered in Lewis's texts goes far beyond anything found in the *Tom Corbett* series. Let me offer just one point of comparison: their portraits of evil.

In the *Tom Corbett* series, evil is entirely identified with alien forces that threaten but never tempt Tom and his friends. The good guys are clearly over here and the bad guys over there. In marked contrast, Lewis offers a far richer image of the seductive power of evil in *The Lion, the Witch, and the Wardrobe*.[7] One of the protagonists of the story, Edmund, is unhappy that the children of his family must move to the countryside to escape the bombing in London. He misses his parents and is especially irritated that his older brother and sister seem to believe they should take his parents' place, telling him and his younger sister how to behave. When he enters Narnia, he encounters the White Witch, the leading protagonist of evil, for the first time. She takes advantage of his hunger and coldness and offers him his favorite candy, Turkish Delight, which warms him up. The more Edmund eats, however, the more candy he desires. The Witch also plays on Edmund's resentment toward his older siblings, promising him that he will rule at her side while they will be mere underlings. As Edmund begins to fantasize about this possibility, he imagines all of the good he would do as a ruler of Narnia. The Witch then plants the hook. If Edmund would have more Turkish Delight and become her partner in ruling Narnia, he must bring his brother and sisters to her if they ever come with him to Narnia. As the story unfolds, we follow Edmund in his betrayal of his siblings and the cause of goodness, as well as his ultimate redemption.

5. Ibid., 2.
6. Carey Rockwell, *Tom Corbett: Space Cadet*, vols. 1–8 (New York: Grosset & Dunlap, 1952–1956).
7. C. S. Lewis, *The Lion, the Witch, and the Wardrobe* (New York: Macmillan, 1950).

Lewis helps his readers imagine the ways evil takes advantage of our immediate needs, deeper sufferings, petty resentments, and desire to do good in order to seduce us to its cause. Our understanding is enriched without sacrificing pleasure, whether we are children or adults. Good literature instructs through delight, as it is sometimes put. It accomplishes this instruction through the story itself, not some hidden message containing the "real" meaning. As Flannery O'Connor once put it, "A story is a way to say something that can't be said any other way. . . . You tell a story because a statement would be inadequate."[8]

Good fantasy literature, like other forms of literature, evokes both pleasure and understanding. Yet this by itself does not take us very far. What are the unique characteristics of fantasy literature that make it such "good company" for the Christian spiritual life? This question confronts us with the difficult task of defining fantasy literature as a genre.

FANTASY AS A GENRE

Genre is often defined as "a type of literature in which the members share a common set of characteristics."[9] The problem is that genres are never clear-cut. This is especially true of fantasy literature, for its most creative authors constantly rework the genres they have inherited. The genre of fantasy is like a fuzzy set in mathematics and logic. It groups members together with common elements but allows much room for degrees of membership.

One of the most widely used ways of describing the common characteristics of fantasy literature builds on Samuel Coleridge's idea that it involves a "willing suspension of disbelief." It introduces characters, settings, and actions not found in our ordinary world, like time travel, magical creatures, beings from other planets, and the capacity to change gender while procreating. The author creates a world in which the fantastic is plausible, requiring readers to suspend disbelief as they enter the world created by the story. Tolkien makes a similar point in a more positive way:

> Children are capable of literary belief, when the story-maker's art is good enough to produce it. That state of mind has been called "willing suspension of disbelief." But this does not seem to me a good description of what happens. What really happens is that the story-maker proves a successful "sub-creator." He makes a Secondary World which your mind can enter. Inside it, what he relates is "true":

8. Flannery O'Connor, *Mystery and Manners* (New York: Farrar, Straus & Giroux, 1990), 96.
9. Lukens, *Critical Handbook of Children's Literature*, 11.

it accords with the laws of that world. You therefore believe it, while you are inside.[10]

Fantasy literature, thus, creates a world of characters, settings, and actions not found in our ordinary world. It includes a variety of subgenres, such as fairy tales, science fiction, epic fantasy, and fantastic stories. Within this broad definition, a further distinction can be made between secondary world fantasy, which creates a fully realized alternate world, and stories of the fantastic, which introduce elements of the fantastic into the world we take for granted. In *The Lord of the Rings*, for example, Tolkien creates one of the richest secondary worlds of modern epic fantasy, a world with a long and complex history, well-developed geography, and various species of elves, hobbits, dwarfs, human beings, orcs, and ents with their own richly developed languages. In contrast, stories of the fantastic retain the "primary" world as the setting of the story and introduce elements of the fantastic not found in everyday life. In the *Twilight* saga, for example, Stephenie Meyer places vampires and werewolves in the familiar world of American adolescent culture. Similarly, in *The Tales of the Otori*, Lian Hearn places characters with quasi-magical powers (the Tribe) in a world based on medieval Japan.

Even this rough distinction between secondary world fantasy and stories of the fantastic must be held loosely. J. K. Rowling quite intentionally overlaps a secondary world of wizards and witches with the world of ordinary human beings. While we can identify common characteristics and rough distinctions within the genre of fantasy, these always must be held tentatively. The authors of fantasy are constantly taking us beyond the familiar, including the conventions of their own field.

FANTASY LITERATURE
AND THE CHRISTIAN SPIRITUAL LIFE

Why is the best literature of fantasy "good company" for the Christian spiritual life? I believe we can identify three contributions that fantasy might make, leading us to read this literature to our children and to offer guidance to youth and adults in choosing their literary friends:

- It nurtures the mythic imagination, helping us view our lives as a moral and spiritual journey.

10. J. R. R. Tolkien, "On Fairy-Stories," in *The Tolkien Reader* (New York: Ballantine, 1966), 36–37.

- It portrays encounters with otherness, helping us learn that the strange and alien are not always to be feared but may be a means of transformation and even a medium of the transcendent.
- It helps us imagine alternate worlds, providing social criticism of the present and nurturing a longing for the "happy ending" of God's promised future.

Nurturing the Mythic Imagination

I noted briefly at the outset the special contribution of fantasy literature to the mythic imagination. What do I have in mind? We gain insight into the role of myth across human societies from the great scholar of comparative religion, Mircea Eliade. In *The Sacred and Profane*, Eliade explores the myths of archaic societies and argues that they accomplish two things when reenacted.[11] First, they take the members of a community outside of profane time into the mythic time of the gods and creation—what Eliade calls *in illo tempore*, "in that time." The reenactments of this liminal time often include the violation of normal social conventions, such as the ridiculing of tribal leaders or the loosening of sexual taboos. Second, the rehearsal of communal myths offers stories explaining the roles, practices, and surrounding geography of the community. Upon returning from sacred to profane time, the members of the community have a renewed understanding of the mythic stories that explain their lives and world.

Over the course of history, virtually every premodern society handed down myths and legends that carried people beyond the profane into the worlds of gods and heroes and heroines, where they were granted a mythic interpretation of everyday life upon their return. Eliade believes that even secular, modern people retain a yearning for the mythic. He writes:

> A whole volume could well be written on the myths of modern man, on the mythologies camouflaged in the plays that he enjoys, in the books that he reads. . . . Reading includes a mythological function . . . because, through reading, the modern man succeeds in obtaining an "escape from time" comparable to the "emergence from time" effected by myths. . . . Reading projects him out of his personal duration and incorporates him into other rhythms, makes him live in another "history."[12]

Fantasy literature is especially well suited to meet this yearning for a mythic imagination. As Vigen Guroian puts it, "Fairy tales and fantasy stories transport

---

11. Mircea Eliade, *The Sacred and the Profane: The Significance of Religious Myth, Symbolism, and Ritual within Life and Culture* (New York: Harvest Book, 1959).
12. Ibid., 205.

the reader into *other worlds* that are fresh with wonder, surprise, and danger. They challenge the reader to make sense of those *other* worlds, to navigate his way through them, and to imagine himself in the place of the heroes and heroines who populate those worlds."[13] Upon returning from these worlds, readers may imagine their lives differently, as more than a simple following of profane roles and scripts but as a moral and spiritual journey.

During my junior year of college, I encountered Ursula Le Guin's *A Wizard of Earthsea* for the first time. It came at an especially important moment in my life. I was struggling with vocational issues, trying to decide whether to apply to law school or seminary. Although I felt nudges of a call to ministry, I had real difficulties imagining myself as a minister. I knew my shortcomings all too well. Weren't pastors supposed to be moral exemplars that embody all the qualities of caring and goodness that I sorely lacked? Le Guin's story allowed me to imagine the next step of my life's journey differently.

A Wizard of Earthsea is a coming-of-age fantasy story about Ged, who lives with his father on the island of Gont in the realm of Earthsea. When Ged's village is threatened by an invasion of Kargad warriors, he hides it by weaving a dense fog with magical powers he did not even know he possessed. He is identified by the great wizard of the island, Ogion, as "mageborn" and becomes Ogion's apprentice. Here he faces and fails his first test. He believes "that as the prentice of a great mage he would enter at once into the mystery and mastery of power."[14] When this fails to happen, Ged grows impatient and leaves Ogion to attend the School for Wizards on the island of Roke. As he embarks on the task of mastering the knowledge and skill of the mages, he is warned by the Master Hand:

> But you must not change one thing, one pebble, one grain of sand, until you know what good and evil will follow on that act. The world is in balance, in Equilibrium. A wizard's power of Changing and Summoning can shake the balance of the world. It is dangerous, that power. It is most perilous. It must follow knowledge, and serve need. To light a candle is to cast a shadow. [15]

Ged fails to heed this warning, and in a duel of magic with an older student unleashes a dark shadow from the world of the dead. He must leave Roke, and as he travels around Earthsea he is pursued by the shadow. Exhausted and despairing, Ged finally returns to his first mentor, Ogion, who tells him that he must turn around and face the shadow if he is to learn its true name. The

13. Vigen Guroian, *Tending the Heart of Virtue: How Classic Stories Awaken a Child's Moral Imagination* (Oxford: Oxford University Press, 1998), 26.
14. Ursula K. Le Guin, *A Wizard of Earthsea* (New York: Bantam, 1968), 16.
15. Ibid., 44.

pursued now becomes the pursuer. Accompanied by his friend, Vetch, Ged follows the shadow beyond Earthsea to the very edge of the world, where they finally come face-to-face. Laying hold of each other, they simultaneously speak the other's name—Ged. Vetch reflects on the meaning of what has happened:

> Ged had neither lost nor won but, naming the shadow of his death with his own name, had made himself whole: a man: who, knowing his whole true self, cannot be used or possessed by any power other than himself, and whose life therefore is lived for life's sake and never in the service of ruin, or pain, or hatred, or the dark.[16]

This brief summary cannot capture the richness of this story's plot, much less the beauty of the world it creates and the depth of its characterization. The meaning is truly found in the story itself, and this will be true of the other stories we explore. But I share enough of the plot to throw light on why this story helped me imagine my own story differently. It helped me realize that an important part of entering the adult world of power and career is confronting one's own shadow. If I was afraid of beginning the journey toward ministry out of a sense of lack and unworthiness, Le Guin's tale deepened my understanding of the real issues I faced and the importance of turning around and naming them with my own name.

As a professor in a seminary, I continue to appreciate what this story taught me and what I hope my students will learn. The journey toward ministry is not a quick apprenticeship in skills and knowledge bestowing ministerial power and success. It is a journey of self-discovery in which those who would lead must first face their own shadow, lest they be driven by hidden fears and longings that will tempt them to misuse their power.

Encounters with Otherness

There is, perhaps, no greater need in the interconnected, globalizing world of late modernity than learning how to negotiate our encounters with otherness. Such encounters are the stuff of everyday life. North American children sit next to classmates born in India and Thailand at school, while we participate in videoconferences at work with people in China and South Africa. Such encounters are indicative of deeper social changes taking place around the world in which the core institutions of modernity—the nation-state and large, hierarchical bureaucracies—are giving way to new forms of social organization. The ambiguities of these changes give us cause to fear,

16. Ibid., 180–81.

not only for our jobs and families but also for the long-term prospects of our world. Are we spiraling downward toward a horrific future? Much recent science fiction has taken a dystopian turn to help us imagine this dark future.[17] But it also helps us reimagine our encounters with otherness and a future that is more hopeful.

Perhaps no author has dealt as creatively with these issues in recent years than the African American, feminist, science fiction writer Octavia Butler. Well-known on college campuses for *The Parable of the Sower* and *Kindred*, Butler offers one of her profoundest explorations of human encounters with otherness in the three-book series *Xenogenesis*. I read the first book of this series, *Dawn*, having just returned from my only trip to Japan.[18] I arrived home both amazed and bewildered by my encounter with Japanese culture. I attributed these feelings to the brevity of my trip and my inability to speak Japanese. Yet the words of my American host, who had lived in Japan for several decades and was fluent in Japanese, continued to haunt me: "I think I will always feel like an outsider here, no matter how many Japanese friends I have. The nuances of relationships and communication often leave me feeling like a child." Reading *Dawn* upon returning home helped me process my encounter of Japanese otherness.

Dawn is a postapocalyptic story beginning several centuries after the earth has been rendered uninhabitable by nuclear warfare. A small number of human beings have been saved by an alien race, the Oankali, who put the survivors in a deep sleep on their ship, which is circling the earth until it can be repopulated. The protagonist of the story is Lilith, an African American woman, who is one of the first to be awakened. The Oankali are hopeful that she will provide help in awakening other humans and convincing them to cooperate with their plan.

A key element of the story is the Oankali's otherness. Covered with tentacles, their very physical form is repulsive to the human survivors. It takes Lilith many hours in the presence of a single Oankali before she is ready to move around the rest of the ship. But the Oankali embody otherness in profounder ways. As a species, they are cooperative, nonviolent, incorporative, and possess superior scientific knowledge. For eons, they have traveled around the universe incorporating genetic components of other species in a process of ongoing self-transformation.

This is the "bargain" the Oankali offer the humans they have saved. In exchange for saving their planet and the chance to repopulate it, the human survivors must join Oankali families and contribute their genes to the creation

17. See Tom Moylan, *Scraps of the Untainted Sky: Science Fiction, Utopia, Dystopia* (Boulder, CO: Westview Press, 2002).
18. Octavia E. Butler, *Dawn* (New York: Warner Books, 1987).

of a new species through cross-species reproduction. As the human survivors awaken, their initial repulsion gives way to a deeper horror. Many believe they are being asked to participate in the demise of the human race and respond with some of the worst qualities of human nature: violence, jealousy, possessiveness, and authoritarian leadership. When repopulation of the earth begins, many survivors escape and form a resistance movement.

The richness of *Dawn* largely revolves around Lilith's response to this situation. She is branded a traitor and collaborator by many of the human survivors, even as she herself harbors deep ambivalence about the Oankali's bargain. Though she adapts and becomes the mother of several human-Oankali children, Lilith refuses to give up her identity as a human being. Later in the trilogy, her son plays a crucial role in negotiating a future for the human resisters, even as he embodies the best features of the new species that is coming into being.

The thematic complexity of the *Xenogenesis* series has given rise to a number of scholarly interpretations.[19] At a personal level, I found it enormously helpful in making sense of my trip to Japan. It served as a kind of mirror that reflected the range of feelings evoked by my encounter with Japanese otherness, from attraction and admiration to fear and, even, revulsion (think food). I also began to wonder if cross-species reproduction in which genes are exchanged is a powerful metaphor of the way forward in our interconnected, globalizing world, a worthy alternative to cultural homogeneity, hegemony, insularity, or clashes. The creation of a genuinely new, global civilization from the "cultural genes" of many societies is a future worth imagining and, perhaps, even working toward. Maybe we will all find ourselves in Lilith's situation. We will only survive if we adapt; we will only adapt if we learn how to negotiate our encounters with otherness.

Imagining Alternate Worlds

One of the most common charges brought against fantasy literature is escapism. Like the entertainment industry, it is portrayed as creating and satisfying desires without really changing anything in the "real" world. This is true of much fantasy literature. Yet it also is true that this literature offers a vantage point from which to see the injustices of our taken-for-granted world and often cultivates a yearning for the "happy ending" in which

---

19. See, for example, Christina Braid, "Contemplating and Contesting Violence in Dystopia: Violence in Octavia Butler's *Xenogenesis* Trilogy," *Contemporary Justice Review* 9, no.1 (March 2006): 47–65; and Patricia Melzer, "Change My Cultural 'Coloring' Again: Anti-Colonial Identities in Octavia E. Butler's Feminist Science Fiction," *International Journal of Media and Cultural Politics* 1, no. 3 (December 2005): 247–61.

healing and justice finally arrive. I draw on J. K. Rowling to illustrate social criticism in fantasy literature and J. R. R. Tolkien to illustrate the longing for a happy ending.

The *Harry Potter* series, I believe, has done more to cultivate a critical imagination among children than any other work of fantasy literature in the past hundred years. Perhaps the most horrific creatures found in this series are dementors, wraithlike creatures covered by long hooded cloaks, hiding faces with no eyes and a large hole where their mouths should be. They feed on the positive emotions of human beings, sucking away happy memories and feelings and leaving them with only their worst experiences. Worse still, they can perform the "dementor's kiss," attaching their mouth to human lips and sucking out an individual's soul. The person remains alive but is stripped of happiness and creativity, with no possibility of recovery.

Rowling introduces dementors in the third book of the series, *Harry Potter and the Prisoner of Azkaban*.[20] They are used by the Ministry of Magic as prison guards on the island of Azkaban and are now being used to guard Hogwarts, the wizarding school attended by Harry and his friends. On the prison island of Azkaban, most prisoners are driven mad simply being near such foul creatures. Their very presence is a form of torture. Yet they are placed in this position by the government of the wizarding world. Harry is particularly sensitive to their presence because of the terrible memories he has of his mother's death as an infant. He works hard to learn the patronus charm, which is the only effective defense against dementors, yet he continues to be debilitated by their presence. In the climatic scene of the book, a swarm of dementors descends on Harry and his godfather, Sirius Black, preparing to administer the dementor's kiss. Though Harry saves them in the nick of time, it is a horrifying scene because we identify so thoroughly with Harry at this point. We feel his absolute terror and loathing as the dementors grow closer, knowing what their kiss would mean.

The second time I taught my course on children's fantasy literature, it was during the early months of the Obama administration. The extensive use of torture under the previous administration was just becoming known. Perhaps more than any other time in the course, the students in my precepts gravitated to a single connection between the *Prisoner of Azkaban* and the world in which they live. Torture is dementor-like, and the fact that it may be sanctioned by the government does not make it right. One young mother in the course was reading this story aloud to her fifth-grade son. She shared her son's question when they finished the book: "Why did the Ministry of Magic let this

20. J. K. Rowling, *Harry Potter and the Prisoner of Azkaban* (New York: Scholastic Press, 1999).

happen?" It is the question we all should be asking—social criticism out of the mouth of a child.

I turn to Tolkien as an example of the way fantasy can evoke a longing for the "happy ending," which speaks to the issues brought to light by social criticism. Tolkien drew attention to this function of fantasy in his lecture "On Fairy-Stories," describing it as the "eucatastrophe," or joyful ending, found near the end of much fantasy literature. Cultivating a longing for the happy ending is one of the most important ways fantasy prepares the way for the gospel. Why is this the case? Tolkien believes that "the Gospels contain a fairy-story, or a story of a larger kind which embraces all the essence of fairy-stories," including "the greatest and most complete conceivable eucatastrophe."[21] He continues: "The Birth of Christ is the eucatastrophe of Man's history. The Resurrection is the eucatastrophe of the story of the Incarnation. The story begins and ends in joy."[22] In other words, the human longing for a happy ending, so often found in fantasy literature, is taken up and fulfilled in the story of Christ. There is much that Christian spirituality has to learn from Tolkien's thoughts on this matter, as well as his handling of the happy ending in his fantasy writing.

Christian spirituality today focuses almost exclusively on providence, on the task of helping Christians to recover an awareness of God's presence in their lives and to discern God's guidance. Too often, however, this emphasis on providence gives little attention to the themes of Christian eschatology: God's promised future for creation and the "eschatological reserve," or ambiguity and incompleteness, of our journey toward this future. Providence without eschatology leaves spirituality vulnerable to the success stories of popular American culture. Those stories suggest that if we pray and trust God, then our lives will be showered with God's blessings, with little sense of the ambiguities of our choices or the cost of discipleship.

No author of contemporary fantasy has depicted the close relationship between providence and eschatology more brilliantly than Tolkien in his trilogy *The Lord of the Rings*.[23] One of the central characters of the story is Frodo Baggins, a hobbit, who is given a mysterious ring by his elderly cousin, Bilbo Baggins. The ring had come into Bilbo's possession on an adventure narrated in *The Hobbit*. Created long ago by the dark lord, Sauron, the ring gave him power over the leaders of the races of Middle Earth to whom he had given lesser rings. Frodo's quest is a journey to the very heart of Sauron's realm, Mt. Doom, the only place in Middle Earth where the ring can be destroyed.

---

21. Tolkien, "On Fairy-Stories," 71–72.
22. Ibid., 72.
23. J. R. R. Tolkien, *The Fellowship of the Ring* (1954), *The Two Towers* (1954), and *The Return of the King* (1955). Quotes here are from the Houghton Mifflin edition (Boston, 2002).

Throughout the trilogy, Tolkien offers many hints that Frodo's quest is guided by providential forces. When Frodo is first given the ring by Bilbo, he is told by the wizard Gandalf, "Behind that there was something else at work, beyond any design of the Ring-maker. I can put it no plainer than by saying that Bilbo was *meant* to find the Ring, and *not* by its maker. In which case you also were *meant* to have it. And that may be an encouraging thought."[24] Later, at the Council of Elrond, Frodo freely chooses to take the ring to Mt. Doom and is told by the elvin lord, Elrond, "If I understand aright all that I have heard . . . I think that this task is appointed for you, Frodo; and that if you do not find a way, no one will."[25]

Likewise, the sparing of Gollum is portrayed as providential several times in the story. Gollum is a hobbit who possessed the ring for many years and had been fouled by its power. He is desperate to have it again. Early in the story, Gandalf speculates that Gollum is "bound up with the fate of the Ring" and that he "has some part to play yet, for good or ill, before the end," though Gandalf does not know what this might be.[26] As Frodo, Sam, and Gollum enter Sauron's realm, the greatest warriors of Middle Earth gather to fight Sauron's armies, which are far superior in numbers and weaponry. But it is clear that the fate of Middle Earth lies in the outcome of a lowly hobbit's quest, not in the clash of warring armies.

In the climatic scene, Frodo reaches the edge of Mt. Doom. All he must do is cast the ring into the fiery torrent raging below. But he cannot. At the very end of his quest, he is overcome by the ring's power. He puts it on and disappears.

Gollum leaps on Frodo and bites off his ring finger. But he loses his balance and falls into the fiery torrent, destroying the ring and himself. Tolkien's story has reached its "happy ending." Middle Earth is saved, and the forces of evil are defeated. But this has not been accomplished through the goodness and power of the hero alone. Gollum has played his part after all. The mysterious forces of providence have turned both good and evil to its final purposes. Moreover, when Frodo returns home to the shire, he is not greeted with a hero's welcome. The wounds of bearing the ring are too deep, and he must leave Middle Earth with the elves and Gandalf for the haven across the sea.

To be sure, Tolkien both creates and fulfills our longing for a eucatastrophe, a joyful ending. But the ending is far different than heroic quests and American success stories. The joyful ending is *not* accomplished through the hero's powers and choices alone. In the end, Frodo is a wounded hero who plays his part in purposes beyond his knowledge and control. He is one of

24. Tolkien, *Fellowship of the Ring*, 55.
25. Ibid., 271.
26. Ibid., 59.

the most compelling models of the Christian spiritual life in contemporary fantasy literature.

I have read and loved fantasy literature all of my life. I hope this essay has captured some of the reasons for this personal passion. But even more, I hope it has expressed some of the reasons I believe the writings of Tolkien, Rowling, and many others are good company for the Christian spiritual life. Perhaps more than any of the arts today, fantasy literature appeals to people at many ages and stages of life. The leaders of Christian communities will do well to partake of the pleasure and understanding this literature brings and to guide those in their care in choosing their fantasy friends wisely.

16

Theological Protest
and the Spiritual Life

BONNIE J. MILLER-MCLEMORE

I have been writing theological protest books for almost twenty years. *Where are mothers*, I asked years ago, in all the scholarly treatises on big topics like God, Christology, and ecclesiology?[1] Surrounded by three young children at the start of my teaching career, I wanted to know how women navigate the undying religious ideals of sacrificial motherhood. And shouldn't motherhood matter to how theologians portray the divine, Christ's atonement, and Christian community? When I discovered that children indelibly mark a mother's voice and powerfully form adults, a second protest arose. *What about children* as subjects, actors, and participants in theological construction? What would Christian claims look like if they did not simply presume the adult as *the* one and only subject?[2] Children also matter to theology. Academic theologians should not do their work without considering them. Children are knowing persons of equal worth in God's eyes, I argued, capable of good *and* evil, wise beyond their years *and* easily broken, gifts that also demand caring labor.

Then I noticed that children turn common conceptions of the spiritual life upside down. A final protest rounded out my trilogy. *What exactly is the spiritual life* for those with complicated mundane family responsibilities?[3] Exactly how do people practice Christian faith in the midst of life's demands? The truncation of spirituality as a practice of silence, solitude, and contemplative prayer, I contended, often excludes children and those who care for them.

1. See Bonnie J. Miller-McLemore, *Also a Mother: Work and Family as Theological Dilemma* (Nashville: Abingdon Press, 1994).
2. See Bonnie J. Miller-McLemore, *Let the Children Come: Reimagining Childhood from a Christian Perspective* (San Francisco: Jossey-Bass, 2003).
3. See Bonnie J. Miller-McLemore, *In the Midst of Chaos: Care of Children as Spiritual Practice* (San Francisco: Jossey-Bass, 2006).

Just as my book title *Also a Mother* can trick readers into assuming it is only about mothers, so also does the subtitle of my book *In the Midst of Chaos: Care of Children as Spiritual Practice* leave the wrong impression that the book is merely about children. Just as the first book is actually about Christian adulthood and not just motherhood, the second book is really on spirituality and misconceptions that make its practice almost impossible for many of us.

QUOTIDIAN SPIRITUALITY

I have watched women weep when they hear that their difficult, sometimes impossible, joy- and tedium-, and anxiety-filled moments with children count as spiritual. Although it seems so contradictory to the message that the church means to send, these women have not heard that their arduous experiences with children matter. Long, slow, subtle formation in Christian community has trained them to exclude as meaningful what is right before them in its mediocre, deadening, and graced moments.

Instead, many women have a sense that if they can only survive these early years of what one developmental psychologist calls the "parental emergency" (which actually lasts a lifetime even if it becomes less urgent and physically taxing), then they will eventually get back to having a real spiritual life. They have imbibed the idea that time with children is a pastime, a waste of time, and time away from praying, feeding the hungry, and visiting the sick—in other words, time apart from the real ministry of the church. Many people believe this despite recent movements and publications affirming everyday spirituality and longstanding religious traditions, such as Ignatian and Benedictine spirituality, that have encouraged the integration of faith into daily life. Spirituality is still seen as something that happens outside ordinary time and space, up on the mountaintop, in the desert, at the retreat center, within formal worship, or within the very private confines of one's inner soul and mind—all places where it is hard to lug children, diapers, laundry, and other assorted household goods.

Women weep when I tell story after story and read passage after passage from contemporary authors and classic theologians of centuries past that expose the absurdity of such assumptions.

I often start with my own turning point, which has become a bit mythic in the retelling. In actuality, it was only one moment among many. But even if I have made more out of it than it merits, it marks a pivotal, even cataclysmic awakening for me.

I was watching my kids in the tub and trying to read a book on the desert fathers, *The Way of the Heart* by Henri Nouwen, I had assigned in my pastoral care class. The book was my feeble effort to link care with spirituality and to enrich my own understanding of the spiritual life. It is a nice book, and it wonderfully retrieves the gift of a monastic spirituality grounded in silence, solitude, and contemplative prayer.

But the book's words could not have felt more alien at the time. New parents joke about barely having time to brush their teeth. The bathroom where I glanced from book to kids was our only full bath. Perhaps the only sanctuary in many homes, this room knew no privacy. The upstairs was built in the round, and this bathroom was located like Grand Central Station with two doors, one opening into our bedroom and the other into a hallway to two more bedrooms. And the doors were *always* open. Kids ran through the threshold on their circuit from bedroom to bathroom to hall and back to bedroom.

Then I read Nouwen's paraphrase of the basic premises of desert spirituality: "The words *flee, be silent* and *pray* summarize the spirituality of the desert. . . . 'These are the sources of sinlessness,' says Arsenics." In fact, "words lead to sin," as the desert fathers say, and silence "keeps us pilgrims" and reminds us of our fleeting nature.[4] My goodness. While this is certainly true in a very real way, it didn't seem so in the din of my jubilant bathing boys. I looked up from these lines to witness one son, not much over a year old, jabbering. For him, wordplay opened up worlds of meaning, power, connection, and even profession of faith.

Don't get me wrong. There were times in those early parenting days and still today that I long for silence, know deeply the place of solitude, and recognize that I chose the teaching profession precisely because of its abundance of both. I did not then and still do not wish to negate how silence and solitude must shape prayer. I simply want to loosen our idealization of these assumptions and expand our spiritual imagination.

What I really want to share with others, however, are the wellsprings of alternative visions in the Christian tradition over which I stumbled like oases in a desert of early parenting. They became a lifeline. Might they be so for others.

I was not alone, I discovered, in questioning the "received tradition," as British theologian Janet Soskice names the reigning model of spirituality that excludes children and those who care for them. Religion professor and spiritual director Wendy Wright was one of the first people I heard raise her own voice in protest years ago when her own children were young: "Few of the great remembered pray-ers of our tradition were married. Few had

4. Henri Nouwen, *The Way of the Heart* (New York: Ballantine, 1981). The quotation is from *The Sayings of the Desert Fathers*, trans. Benedicta Ward (London and Oxford: Mowbrays, 1975).

children." To attain spiritual heights, one had to subdue the body, seek solitude, and live a life of poverty. Those most esteemed in Christian history as
models of the spiritual life resisted matrimony, decried children, cut family
ties, and extended love dispassionately to all. They spoke of the spiritual life
as a "journey, a going away to somewhere else, a ladder ascending from earth
to heaven, or a pilgrimage to destinations far beyond earth's (and family's)
purview."[5] On each count, Wright's life departed radically. She was immersed
in intimate relationships of bodily import. She knew sexual desire as essential
to love. She had found divinity through birth and nursing, pursued material
goods for the nurture of children, and put down roots in a home built to
anchor loved ones in one place.

Soskice offers her own vivid illustration of the limitations of the received
tradition, recounting the counsel of three priests to a young, exhausted Anglican mother who found her devotional life in disarray after the birth of her
first child:

> The first told her that if the baby woke at 6.00 A.M., she should rise at
> 5.00 A.M. for a quiet hour of prayer. The second asked if her husband
> could not arrange to come home early from work three times a week
> so that she could get to a Mass. This advice proved threatening to
> life and marriage. The third told her, "Relax and just look after your
> baby. The rest of the Church is praying for you."[6]

This tale of three priests never fails to evoke laughs, gasps, and nods of
recognition when I share it with knowing parents. They have heard similar
words and felt the pressure to buck up and get their spiritual life in order, or
to give it up entirely until their kids grow up. They know how difficult the
suggestion is to rise early and regularly for those already stretched and living
with the unpredictability of children. And they know the hazards of negotiating for more time. They have had their own bitter arguments competing with
partners for this scarce resource. The final suggestion is the best of the bunch.
It rings true to the Christian commitment in baby baptism and dedication
that the community support both parent and child in sustaining a life of love
and service. But even here the remark cannot help but suggest, even if only
indirectly, that children and parents are "Christians on idle," as Soskice says,
taking some years off while others seek God on their behalf.

Fortunately, there are many in the Christian tradition who know this is not
true. When a friend and colleague of sixteenth-century Reformation leader

---

5. Wendy M. Wright, "Living the Already but Not Yet: The Spiritual Life of the American
Catholic Family," public lecture, University of Tulsa, March 21, 1993.

6. Janet Martine Soskice, "Love and Attention," in *Philosophy, Religion, and the Spiritual Life*,
ed. Michael McGhee (Cambridge: Cambridge University Press, 1992), 62.

Martin Luther told Luther proudly that he had placed a cherry bough in his dining room to remind him of God, Luther replied, "Why don't you think of your children? They are in front of you all the time, and you will learn from them more than from a cherry bough."[7]

Jesus is great. But "what a friend we have in Luther," I thought when I came across his words. I even dub him the "father" of the rejoining of the holy and the mundane at the root of spiritual life. Here is a male theologian who says he found God in stinky diapers. He could never have made such claims without boisterous and hardworking Katherine von Bora at his side, a nun in the reform movement who pulled him into marriage and did more than her share to deepen his ideas about vocation. They both recognized domestic work as a "holy, godly, precious" part of the Christian life. Marriage and children are every bit as much a "school for character" or training ground for virtue as the monastery. Siblings are our "first neighbors." And on the parable of the Last Judgment in Matthew 25:31–46 ("For I was hungry and you gave me food"), Luther boldly proclaims, "How many good works you have at hand in your own home with your child who needs all such things as these like a hungry, thirsty, naked, poor, imprisoned, sick soul!"[8]

I bet few parents hear Matthew 25 without self-reproach, sure they should get out of the home and go somewhere else—prison, hospital, homeless shelter, food pantry—to meet Christ and do God's work. But Luther christens parents "apostles, bishops, and priests to their children."[9] The adult who engages in the Christian nurture of children is carrying out, as historian William H. Lazareth puts it, "a far better work in God's sight than all the current pilgrimages, sacrifices, and cultic ceremonies combined."[10]

How have Christians managed to overlook this? Catholic medievalist scholar Elizabeth Dreyer describes caring for kids as the "ascetic opportunity *par excellence*." Traditionally, asceticism referred to the use of disciplines of self-denial and world renunciation, such as celibacy and fasting, to draw closer to God. Dreyer turns this usage on its head. If regarded from the right angle, a parent's daily life has an oddly haunting resemblance. Unbidden and unexpected, opportunity arises for a similar kind of disciplined religiosity: "A full night's sleep, time to oneself, the freedom to come and go as one

7. Quoted by Roland Bainton, *Here I Stand: A Life of Martin Luther* (Nashville: Abingdon Press, 1950), 302.

8. Martin Luther, *Luther's Works*, ed. Jaroslav Pelikan and Helmut Lehmann, 55 vols. (St. Louis: Concordia, 1955–1986), 44:85; and Luther, "The Estate of Marriage," in *Luther's Works*, ed. Walther I. Brandt and Helmut T. Lehmann (Philadelphia: Muhlenberg Press, 1962), 46.

9. Luther, "The Christian in Society II," in Pelikan and Lehmann, eds., *Luther's Works*, 45:46.

10. William H. Lazareth, *Luther on the Christian Home: An Application of the Social Ethics of the Reformation* (Philadelphia: Muhlenberg Press, 1960), 131.

pleases—all this must be given up. . . . Huge chunks of life are laid down at the behest of infants. And then, later, parents must let go."[11] Here, in this one depiction, she captures the whole spectrum of the formative cycle of spiritual life and parenting. I cannot say how relieved I felt when I first came across these words several years ago.

There are plenty of books today on everyday spirituality. The idea of finding the divine in the quotidian is commonplace these days. My own understanding departs from this trend in at least two ways. Most books on the spiritual life almost inevitably leave readers feeling like we just have one more thing to do. I work actively against this. The last thing those caught in the demands of family life need is one more exercise to implement, one more task to execute, one more ideal to live up to. Parenting is guilt-inducing enough without this. If anything, I want to lighten the load by offering a child-friendly, caregiver-supportive, non-elitist understanding of faith and theology. I want people to see what they are already doing and do these practices with greater intentionality, awareness, respect, care, and reflection. Nobody excels in all practices. Everyone has to start somewhere. So I pick favorites and invite others to do the same. The practices I name—pondering, playing, reading, loving, doing justice, blessing, and letting go—are illustrative, not exemplary. They are named to provoke imagination about one's own life and the grace to see God within it when we are honest about the difficulties and attentive to the gifts.

There is another important difference between my approach to the spiritual life and the pile of books on everyday spirituality: doing justice stands at its heart. For my book *In the Midst of Chaos*, the chapter on doing justice was both the hardest to write and the most important. Popular New Age spirituality often ignores the mandate undergirding almost all institutional religious traditions to care for the neighbor and the marginalized. But Luther's interpretation of Matthew 25 is no excuse for indulging in one's own children to the exclusion of others, a natural proclivity and a rampant temptation among parents with means today. As Luther himself would agree, his claim should not be used to justify lavishing love on one's own family alone. At the heart of the Christian message stands the mandate to love all children.

How does one balance intimate love of particular people in one's family with general love for humankind to which Christians are called? Does following Christ mean leaving family behind? This choice, this division in human love, is precisely what has led many religions to define the spiritual life as pursued apart from families—in celibacy, for example, or later in the life cycle.

---

11. Elizabeth Ann Dreyer, "Asceticism Reconsidered," *Weavings: A Journal of the Christian Spiritual Life* 3, no. 6 (1988): 14.

But families have their own distinctive contributions to make to the demand to follow Christ. Even if they sometimes resurrect obstacles, the intimate love of others in families is not automatically juxtaposed to love of others. In fact, the "most distinctively Christian moral virtue" or family value, according to Catholic ethicist Lisa Cahill, is taking the love encountered most deeply in families and turning it outward, seeking the well-being of those beyond natural family boundaries.[12] That is why theologians such as Rodney Clapp and Cheryl Sanders identify the Christian home as a "mission base."[13] The spiritual life in families rests on turning the love of self outward to others. The particular love of households must be shared with the household of God. And parents stand on the threshold, ushering children back and forth.

THE ACADEMIC LIFE, THE SPIRITUAL LIFE

If I am only writing a trilogy, I'm done. But I have one more itch. Maybe I always will. How does one sustain an academic life *and* a spiritual life? Stereotypically, under the reign of modernity, the academic and the spiritual life are antithetical. The academic life values critical thinking, analysis, debate, and individual freedom in the exchange of ideas. The spiritual life prizes faith, mystery, community, justice, passion, and love. I am guessing that many people reading this book—if you appreciate the intellectual act of reading itself—wonder about this tension. Most of my fellow authors in this book have been as fundamentally formed by the academy and its logic of reason and science as by the particular logic of religious communities. But we so seldom talk about this ambiguous formational process. Why? The relationship between the academic and the spiritual life, I have discovered, is much more ambiguous and complicated than simple opposition or antagonism. The academic life enriches *and* nearly destroys the spiritual life. Few people have tried to probe and understand this because it is not an easy dynamic to grasp and appreciate.

The modern academy teaches scholars to hide the personal desires that motivate their work, especially the spiritual longings. This is less true today as postmodernism reveals the biases and values that color even the most objective of sciences. But academicians in theological institutions are almost inevitably a divided lot caught between belief and learning. Modernity heightens

12. Lisa Sowle Cahill, *Family: A Christian Social Perspective* (Minneapolis: Fortress Press, 2000), 48.

13. Rodney Clapp, *Families at the Crossroads: Beyond Traditional and Modern Options* (Downers Grove, IL: InterVarsity Press, 1993), 155; Cheryl J. Sanders, *Ministry at the Margins: The Prophetic Mission of Women, Youth, and the Poor* (Downers Grove, IL: InterVarsity Press, 1997), 72.

this division but is not its only source. The tension surfaces in other places across the tradition, such as the Greek ranking of spirit over body in early Christianity or the triumph of doctrinal over spiritual theology in the medieval era. No wonder so many theological schools today post Charles Wesley's well-known quote on doorposts and Web sites, "Unite the pair so long disjoined, knowledge and vital piety," itself a warning and reminder that the split has a history that goes back past the eighteenth century. People repeat this slogan because they know seminaries are torn and hybrid institutions, weaving drunkenly back and forth from arguing to believing in ways other institutions of higher education do not.[14] The rest of the academy is tempted to judge us anti-intellectual. As a response, many Protestant schools in particular have historically neglected attention to their spiritual influence over students even though they admit and even affirm the mix of skill, knowledge, and formation that characterizes curriculum. President Serene Jones of Union Theological Seminary observes, "Faculty at many seminaries are more scholars about faith than imparters of it. Students, as a result, do not always have mentors who can guide them on a journey that is both intellectual and spiritual." Even as Jones flags her appreciation for the spiritual, she is compelled to stress that it need not undermine "intellectual rigor," the age-old Enlightenment fear.[15] We seldom talk about how hard it is to walk this line as faculty who are inevitably caught between intellectual and spiritual leadership.

I am a product and emblem of this division. I did not set out to write an essay, much less a book on the spiritual life. I inadvertently backed into it. By nature and religious tradition, I resist thinking of myself as particularly spiritual. On any given day, I am more likely to want to disabuse someone of the notion than try to demonstrate it. "I am *not* holier than thou," I want to say. And to the passenger seated next to me on the plane who has made the mistake of asking what I do, I might say, "Just because I teach theology doesn't mean I'm ready to evangelize you or that I am receptive to your own attempts at evangelism, for that matter." In my own field, I see the value of the term *spiritual* care as more inclusive than *pastoral* care, and I understand why some people prefer to call themselves *spiritual* rather than religious, which they interpret as limited by institutional affiliation and tradition. But I am not enamored by either adjective. *Pastoral* feels parochial, limited by its immediate connotation to pastors, parish, and comforting shepherds in green

14. See Daniel O. Aleshire, *Earthen Vessels: Hopeful Reflections on the Work and Future of Theological Schools* (Grand Rapids: Wm. B. Eerdmans, 2008), 5, 83.

15. Quoted in Genine Babakian, "A Fantastic Moment," *Faith and Leadership News*, Duke Divinity School, http://www.faithandleadership.com/profiles/fantastic-moment, February 16, 2010; accessed on June 24, 2010.

meadows. *Spiritual* seems unearthly, juxtaposed to material bodies and every-day life. Overly pious portraits of the spiritual life irk me.

This aversion rises partly out of my hometown Protestant upraising in a Midwest middle-of-the-road Christian Church (Disciples of Christ) congre-gation, a religious tradition described by one scholar within it as "reasonable, empirical, pragmatic."[16] This nineteenth-century, American-born, Second Great Awakening tradition adopted rather uncritically Enlightenment argu-ments for religion as a rational choice. It also adapted the frontier view of religion as a means for changing the world. I cannot completely escape these roots. By osmosis as much as overt teaching, I learned that Christian disciples demonstrate their faith by living it out, professing it through action more than through pious words or spiritual practice. I chose a graduate program in a university divinity school that focused on intellectual debate and did not demand public profession of faith. I have kept a distance from semi-naries of my own tradition and prefer teaching in contexts like my current graduate institution, where research and religious diversity trumps Christian confession.

So when a wonderful colleague complained recently about the avid Christians in her classes who refuse to think critically about scriptural and historical resources, I completely understood. "'I *believe* this, I *believe* that.' That's all I hear my students say," she objected. "I want them to say 'I *argue* this, I *argue* that.'" She teaches in biblical studies, an area that never fails to unsettle students. And she teaches undergraduates in the conservative South. In the words of another faculty member who teaches in the same part of the country, it is important to establish a "high wall between academic study and pious testimony." "I won't open the door to the proselytizers and those who can only accept one religion," he says.[17] This makes perfect sense. Education in theology and religion is not induction into belief. That is the aim of religious communities. And the academy is not usually a religious community.

Yet I know arguing isn't enough for faculty and students in theological education and for Christians whom they serve. So I spend time in courses in pastoral theology and care rebuilding faith. Spiritual questions shape the classes I teach and the books I write. A lot of faculty go to graduate school in religion seeking a deeper spiritual life even though most of us do not admit it. According to the previous executive director of the largest academic asso-ciation of faculty in religion, for every member who is suspicious of religion,

16. W. B. Blakemore, "Reasonable, Empirical, Pragmatic: The Mind of Disciples of Christ," in *The Reformation of Tradition*, ed. Ronald E. Osborn (St. Louis: Bethany Press, 1963), 173–78.

17. John D. Barbour, "The Place of Personal Faith in the Classroom," *Religious Studies News*, March 2009, 21, citing a friend.

there are more "whose spiritual sensibilities and religious commitments set a context for their intellectual reflections."[18] This is true for our students also. "Students don't generally go to seminary or divinity school to get a better job," observed a recent book review. "They go there because they feel called to pursue something of higher meaning in life."[19] Indeed, as practice theorists have begun to point out, academic theology is itself a practice with its own rituals, rules, and spirit-forming *habitus*. We could even say that studying religion is a new religious form in postmodernity. That is, it is a way to sustain deep reflection on fundamental questions about life. So it is no surprise that religious historian Karen Armstrong confessed in a recent interview on public radio, "My study *is* a form of contemplation."[20]

Education is often a means to resolve ambivalent relationships with conservative and destructive religious communities that have malformed and hurt students. When I taught a class on spirituality and pastoral care last spring, almost everyone in the room had come to our nondenominational university divinity school out of religious contexts that had harmed them. They talked about the dysfunction they had experienced and their desire to find alternative understandings of spiritual life that did not repeat these patterns. Those disenfranchised from religious traditions come to theological education to resolve this. Education that sets aside or temporarily brackets enforced confession of particular beliefs can become an incredible place of spiritual freedom and healing. So paradoxically, undoing, questioning, analyzing, demythologizing, and uncovering pave the way for the rebuilding of faith. Once again, because I teach in pastoral theology, I often find myself helping students undo *and* redo, unearth *and* reclaim. I tackle the hermeneutic of suspicion, but I connect it to a hermeneutic of appreciation.

Spirituality has been, in other words, a latent theme in my work all along. It emerges partly out of how I do theology and where my work is located in the theological curriculum. Pastoral theology is often the least understood area; doctoral study in religion and psychology is a fledgling enterprise found in only a handful of graduate universities. But this area of study has afforded me a place to explore religious experience and subjectivity, basic elements in the spiritual life that often seem like an afterthought in other curricular areas. When anthropologist Marla Frederick engages in an ethnographic study of eight black women and religion, she uses the term *spirituality* to describe her focus. She defines it as "women's expressions of faith" in and beyond the

18. Barbara DeConcini, letter to the editor, *Christian Century*, July 31–Aug. 6,1997, 763.

19. Dale T. Irvin, "Precarious Institutions (review of Daniel O. Aleshire's *Earthen Vessels*)," *Christian Century*, February 24, 2009, 42.

20. Karen Armstrong, interview with Terry Gross, National Public Radio, September 21, 2009.

church—"their understanding of God and God's work in their day-to-day lives."[21] Spirituality is a term used to talk about daily, lived religious experience, the same subject the discipline of pastoral theology has studied for years.

In each case in the trilogy with which I began, I have been searching for a kind of lived theology or spirituality that matters in the midst of life. "Spirituality" or "the spiritual life" is simply a term to use when talking about how one attempts to live a life of faith with integrity. If I have one more protest book to write, it will be about the dire need to reclaim theology as an everyday embodied practice of everyone in the Christian community. There is an important parallel here between my earlier work on spirituality and children and this protest on theology and all Christians. Just as I sought to return spirituality to children, mothers, and people in the midst of complicated mundane lives, so also am I now interested in reclaiming theology as a practice for all Christians in every walk of life.

I never learned to pray easily or spontaneously in public. I seldom make verbal claims about God's influence in my life. I wish I had better disciplines of prayer, Scripture reading, and worship. I am not sure I have the spirituality needed to teach a class by this name or raise children in faith. Yet even as I confess spiritual hesitation and shortcoming, I know on another level that my life as a whole is driven by deep spiritual convictions. Just as the quotidian opens up to the divine in parenting, so also do the mundane practices of academic life—reading and writing in particular—have spiritual potential.[22] Just as splits between intellect and belief have occurred since time began, so also have people found amazing ways to join them. This was evident as my spirituality class read through diverse texts in Christian history—reformer theologian Karl Barth's little book *Prayer*, for example, and contemporary feminist theologian Marjorie Procter-Smith's *Praying with Our Eyes Open*.[23] Here are scholars of the church subverting the academic spiritual split by starting and ending theology in prayer. For the ancients and the medieval, according to Catholic theologian David Tracy, philosophy and theology demanded not only theoretical reflection but also spiritual exercises to hone attention,

---

21. Marla F. Frederick, *Between Sundays: Black Women and Everyday Struggles of Faith* (Berkeley: University of California Press, 2003), 4.

22. See Stephanie Paulsell, "Writing as a Spiritual Discipline," in *The Scope of Our Art: The Vocation of Theological Teachers*, ed. Gregory Jones and Stephanie Paulsell (Grand Rapids: Wm. B. Eerdmans, 2001), 17–31. Paulsell, David Tracy, and others often cite in this regard Simone Weil, "Reflections on the Right Use of School Studies with a View to the Love of God," in *Waiting on God*, trans. Emma Craufurd (New York: Harper & Row, 1951).

23. Karl Barth, *Prayer*, ed. Don E. Saliers, trans. Sara F. Terrien (Louisville, KY: Westminster John Knox Press, 2002); Marjorie Proctor-Smith, *Praying with Our Eyes Open* (Nashville: Abingdon Press, 1995).

deepen humility, and compel love. The "devastating separation of spirituality and theology in theological education," he insists, "must be undone."[24]

Undoing a split that runs straight through us all won't be easy. I'm convinced that those of us in the academy should tread lightly when speaking about the spiritual life. Sometimes the sheer pace and pressure of education alone ruin spiritual health. But more important, we should admit that knowledge disturbs faith. And it disrupts community, as human origin stories about the fall suggest. Plain and simple, science disenchants, as founder of modern sociology Max Weber famously observed. Few of us find our way easily through this disenchantment to some kind of solid second naiveté, even if we have able guides like philosopher Paul Ricoeur and the faithful of our own particular communities. We should recognize how unsettling our biblical and theological research is to our students and ourselves. Education makes it hard for us to participate in religious communities. It surfaces criticisms and perspectives that lead to dissatisfaction and disappointment. And we need to continue to ask ourselves what we can do to help students face the challenge of translation and re-enchantment as they move from classroom to religious communities. But if it is in the nature of the academic spiritual life to unsettle *and* reconvict, disturb and transform at the same time—and I believe it is— then perhaps these kinds of complicated moves are all in a day's work.

24. David Tracy, "Traditions of Spiritual Practice and the Practice of Theology," *Theology Today* 55, no. 2 (July 1998): 240.

17

Spiritual Discipline

HOMER U. ASHBY JR.

As I reflect on the spiritual life—my spiritual life—there are two definitions of spirituality that have influenced my teaching, pastoral counseling, and personal life. The first is by Nelson Thayer: "In the most general sense, spirituality has to do with how we experience ourselves in relation to what we designate as the source of ultimate power and meaning in life, and how we live out this relationship."[1] I have altered Nelson's definition somewhat and have composed the following definition that best expresses my own perspective on spirituality: the establishment *and maintenance* of a relationship with the ultimate source of power and meaning. For me, life in the spirit is not a one-time established reality but an ongoing relationship that requires constant attention and nurture. And for me there is one ultimate source of power and meaning: God. The second definition comes from Urban Holmes. It is somewhat cumbersome, but in its cumbersomeness I find a completeness that warrants full adoption:

> Spirituality as (1) a human capacity for relationship (2) with that which transcends sense phenomenon; this relationship (3) is perceived by the subject as an expanded or heightened consciousness independent of the subject's efforts, (4) given substance in the historical setting, and (5) exhibits itself in creative action in the world.[2]

For me, the spiritual life is rooted in a relationship with God. God is spirit, and to be in relationship with God is to live life in the spirit. At its heart

---

1. Nelson Thayer, *Spirituality and Pastoral Care* (Philadelphia: Fortress Press, 1985), 13.
2. Urban Holmes, *Spirituality for Ministry* (San Francisco: Harper & Row, 1982), 12.

the spiritual life is a life of relationship. It is never a solitary or individual existence. Life in the spirit seeks to know and to be known, to influence and be influenced by, to link one's life with an ultimate other. A relationship with this ultimate other transcends sense phenomena. That is, the knowing, the influencing, the linking are not limited to what we can taste, see, smell, hear, and touch. The transcendent nature of this spiritual relationship is twofold. On the one hand, the encounter with the ultimate other cannot be reduced to a taste, an object observed, a smell, a sound, or a physical sensation. At times we might say that a dish we eat is "divine" or that a piece of music sounds "heavenly," but the fact of the matter is that our relationship with the ultimate other can never be fully realized in these concrete forms. On the other hand, we often find that the establishment and maintenance of a relationship with the ultimate other comes as a result of our senses. We know the love of God through the provision of food for us to eat. Our relationship with the ultimate other is restored when we are blessed to hear words of forgiveness or reconciliation. Sense phenomena can be a means through which we are transcendently linked in relationship with the ultimate other. Those things that we concretely sense can be conduits to transcendent spirit, although they cannot assume the ultimate power and meaning found in transcendent spirit. To claim such is idolatry.

The spiritual life is a *way of life* that takes seriously the need for transcendence and ultimacy in one's life. Thus, one is always looking for ways to bring this way of life to bear on one's daily activities so as to infuse them with power and meaning. Spiritual disciplines, then, for me, are the way in which I intentionally maintain my relationship with God and live the spiritual life. Spiritual disciplines are both a set of attitudes as well as concrete activities that I engage in on a regular basis. The relationship between the attitudes and the activities is such that the attitudes are made manifest in the concrete acts. Let me give an example. One of my spiritual attitudes is to think positively. I try not to do this in a Pollyannaish kind of way (the assumption that there is no pain, suffering, or sorrow but only good) or in a reductionist way (if life gives you lemons, then make lemonade). Rather, I try to look for the deeper meaning in all of life's events and draw upon those transcendent resources (power) that are needed to meet the challenge. My recent encounter with bladder cancer is a good example. In February 2009 I noticed blood in my urine. A trip to the local emergency room could not diagnose anything specific, but I was referred to the urology department. A month later (it took that long to get an appointment) a cystoscopy revealed that I had bladder cancer and needed surgery right away. So on Good Friday I had surgery to remove cancer tissue from my bladder. I was blessed that the cancer was caught early and that it was not an invasive kind. A three-month follow-up indicated that

I was still cancer-free, but I will have to undergo routine checkups for the remainder of my life.

One element of a positive attitude is how one interprets the events of one's life. I did not ask the "why" question, nor did I see the occurrence of the cancer as a punishment or judgment by God. I did acknowledge that depending upon what was found, the cancer diagnosis might lead to the end of my life. But even there my thoughts centered more on the blessings that I have enjoyed in life up to that time.

Another general spiritual discipline that I regularly exercise is that of trying to maintain good health. Right after college I gained a lot of weight. I shot up from 220 pounds to 260 pounds. I carried those extra pounds for almost twenty years. Then, as a part of a health initiative sponsored by the Presbyterian Church, I started a weight management program. Over the course of the next year I lost sixty pounds. That was in 1987. Since then I have kept the weight off. How did I take the weight off? Basically it was the tried and true method of eating less and exercising more. I employ a disciplined practice of eating the same thing every day for breakfast and lunch. For breakfast I eat an orange and a bowl of oatmeal. For lunch I eat a muffin (which I bake), an apple, and a low-fat yogurt. For dinner I eat a variety of things, but not too many fatty foods. My exercise regimen is primarily comprised of swimming. I try to swim at least four or five times a week. With at least 50 percent blockage in two of my heart arteries and the appearance of cancer, I am doing what I can to take care of the gift of life God has given me. God did not give me a challenged heart. My genes are the cause of that condition. Nor did God give me cancer. However, God has empowered me to do what I can to resist further heart disease and survive cancer's initial assault.

A third general spiritual discipline I employ is maintaining an even keel emotionally. Early in my life I witnessed the negative outcomes of emotional excess. I was in sixth grade. On the way home from school I noticed that there were a number of police cars and an ambulance parked at the end of an alley behind a row of houses. Soon a stretcher bearing a body covered with a gray blanket emerged from the alley. On the blanket there was a bloodstain where a bullet had entered the chest of the man on the stretcher. Apparently two brothers, both in their late teens, had gotten into a fight. One brother located the father's gun and shot the other brother. Soon after the one brother was placed in the ambulance, the other brother was escorted down the alley and placed into a police car. The one lesson I came away with that day was that anger and hatred can have tragic consequences.

I also witnessed enough abuse and violence in my own family to convince me that I want to rein in impulses to hurt or injure. I do get angry. But I try to address what has frustrated or angered me so that I do not harbor it for long periods of time. Friends, colleagues, and acquaintances have often commented on my calm. In my vision of the realm of God, the resolution of conflict is more successfully achieved in nonviolent ways. It is that general attitude that led me to seek a conscientious objector discharge from the army after having been commissioned a second lieutenant.

A final general spiritual discipline for me is being solution-focused. This is a spiritual matter for me for a simple reason: God is not honored by how many problems we can create or fail to solve; rather, God is honored by the ways in which we engage in renewal, transformation, and reconciliation leading toward outcomes that reflect abundant life. Such outcomes often require God's transcendent power and imagination. If we want to live lives that are more than just mere survival—if we want to live out the promise of abundant life—then joining with God is a necessary discipline. It is spiritual because it more often than not requires more than we can ordinarily muster on our own. Anyone who has participated in a 12-step program, or engaged in a forgiveness process with an enemy, or achieved success in overcoming personal demons and shortcomings knows this.

What I have written thus far is a kind of prolegomena to my reflections on my spiritual life as lived out in three areas: teaching, pastoral counseling, and personal living. It is to these three topics that I now turn.

TEACHING

For twenty-seven years I taught pastoral care and counseling at McCormick Theological Seminary in Chicago (from 1979 to 2007). My courses tended to focus on the spiritual dimensions of pastoral care, with a particular emphasis on the spiritual life of the pastoral caregiver. I certainly taught theory and skills of pastoral care and counseling, but the theory and skills were always seen in light of certain spiritual disciplines. In this regard I was influenced by Alastair Campbell's understanding of pastoral care: that the life experience of the pastoral care provider has as much (if not more) to do with the successful outcome of the caregiving as any skill, title, or technique the caregiver employs.[3] This life experience includes the spiritual challenges and spiritual dilemmas faced by the caregiver. What the care receiver seeks is someone who, like her, has faced such challenges *and* can bring to the care enterprise a witness to what has been important for the caregiver in grappling with life's challenges. The person in need of care has exhausted all of her own power

3. See Alastair Campbell, *Rediscovering Pastoral Care* (Philadelphia: Westminster Press, 1981).

and meaning-making capacities but still finds herself in distress. Her unspoken question is, "What have you found helpful, meaningful, empowering in your life struggles?" In that she has come to a pastoral counselor (or other minister), the question might best be stated, "Is there a word from the Lord?" Apart from the degrees on our wall, a technique we read about in a textbook, or skills we developed in a seminar practicum, what do we have to offer? Ideally, what we have to offer is a witness to the hope that we found outside of ourselves in the practice of our spiritual disciplines. What we have to offer is a witness to strength that we once thought we never had. What we have to offer is a larger metanarrative that expands the narrow personal narrative and gives it new meaning.

In some cases we might bear this witness through our own experience, being careful to avoid the explicit or implicit statement "I know just what you are going through; the same thing happened to me." It is better for us to sit with courage and faithfulness with those in distress and thereby embody hope, better to sit and share in the bearing of pain and suffering and thereby lend strength, better to give an interpretation of the current moment in light of a larger story, so as to give new and deeper meaning to the current moment. And where do we get this hope, strength, and expanded meaning? From the exercise of spiritual disciplines in our own lives that nurture these spiritual gifts within us.

In a similar vein, whenever I taught my introductory course in pastoral care, I included in the first class a reading of 1 Corinthians 13:1–3. There Paul claims that any caring act we do without genuine love is worthless. Without love, our concern for the other person comes across as false and inauthentic. It would have been better if we had not offered a helping hand than possibly to exude an attitude of duty or bother. But sometimes as caregivers it is difficult to offer care that is fully genuine and authentic. At times we are tired. Sometimes we find it hard to be caring toward certain people. At still other times we are unsure of what can be helpful. Paul encourages us to draw on the love of God as a resource when we encounter the limits of our capacity for care.

Over the weeks of the course I would try to instruct students in how that loving relationship with God might enhance their capacity to care. God may encourage us to engage in some self-care, so as to increase our caring resources for others. Or God might encourage us to accept our limits as a caregiver and refer someone to another caregiver. Or, through prayerful reflection after a confusing caregiving session, we might ask God to illumine what transpired and how best to care for the person the next time.

At the heart of my teaching was the notion that the nature of the "work" we do as pastoral caregivers is to help persons move from a life of mere survival to abundant life. In class I would straddle my legs between two points. One foot stood on the place where persons found themselves. The other foot stood on the place where God intended for them to be (abundant life). What we as pastoral caregivers and pastoral counselors do is to act as the bridge or connection between those two points, without relinquishing either place in the process. To stand with persons only at the place of where they find themselves (a place of pain or struggle) is to offer a hopeless presence. To stand with persons only at the place of where they ought to be is to point out their inadequacies or limitations. To truly care for persons, I would instruct, is to simultaneously immerse ourselves in their current distress *and* their desire for relief and release. The spiritual discipline of pastoral care requires us to be in two places at the same time with those for whom we care. Such a dual presence can only be accomplished with the transcendent power of the one who represents ultimate power and meaning.

In order to make the spiritual discipline of relating to God on a regular basis more concrete, I began each class meeting with a song, a reading from Scripture, and a prayer. The song was usually an African American spiritual or gospel song. My intent was to say that whatever we do as pastoral care providers has as its origins our relationship with God. Our learning and our practice of pastoral care are rooted in the praise of and communication with God. Having reestablished our relationship with God, we were ready to have revealed to us in that class what God would have us know, as students and teacher.

A part of my academic work included research and writing in the area of pastoral care and counseling. There, too, I reflected on the ultimacy and transcendency of human transformation, both individually and socially. In my book *Our Home Is over Jordan*, I argued that the future deliverance of African Americans would depend on their capacity to conjure a place different from the current stagnation in which African Americans are embedded.[4] Forty years after the civil rights movement of the 1960s, African Americans still find themselves on this side of Jordan. Yes, we have a president of African descent. However, compared with their white counterparts, African Americans as a group are not making proportionate gains politically, educationally, and economically. I suggest that our conjuring culture needs to conjure a vision of successful crossing of the Jordan, so as to claim the promises of God valiantly fought for in the '60s. We must become a Joshua people whose reliance on the Lord will ensure victory. Apart from God's power and vision, African Americans will continue to be stalled on this side of Jordan in a prolonged extension of the wilderness wandering.

4. Homer Ashby, *Our Home Is over Jordan: A Black Pastoral Theology* (St. Louis: Chalice Press, 2003).

PASTORAL COUNSELING

In my role as a pastoral counselor, I see God as my co-counselor. It is in this co-counseling relationship that I am empowered and find a fuller meaning in my counseling. In those moments when I am unsure about where the counseling is headed, or unsure of what if anything I need to do or say, God bolsters my confidence. God sparks my imagination to see and hear beyond the actual words that are spoken. The larger narrative in which the counselee's story is being told emerges in the light of God's action in the world. It is God who helps transport me out of my own more narrow perspective to have accurate empathy for another.

In addition to the spiritual discipline of intentionally relying upon God as co-counselor, I also orchestrate spiritual disciplines in the counseling itself. Many of my pastoral counseling sessions include prayer. References to the Bible are often used to better understand a dimension of life or relationships. I sometimes ask counselees to think about their own life experience as reflective of a person's story in the Bible. I view homework assignments as spiritual disciplines in that I am asking counselees to engage in practices that transport them from their common behavior to uncommon behaviors that more closely approximate abundant life.

My good friend and colleague, Ed Wimberly, has written extensively on how pastoral care and counseling is an effort to help persons become reconnected to God, to others, and to themselves.[5] I view in Wimberly's work the belief that a right relationship with God leads to a right relationship with others and oneself. If we can help counselees recognize that they are not self-sufficient, then they may more easily turn to God as a reliable resource on which to depend. If we can help pastors and others renew their original sense of call from God, then we may assist them in renewing their commitment to that call and be energized in the process. Wimberly's emphasis on the relationship with the transcendent other as a crucial ingredient in reconnecting with others and with oneself was a theme I repeated regularly in my teaching. For me, the vehicle for this kind of relationship building is in the relationship counselees have with their counselor.

I was careful to warn students that they were not God and that the relationship they had with counselees was not the same as the God/counselee relationship. Rather, the counselor/counselee relationship points to the God/counselee relationship. Counselees often relate to the counselor as if the

---

5. See Edward Wimberly, *Recalling Our Own Stories: Spiritual Renewal for Religious Caregivers* (San Francisco: Jossey-Bass, 1997); Wimberly, *Relational Refugees: Alienation and Reincorporation in African American Churches and Communities* (Nashville: Abingdon Press, 2000); Wimberly, *Claiming God—Reclaiming Dignity: African American Pastoral Care* (Nashville: Abingdon Press, 2003).

counselor is a significant person (e.g., a parent, sibling, or partner) in their current or earlier life. This transfer of emotional connection is called transference. In the transference that occurred in my counseling sessions, counselees asked questions, made requests, revealed wishes, expressed needs, made confessions, gave thanks, and spoke truth at a deep level to that ultimate source of power and meaning with whom their pain sought to connect for healing and growth. In my teaching, I have tried to help students listen for these drives for connection or reconnection that often link with transferences, and to encourage students in how to guide their counselees.

PERSONAL LIFE

I have always felt blessed by God. It is not that I have been spared hardships and challenges in life. I have already alluded to some of these. And I realize that whatever I have encountered in life does not measure up to the pain and suffering some of my fellow human beings throughout the world have endured. Thus, it is much easier for me to say that I have always felt blessed by God. The witness that I want to make is that beyond my own efforts or deserving God has blessed me. And in spite of the difficulties that I have had, God's blessing has been a constant presence in my life. Hence, my personal experience of the spiritual life has been that God has been an ever present help in times of trouble. I have tried to stay connected with God by various means: through the care of my body as a spiritual disciple of gratitude for the gift of life; by looking for God's blessing and meaning in the course of the day; through adopting a character of moderation; and by attempting to see in whatever challenge comes my way the opportunity to declare in the words of James Cleveland, the gospel singer, "Everything will be alright!" The spiritual discipline I try to maintain in my relationship with God is one of discerning how God is working in my life to make things all right. If in this relationship God communicates with me, I seek to know the good news that God is trying to convey. If, as with Joshua, God has already declared that I have the victory, my spiritual life is an effort to walk with God in such a way as to live into that victory. For me, the spiritual disciplines that constitute the essence of the spiritual life are less concrete actions or activities, although these are important, and more the attitudes that one adopts in relationship to God. When I live my life intentionally seeking to maintain this positive, grateful, moderate, and abundant life–focused attitude, then I am engaged in disciplines that are drawing on power and meaning that, for me, can only be found in a relationship with God.

18

Reading St. Therese*

STEPHANIE PAULSELL

In the late summer of 1970, the year I was to enter the second grade, my hometown closed the schools. The last week of August came and went, and we children all remained at home.

During the sixteen years since *Brown v. Board of Education*, my hometown of Wilson, North Carolina, had moved with slow reluctance toward integration. It was twelve years after the Supreme Court ruled the concept of "separate but equal" unconstitutional before Wilson took its first steps toward integrating its schools, and, even then, Wilson, like many other towns and counties in the south, did only the minimum: it offered school choice, but it did not actively assign children to different schools. Finally, the courts insisted: the Wilson Public Schools must integrate. My hometown responded by shutting the doors of all its schools and locking them tight.

When the town refused to give our parents any indication of when the schools would reopen, my parents sent me to a Roman Catholic school named for St. Thérèse of Lisieux, a saint who lived in France in the late nineteenth century, a Carmelite nun who entered a monastery at the age of 15, died of tuberculosis at age 24, and became famous for her "little way" to God.

St. Therese Catholic School was already integrated. Many of my African-American classmates arrived each morning in a yellow school bus that said "Saint Alphonsus" on its side. The school was run by the Sisters of Providence: Sister Mary Griffin was our principal, and Sister Mary Ann was the second-grade teacher. They lived in a convent, a big white house, next to the school.

*This essay was originally published in the *Harvard Divinity Bulletin*, Summer/Autumn 2010, vol. 38, nos. 3 and 4.

Sister Mary Griffin and Sister Mary Ann became friends of our family. They played their guitars and sang in our living room on the evenings when my dad's students came to dinner; they joined in on the long discussions of prayer and theology and the Vietnam War going on at our dining room table or in our backyard; they let my dad's students do their laundry at the convent. I wanted to be just like them, and one evening, while everybody was sitting around talking, I crawled up into Sister Mary Griffin's lap and poured out my desire to become a Roman Catholic. Later, when we were all standing around in the front yard, my dad picked me up by one arm and one leg and swung me in circles. "You want to be a *what*?" he laughed while I giggled uncontrollably. That's how so many of those evenings ended, with all of us laughing in the yard as the dusk deepened into darkness.

At school, Sister Mary Griffin and Sister Mary Ann taught us and disciplined us and played with us. Every day at recess, someone would plug a 45 rpm record player into the outdoor socket. I remember Sister Mary Griffin coming outside to dance with us to the music of the Jackson 5, swinging her head, with its tight cap of hair, to the beat.

The other thing we did at recess was to climb around on the shrine of St. Therese until Sister Mary Griffin and Sister Mary Ann made us stop. The shrine was made of stone and held within it a statue of "the little flower," as St. Therese was often called. But there was also room for a small child or two in the niche that held her. It was hard to resist climbing into that shrine. The sisters had to shoo us out of it every day.

The public schools opened about three months late that year, and busing finally began. At the end of the year, the Sisters of Providence—including my beloved Sister Mary Griffin and Sister Mary Ann—were sent away from our diocese. When I entered the third grade, yellow school buses appeared all over Wilson, and I attended a formerly-segregated school for black children on the southeastern edge of town.

My days at St. Therese were over, but St. Therese entered my life again a few years later, in 1975. My dad had a copy of a brand-new translation of the original manuscripts of her autobiography, *Story of a Soul*, and he loaned it to me. It was a big gray book with a sketch of the saint on the cover. The print looked almost like typescript, as if the translator had been so eager to make it available to English readers that he couldn't wait for a fancier printing press to do the job. Inside were photos of St. Therese herself. She had a face like an apple, round and full, and eyes that seemed to look out of the page and straight into me.

In her autobiography, Therese tells a story about being loaned a book about the spiritual life by her father when she was fourteen years old. "This reading," she writes, "was one of the greatest graces in my life. I read it by the window . . . and the impressions I received are too deep to express in human words."[1]

That's what reading St. Therese's book was like for me. Her book carved out a little place of solitude inside me, a place I could go to meet her, a place I could go to meet God. Reading her book, I could feel God shining on me, like a light from a distant star.

What did I love about her? I loved her account of playing "hermits" with her sister Marie. One would pray while the other worked in the garden; then they would switch, all in total silence. I loved the way she would build little altars in niches in the walls of her house. I loved the way she imagined herself as a little ball the child Jesus picked up and played with from time to time. I loved that she had thrown herself at the feet of Pope Leo XIII during a papal audience in which she had been told not to speak to beg him to allow her to become a nun, and I loved that she tried to turn the smallest interactions with family and friends into opportunities to cultivate love and holiness. I loved that she used italics and capital letters and exclamation points so liberally that her words seemed to leap off the pages. I loved her accounts of the feast days she observed with her family, the processions she participated in with her church. I loved that she prayed for the criminals she read about in the paper, hoping that they would turn toward God and seek forgiveness for their sins. I began to comb through the *Wilson Daily Times* looking for criminals of my own to pray for.

St. Therese's "little way" did not seem, to me, little at all. It seemed huge, spacious, full of places to explore—large enough, certainly, for me.

Elementary school gave way to high school and high school to college, and I found new books to read, new writers to admire. When I was a junior in high school, members of the Ku Klux Klan and a local neo-Nazi group in Greensboro, North Carolina, murdered five members of the Communist Workers Party. They shot them down in the street, in front of rolling TV cameras, and were found not guilty by a jury of their peers. When I arrived in Greensboro for college two years later, I was befriended by the widow of one of those murdered CWP members, and my political education began in earnest. The books I read from my dad's shelf in those years were Dorothy Day's *The Long Loneliness* and Thomas Merton's *Conjectures of a Guilty Bystander*; from my mom's, the writings of Virginia Woolf. If I'd thought about it, I'd probably have thought that St. Therese's "little way" wasn't up to the challenges of our day. (I was ignorant of the fact that Dorothy Day herself loved St. Therese and had even written a biography of her.) What our world needed was a big

---

1. *Story of a Soul: The Autobiography of St. Therese of Lisieux*, trans. John Clarke, OCD (Washington, D.C.: ICS Publications, 1975), 102.

way out of the mess we had made: a change of consciousness, a conversion on a massive scale. Revolution. What did St. Therese's pious musings have to say to the world I lived in? I had a warm memory of St. Therese, but I didn't read her, or seek her out, during those years. It wasn't until graduate school that I encountered St. Therese again.

In a seminar on Christian women mystics, I found her on the syllabus. So much of what I was learning in graduate school was deeply unfamiliar, and I was glad to see the name of a writer I remembered knowing and loving. I mentioned to a friend, a former Roman Catholic nun, that I was excited to get to read St. Therese again. "Ugh," she said. "The little flower. She was crammed down my throat in the convent. We were all supposed to be like her, and who would want to be? I'll be glad if I never read her again."

This shocked me, the idea of St. Therese as a tool of oppression. But my memory of loving St. Therese as a child was still strong, and I turned to *Story of a Soul* with excitement.

I didn't have my Dad's old copy, the one I'd read as a child, so I bought a new copy in the bookstore, one without the photos of Therese. And I found that no one—not my teacher nor my fellow students—called her "Therese." They called her "Tay-rez,", using the French pronunciation of her name: Thérèse Martin, Thérèse de Lisieux. As impossible as it was for me to imagine the school I attended in Wilson, North Carolina, as "Sainte Thérèse" Catholic School, I tried to get used to the sound of this new name, the feel of it in my mouth. And so, with an unfamiliar edition of her book, addressing her with a new name, I set out to reacquaint myself with the saint I loved as a child.

In an essay on reading, the cultural critic Sven Birkerts remembers loving Jack Kerouac's novel, *On the Road*, as a young man. But when he returned to it years later, he found that "whatever magic had been there now survived as only a memory of magic."[2] That pretty much sums up my experience of reading Therese's book as a twenty-four year old. The italics and capital letters and exclamation points that had made her text come to life for me as a child seemed rather immature now, reminding me of the loopy handwriting of little girls who dot their "i's" with hearts. She seemed overly obsessed with tiny domestic dramas in her home and in the convent, to which she attached cosmic importance. For example her description of her great "conversion" on a Christmas evening when she was thirteen years old. The family had just returned from midnight mass, and her father, cranky and tired, expressed annoyance with Therese for her continued child-like love of opening presents

2. Sven Birkerts, *The Gutenberg Elegies: The Fate of Reading in an Electronic Age* (New York: Fawcett Columbine, 1994), 104.

after the service. Looking at her slippers filled with presents in front of the fireplace, he grumbled, "Well, fortunately, this will be the last year!"[3]

Ordinarily such a rebuke would have sent Therese into spasms of crying– "I was really unbearable because of my extreme touchiness,"[4] she writes. But that Christmas night, she says, Jesus changed her heart. "Forcing back my tears," she writes, "I descended the stairs rapidly; controlling the poundings of my heart, I took my slippers and placed them in front of Papa, and withdrew all the objects joyfully. . . . Having regained his own cheerfulness, Papa was laughing. . . . I felt *charity* enter into my soul, and the need to forget myself and to please others; since then I've been happy!" she writes.[5]

Well, what kind of conversion is this? Especially when compared with Paul's being knocked from his horse on the road to Damascus, or Augustine's hearing the voice of God in scripture and leaving his wild ways behind? She's really just describing the kind of self-mastery that we all have to learn in order to grow up. Ordinary. Unremarkable.

And weren't those fervent prayers for the murderers she read about in the paper sentimental at best and macabre at worst? And didn't it seem like she wanted to enter the Carmelite monastery at age 15 so that she could be with the big sisters who had raised her after her mother died and had entered the convent before her? And what about that passage where she talks about being splashed by dirty water in the laundry room by a nun who wasn't taking care with her task? Is her choice not to wipe her face so as not to make the other nun feel badly really a way to holiness? "My dear Mother," she wrote to her prioress about this episode, "you can see that I am a *very little soul* and that I can offer God only *very little things*."[6] I'll say. With all that God has to think about in the great, suffering world, did she really think God noticed how she responded to being splashed in the laundry room?

When I read St. Therese as a child, her words had opened space around me, above me, below me. I grieved that I couldn't return to that space, "the great cathedral space which is childhood," as Virginia Woolf once put it. St. Therese had set my feet in a broad place when I was twelve, but when I was twenty-four, she herself seemed to me utterly hemmed in—trapped by her piety, by her times, by her culture, by her gender. Like a lot of my classmates, I was searching among the women mystics of Christian history for models, for mentors. I found it much more comfortable—not to mention more intellectually and politically respectable—to read the saint for whom St. Therese had been named: St. Teresa of Avila, the great Spanish mystic of the sixteenth

3. *Story of a Soul*, 98.
4. Ibid., 97.
5. Ibid., 99.
6. Ibid., 250.

century. Now there was a saint: a reformer of her religious order, a founder of monasteries, a teacher, a mystic, an interpreter of scripture who clashed with the Inquisition. In St. Teresa's childhood, she ran away from home with her brother to seek martyrdom rather than looking for ways to make the littleness of her life holy. She wanted a big life, an "epic life," as the novelist George Eliot later put it when she invoked St. Teresa in the prologue to *Middlemarch*. Her namesake, St. Therese, seemed but a pale imitation of her—St. Therese, the little flower, the child.

It is a tribute to the power of childhood memories that, twenty years later, I've found myself wanting to return to St. Therese, to read her again. I couldn't bear, though, to read the copy of the book I'd read for my seminar twenty years ago. I felt that I needed to read the same book I'd read as a child, the very one. I needed the relic, the thing itself. Visiting my parents a few summers ago, I looked all over my dad's study for that book, with no luck. But then, a few months later, I found an edition almost exactly like the one I'd read as a child in the bookstore of the Trappist monastery in Spencer, Massachusetts. The typeface was nicer, but the chapters were laid out on the page exactly as I remembered, and all the photos were there. It's hard to describe what it felt like to find that book. "This is *it*!" I exclaimed to my husband and my daughter. They smiled patiently, and, I'm pretty sure, rolled their eyes behind my back. "Are you *obsessed* with her, Mom?" my nine-year-old daughter asked me.

I began reading the book slowly but soon picked up steam, because I couldn't put it down. And I heard things in her writings that I hadn't, somehow, heard before.

I heard her desire to be a priest, for one thing. How had my young feminist self missed this? Her frustration that she cannot be a priest juts to the surface throughout her writings and even through others' remembrances of her. How I wish I were a priest, she would say, so that I could preach a good sermon on the Virgin Mary! She felt that one rarely heard a good sermon on the Virgin Mary–preachers tended to make her perfect, unable to be imitated, remote. Therese was drawn to stories of Mary's humanity, like the one in the second chapter of the gospel of Luke, where Mary doesn't understand what Jesus means when he says to her, after she had lost him after the Passover festival in Jerusalem, "Did you not know that I must be in my Father's house?" It's not perfection that attracts Therese to the mother of Jesus; it's Mary's ability to remain faithful and loving even in the face of events she doesn't understand.

In a letter to her sister Marie she wrote, "I feel in me the *vocation of* the PRIEST. With what love, O Jesus, I would carry You in my hands when, at my voice, You would come down from heaven. And with what love would I give you to souls! But alas! While I desire to be a *Priest*, I admire and envy the humility of St. Francis of Assisi and I feel the *vocation* of imitating him in refusing the sublime dignity of the *Priesthood*."[7]

I love that; she'll *refuse* the priesthood, not be denied it.

Not only did she want to be a priest, but she also longed to be a missionary. She had hoped that God would let her live so that she could go to the Carmelite house in Hanoi. Unable to fulfill that goal, she corresponded with a young missionary priest and supported him with her prayers. In a letter to him, she assures him that her death will not separate them. When I die, she wrote, "there will no longer be any cloister and grilles, and my soul will be able to fly with you into distant missions. Our roles will remain the same: yours, apostolic [labor], mine, prayer and love."[8]

I was also surprised to find, reading St. Therese this time around, that she spent the last year and a half of her life in what St. John of the Cross once called "the dark night of the soul." On the night before Good Friday in 1896, Therese had a coughing fit in the night, and when she awoke the next morning, she was covered in blood and knew that her dying had begun. She was at first filled with joy at the thought of leaving this earthly exile and joining Jesus in heaven. But by Easter Sunday, that joy was gone, and it never came back, ever.

St. Therese died in 1898, quite young, at 24. But if she had lived as long as some of her sisters lived, my lifetime might have overlapped—a little—with hers. She lived in an in-between time—in between a culture suffused with Catholic Christianity and its practices and a culture which would question the very existence of God. It was a time of great scientific and technological advances—the time when Marx, Freud, Darwin, and Nietzsche were doing their groundbreaking work. Although she was cloistered in a monastery, she was not immune to the great questions of her age. When faced with her imminent death, she fell into a trough of doubt and fear. She said it was like living in a country upon which an impenetrable fog had settled; try as she might, she could no longer make out the joyful confidence she had had in God's love and care and promises. It was a night, as she put it, of nothingness.

But even in this night of nothingness, even with her vision of God's love obscured, she stayed turned toward God, and she kept loving. Even though I no longer have the joy of faith, she wrote, I am trying to carry out its works.

It took St. Therese a year and a half to die. She never regained the joy of her faith and the consolations it had once provided. But she never stopped loving God either. She was living in the midst of what the philosopher Simone

7. Ibid., 192.
8. Mary Frohlich, *St. Thérèse of Lisieux: Essential Writings* (Maryknoll, NY: Orbis Books, 2003), 164.

Weil calls "affliction"—an uprooting of life, in which God can seem entirely absent. "The soul has to go on loving in the emptiness," Weil writes, "or at least to go on wanting to love, though it may only be with an infinitesimal part of itself. . . . If the soul stops loving it falls, even in this life, into something almost equivalent to hell."[9]

Christ loved like this on this cross, Weil says. The one "whose soul remains ever turned toward God though the nail pierces it finds himself nailed to the very centre of the universe."[10] This, Weil writes, is the place where the arms of the cross intersect; it is the true center of the world; it is God.

This is where Therese Martin, 23, 24 years old, lived for the last year and a half of her life. Nailed to the center of the universe, with her face turned toward God, she remained determined to make her whole life, up until her last living breath, an act of love.

Now St. Therese's "little way" no longer seems so little. I even have a renewed appreciation for her Christmas conversion. Yes, it is a story about growing up, about maturing, about moving from an exclusive focus on oneself and one's feelings to noticing the effect of one's choices on others, to putting the feelings of others before one's own. Yes, and what better definition of conversion could there be? And how had I ever thought this was a simple change in her life, that it had nothing to do with holiness? That only shows how much I need to be converted.

St. Therese's "little way" is cherished by millions of people around the world because it is a way of holiness that anyone can pursue. Seeking to make every interaction, no matter how ordinary, an opportunity to love more deeply, she prepared herself to keep loving, even in the face of doubt and suffering and death. Her little way invites us all to take the small steps that make the big steps possible. In my hometown, we needed the courts to take a big step, to insist that we integrate our schools. But without the little way of children cultivating friendships on the playground, of black parents and white parents choosing to send their children to integrated schools, it would have been hard for the big changes of those years to have taken root.

When I visited my parents the next summer, the old copy of St. Therese's autobiography was back on my dad's shelf in his study. (Where had it been last summer? Only God and St. Therese know. Maybe it had been there in front of my eyes the whole time, and I just couldn't see it.)

It has my dad's name in the front, and also mine. And it has some underlining that is most definitely mine. I turned every page to see what had struck me when I was twelve. I laughed out loud to see my unsteady pencil marks

9. Simone Weil, *Waiting for God*, trans. Emma Craufurd (New York: G. P. Putnam's Sons, 1951), 70.
10. Ibid., 81.

underneath the words "*Martyrdom* was the dream of my youth. . . . I would die flayed like St. Bartholomew. I would be plunged into boiling oil like St. John. . . . With St. Agnes and St. Cecelia, I would present my neck to the sword."[11] I laughed because I am the person I know *least likely* to seek martyrdom, or to want to suffer in any way, for any reason. I have no memory of desiring this as a twelve-year-old. What did I love here? Why did I mark this passage? It's her passion, I think, her desire to do all for God—to leave nothing out—that I think I loved.

There were a few other passages underlined or marked, mostly passages with lots of exclamation marks and italics. But there was one passage that stopped me in my tracks. In the back flap of the book, I found the words "page 87" written in my handwriting. And when I turned to page 87, I saw underlined in heavy pencil these words: "I felt it was far more valuable to speak to God than to speak about Him, for there is so much self-love intermingled with spiritual conversations!"

I felt that I was receiving a message to my middle-aged self from my twelve-year-old self. Or perhaps a message from St. Therese herself. There's not a single bit of italics anywhere in that sentence (although there is an exclamation point), but I felt it as if every single word had been italicized. Being in the religion business, I spend a lot of my hours and days talking about God and having "spiritual conversations." But how much time do I spend speaking *to* God? How much time do I spend in prayer? I heard those two young girls—myself as a child and Sister Therese of the Child Jesus—ask me: don't you remember? Don't you? Hand in hand—in cahoots, even—they whisper the word that Therese knew was at the heart of everything: love. More love.

11. *Story of a Soul*, 193.

PART III

Preachers

19

Practicing Spirituality in the Middle

THEODORE J. WARDLAW

While spending a weekend recently with out-of-town friends, I encountered a framed poem hanging on the wall of their guesthouse. It is by Barbara Crooker, one of their favorite poets—and now one of mine. The poem is titled "In the Middle."

> In the middle
> of a life that's as complicated as everyone else's,
> struggling for balance, juggling time.
> The mantle clock that was my grandfather's
> has stopped at 9:20; we haven't had time
> to get it repaired. The brass pendulum is still,
> the chimes don't ring. One day you look out the window,
> green summer; the next, and the leaves have already fallen,
> and a grey sky lowers the horizon. Our children almost grown,
> and parents gone, it happened so fast. Each day, we must learn
> again how to love, between morning's quick coffee
> and evening's slow return. Steam from a pot of soup rises,
> mixing with the yeasty smell of baking bread. Our bodies
> twine, and the big black dog pushes his great head between;
> his tail is a metronome, ¾ time. We'll never get there,
> Time is always ahead of us, running down to the beach, urging
> us on faster, faster; but sometimes we take off our watches,
> sometimes we lie in the hammock, caught between the mesh
> of rope and the net of stars, suspended, tangled up
> in love, running out of time.[1]

---

1. Barbara Crooker, "In the Middle," in *Radiance* (Cincinnati: Word Press, 2005), 65. Reprinted by permission.

The poem there in that guesthouse, with its panoramic views of a beautiful lake, caught me, well, in the middle—in the middle of a head buzzing
with agendas, in the middle of a weekend where I was visiting area donors to
Austin Seminary, preparing for a church school class, working on a sermon
to preach on Sunday at two services, and thinking not so much about the
geese landing and taking off outside and the beaver swimming by as about the
things awaiting me in my office the following Monday. My desk in that place
groans, after all, with the chronic weight of faculty politics, the preliminary
details of a much-desired comprehensive capital campaign, next year's budget
to build and this year's budget to cut, an enrollment to increase, an anxious
denomination, and a stack of constituencies to attempt to satisfy. The poem
nailed me to the wall with its diagnostic judgment of my age, and, finally, my
whole life.

Magisterial Protestant that I am, I have always, somehow, navigated away
from any edges and out to the middle. In my family I was formed, and in
my theological education I was later schooled, in a sort of transformational
Calvinism that lifted up a notion of God who cared about and was invested
in everything—not just our souls or our prayer life, but everything! It was
either my father or some seminary professor who first extolled in my hearing how John Calvin was as interested in the sewers of Geneva as he was its
schools and hospitals. Years later, I would hear Fred Craddock, the noted
homiletician, say something to the effect that there is not one square-inch in
all of creation where, if you look hard enough, you can't find carved there the
initials of God.

In my growing-up years, in the abstract at least, this was the way of seeing
cultivated in me. Through this way of seeing, I learned that there was something noble about the possibility that all living things and all social systems
mattered immensely to God. I still believe this. What's different now, however, is that I also believe that this God is far less mannered and well-behaved
than the God of my childhood—the God who accepted gratefully the quali-
fied weekly praise of the Rotarians, who smiled at the blessing of every bar-
beque pit, who winced uncomfortably, maybe, but didn't really do much else
in the face of the dramatic racial injustices that tracked my boyhood years.

THE SPIRITUALITY OF THE CHURCH

In fact, my first conscious memory of the use of the word "spirituality" in my
childhood had to do with an incident in which, for the first time in my life,
I heard invoked a strange doctrine that Southern Presbyterians had invented
during the Civil War: "the Spirituality of the Church." With our national

denomination split in 1861 by arguments over slavery versus abolition, Presbyterians in the South forming a new church—the Presbyterian Church in the Confederate States of America—adopted this doctrine, a Reformed heresy if ever there was one, to explain why the church should not tackle such difficult social problems from the pulpit. Similar, I suppose, to how the historic Lutheran notion of "two kingdoms" was sometimes practiced, this doctrine staked off for my church a sort of spiritual "playing field" beyond which pastors and church people need not concern themselves. With the great matters of conscience of the nineteenth century (and later the twentieth century) being thus relegated to "secular playing fields," a Southern Presbyterian's ethical eyesight was conveniently averted by the church's constitution.

A century later, when I was eight or nine, this doctrine of the Spirituality of the Church forgave in advance any Presbyterian minister too timid to lift a voice against the segregated water fountains, hotels, doctors' waiting rooms, schools, churches, and sides of town that I vividly remember. My father, a prince of a minister, was hardly a social prophet. He did not go to Selma, and he never, to my knowledge, preached on the topic of civil rights. For the most part, he kept his social convictions within the confines of our home, and, even there, he did not reveal them readily.

But I can speak of two exceptions. Given the impossibility in the South of even politely discussing such matters, these exceptions were downright heroic. The first occurred when we were living in Atlanta, before we had moved to Kingstree, South Carolina, the town of my late elementary and middle school years. In the face of political opposition to the idea that Atlanta's public schools should be desegregated, some of that city's religious leaders—the Catholic bishop, a Reform Jewish rabbi, the dean of the Episcopal cathedral, some large-church pastors, and the president of Columbia Theological Seminary—drafted a public statement encouraging such desegregation. Called "The Ministers' Manifesto," it was published in the *Atlanta Constitution* and drew a great deal of public attention. My father was one of its signers. It was ridiculed by the Georgia governor and by U.S. Senator Richard B. Russell Jr. for promoting the "mongrelization of the races," and only the Lord knows what private invectives fell on those willing to so stick their necks out. Nevertheless, the desegregation that the manifesto called for became the status quo in just a few years. I wonder now if my father's signing that document led to his leaving his parish in Atlanta in order to move our family to Kingstree—a small, county-seat town in the Lowcountry of South Carolina.

Even there, the political winds were blowing. An African American man, a dentist, announced his candidacy for a seat in the South Carolina House of Representatives. The white Protestant establishment of that town was furious. I remember hearing arguments about this matter emanating from front

porches as I rode my bike up and down the streets of my side of town. I
remember too that on the Sunday prior to Election Day in Kingstree, all of
the white ministers were to announce from their pulpits that their people
should be sure to get out and vote so as to guarantee the defeat of this dentist. My father did not make that announcement. I remember watching him
shaking hands on the church's portico that Sunday following worship and
witnessing one of his red-faced parishioners unleash a profanity-laced diatribe
against him, which culminated in my father's being called a "nigger lover." I
asked my father later why he had not made the announcement. With a reso-
lute twinkle in his eye, he responded, "Because it would have violated the
Spirituality of the Church."

MY EARLY SPIRITUALITY:
A MIDDLE-OF-THE-ROAD GOD

The God to whom I was introduced in my childhood was not just a God in
the middle, but, by and large, also a God in the middle of the road. As interested as this God was in every square-inch of the world, at least in theory,
this God seemed to prefer the middle of any issue or argument to its edges or
its margins. It took me a number of years, and countless conversations with
people coming from this or that edge or margin, to understand how "middle
class" the value of "middle" really is. So often accompanied by the rhetoric of
compromise as an always-to-be-most-desired good, of "there are always two
sides to any issue," the value of "middle" can ultimately imagine itself somehow purer than the cases made on the margins.

During the summer before I entered the fifth grade, while we were vaca-
tioning at our summer cottage in Montreat, North Carolina (a kind of cross
between Chautauqua and Coney Island for Southern Presbyterians), my
mother and father took me with them to hear a speech given by Martin Luther
King Jr. in the Montreat Auditorium. This was during an era in which African Americans who decided to attend one of Montreat's many conferences
would not have been allowed to eat in the main dining hall but rather in the
kitchen, near which there was an old building provided for African American
worship. This worship took place on Sunday afternoons, at an hour when the
many family servants would have finished preparing, serving, and cleaning up
after the Sunday dinners of numerous cottage owners they had accompanied
on vacation. It was an era only a few years removed from the time when public buses bringing visitors to Montreat stopped routinely at the gate of the
conference center so that African Americans on these buses could disembark
and walk the rest of the way to their destinations. Surely I was aware of this

zeitgeist, at least in some corner of my subconscious, as I sat amid the nervous excitement of more than a thousand people waiting for King's arrival. Years later, I would learn of the death threats called in from people all over that portion of western North Carolina, and of the back-room machinations that attempted to persuade Montreat's leadership to withdraw King's invitation. Yet sitting there that night, there was the sense that all of us gathered had an appointment with destiny.

The first thing that particularly captured my attention that night was King's dramatic arrival amid a flurry of Buncombe County sheriff's cruisers—all lit up, sirens blaring, screeching to a halt just outside the auditorium door near which we were sitting—and the way in which, surrounded by officers and private security, King was whisked into the auditorium and up to the speaker's platform. This is an important man, I thought to myself. The second thing that captured me that night was his preaching. I had never heard, in person, such magnificent oratory. Nor had I ever heard a large audience of Presbyterians self-forgetful enough to shout "Amen!" and to clap joyously at the end of this or that gorgeous cascade of biblical and homiletical imagery. I remember his concluding words—what I know now to have been the familiar conclusion to many of his speeches—and how a chill ran up my back when he said them: "Free at last, free at last, thank God almighty that I'm free at last!" Later, as we all walked through the summer darkness back to a multitude of cars in the parking lot, I heard comments like "Great message!" and other murmured approvals from many people, some of whom were in the process of changing their minds that night. But I also heard, here and there, a complaint: "He was trying to suggest that all of the racial problems we're living through right now are somehow *our* fault." If there are, indeed, *always* two sides to any issue, many lovers of the middle that night—people trained to embrace occasional withering ethical compromises—were desperately trying to figure out the *other* side of *this* issue. I imagine them walking back to their cars nursing an argument something like this: "Maybe the capture and enslavement of hundreds of thousands of people, the breaking up of their families and tribes, and their removal from one side of the world to the other so that they could either live in a strange land in obedience to their masters for the rest of their lives or die defying such obedience was, in the end, a *good* thing."

DISCOVERING A GOD OF THE MARGINS

Years would go by before I discovered in some depth what is magnificent and good about the uncompromising spirituality of the margins.

Beyond high school, college, and seminary, it was in New Haven—in my wife Kay's and my first year of marriage—that we had our first sustained and reverent conversations with deeply spiritual people who would have been described by any South Carolina newspaper as "extremists." Fellow students at Yale Divinity School, some of these people became friends of ours. For the most part, they were radical, Daniel Berrigan-like inhabitants of a Catholic counterculture. I had never met people more richly formed by such paragons of Christian spirituality as Thomas Merton and Dorothy Day, and in frequent conversation with Henri Nouwen—then a virtual phenom at Yale. They were not troublemakers or rabble rousers. They were simply, well, spiritual—*and* religious. They loved their church, they were fed regularly at its table, they prayed with discipline, and they put their bodies on the line. Once, Kay joined them in a demonstration at a Connecticut military installation where a Trident submarine was in dock (I "couldn't" go—I "had" to work on my master's thesis—but now I believe I was clinging reflexively to life in the middle, where surely there was some not-yet-grasped acceptable compromise between war and peace). Some demonstrators there that day were arrested, but these joyful peacemakers came back to our apartment at the end of the day—all present and accounted for—and shouted up to the windows of my study, "No more nukes, no more nukes!"

In class once, Henri Nouwen spoke of the deep roots of monasticism. As a resident of the most Protestant state in the country, I hardly knew a thing about monasticism. A professor of mine at Union Theological Seminary in Virginia had once reminded me in response to a question I had asked him about monasteries, "You know, Mr. Wardlaw, John Calvin once said that the whole world is a monastery." That was good enough for me—the notion that to particularly sacralize anything (like a specific monastery) was also, perhaps, to desacralize everything else (like, say, the whole world), and who would want to risk that? But now, Nouwen was complexifying my understanding of monasticism. He noted that monasteries were, from perhaps our angle of vision, marginal places, places on the edge of relevance. But, he went on, from another angle of vision monasteries—where monks prayed constantly through the hours of the day—were in fact at the very center of the world and the reason that the world was still intact. The world, he suggested, *was held together by the ongoing diligence of Christian prayer.*

From my accustomed place in the middle, monastics praying their way from Matins to Compline, day by day and year by year, were irrelevant; they had simply opted out of life, praying while the rest of us had our hands on various very important levers. But from their angle of vision they were praying constantly at the center of the universe. I was the one who was marginalized—I with my premature certainties about how the world works, I with my pathetic secret confidence in Trident submarines and political parties and a pragmatic "you scratch my back and I'll scratch yours" way of living.

Years after our time in New Haven, I was serving an urban congregation in Atlanta. It was the very definition of a center-city church—across the street from the Georgia Capitol, virtually next door to City Hall on one side and, on the other side, just a hundred yards or so from the zero milepost of the original railroad that brought Atlanta into being. Homeless people, state legislators, parents dropping off or picking up their children at the child care center, persons needing health care at the church's ambulatory health center, folks entering the chapel to pray or to attend a weekday service—these people, plus, of course, the church's parishioners, were forever populating the church's halls. It felt sometimes like an ecclesial Grand Central Station.

On one occasion, Kay, who was visiting a monastery outside Atlanta, called me and said, "Grab the girls and come out here right now. You won't be sorry." At that time our two daughters were young—Shelby a toddler and Claire still a babe in arms. Without arguing, I did exactly what Kay said. I retrieved Shelby from the church's child care center and Claire from the sitter, and we drove the thirty or so miles to the Monastery of the Holy Spirit, outside Conyers, Georgia. It was a place where, across later years, Kay and I would each spend short seasons of quiet time. On this particular afternoon, though, Kay wanted us all there together because it was a day immersed in springtime beauty. Azaleas and dogwoods alive with color sparkled everywhere, especially against the backdrop of a shimmering pond near the monastery chapel. Upon arriving there and before we connected with Kay, the girls and I walked over to the pond to watch the ducks. Out of nowhere appeared this Cistercian monk—at first glance, an apparently unhinged man in a coarse, brown cassock—who walked straight up to me and put his hands on Claire's head, then on Shelby's head, and then on mine. Looking straight into our eyes, one by one, he simply said, "Jesus loves you."

That's not a bad three-word summation of the gospel—which I, as a preacher, have been charged with proclaiming for over three decades now—but, on that occasion, I heard it as if for the first time, and tears leapt out of my eyes. Was that setting irrelevant? Was it marginal?

Early in my ministry at that urban church in Atlanta, Central Presbyterian Church, I went to an evening service at the historic Ebenezer Baptist Church, a living monument to the civil rights movement if ever there was one. It was the church which Daddy King led before his son Martin, and it presided over Auburn Avenue, the economic center of Atlanta's black establishment. In those days, before the stunning new church was built across the street, the relative modesty of the original building could catch a first-time visitor off guard. Ushers directed me up to the sanctuary on the second floor, and I was struck by the unadorned intimacy of the place. A sturdy pulpit stood on a dais, and artificial light from the stained-glass window depicting Jesus praying in Gethsemane shone down upon it. There were sprays of flowers here and there, but otherwise not much ornamentation. I sat in the balcony, and as the church filled up the Hammond organ began an opening voluntary. Soon, the Rev. Dr. Joseph L. Roberts Jr. and an entourage of associate ministers and musicians filed in. The hymns were sung, for the most part, in first-person singular, and the sermon was a stirring one (if God has a voice like Joe Roberts, I won't be disappointed) about a theme related to a Christian's personal piety. The choir's anthem that evening was titled "He's All Right with Me."

This was the cathedral of civil rights, a shrine of social activism, and there was not one petition circulated in the service, not one manifesto read out loud by a church officer, not one march organized at the end of it all, and, for that matter, not one pronoun in the first-person plural. I asked someone after the service, "How can it be that this church, which stands for the collective civil disobedience of thousands of oppressed people tired of waiting another moment for a justice long delayed—how can it be that this church, in the language of its worship, expressed a sort of piety marked by the personal pronouns "I" and "me"? The man smiled at me and said, "We can afford to talk like this in the sanctuary because of all the things we know are going on down in the basement."

He was talking about the profound link between a deeply personal faith and the actions of justice and mercy that such faith fuels. Was that language irrelevant? Was it marginal? No.

A MORE MATURE SPIRITUALITY: LIVING AND LEADING OBEDIENTLY IN THE MIDDLE

In my own spiritual journey, haphazard as it has often been, I have learned, sometimes kicking and screaming, from the voices coming from what we often define as the margins. Nonetheless, it has been my lot—and more recently, I've even been willing to say my *vocation*—to live in what those very voices themselves define as the middle, caught, as Crooker says, "between the mesh of rope and the net of stars."

Last year, I was asked to participate in a study of seminary presidents conducted by Auburn Theological Seminary's president, Barbara Wheeler, a dear friend and one of this generation's brightest lights with respect to the landscape of North American theological education. The study included a multiple-choice instrument. Although I don't remember any of the questions accurately, I experienced their net effect as somehow ferreting out of me every ounce of frustration I often feel in my work. The general gist of the questions was as follows. Do I often feel lonely? Yes. Is it the case that I frequently sense that the faculty has little understanding of the scope of my job? Yes. When I stepped into my position, did the board essentially just throw me the keys to the *Titanic*? Yes. (For the record, nothing resembling this question was on the instrument.) Is the task of fund-raising often very frustrating? Did you sometimes inherit less-than-effective staff? Do you feel overwhelmed by the swirl of agendas within your various constituencies? Are there serious liabilities in your work? Do you suffer in this work? Yes. Yes. Yes. Yes. Yes. Page after page, I felt myself digging into a deeper and deeper hole of despair. Then came the last question, which was something to this effect: If you could leave now to do some other kind of work, would you? My mouth went dry and my hands shook for maybe a few minutes until, steadily and deliberately, I checked the box that said "No."

When the study was completed, Barbara offered a fascinating presentation of its results to a gathering of seminary presidents from the United States and Canada. She said many things that were important, but one thing in particular was most important to me: this job is frequently a kind of ascetical practice, but it has the capacity to make one a better person. "Ultimately there is joy in obedience," Barbara said. "You don't always enjoy yourself, but your efforts are often their own very satisfying reward."[2]

Ultimately there is joy in obedience! That's the payoff for those of us who strive for some sort of spiritual practice in the middle of whatever it is that we do. It is joy!

For over a year now, I have been meeting once a week at 7:30 a.m. for an hour and a half with a small group of men engaged in various ministries. We are now sewn at the hips, all within a decade or so of one another in terms of age, and bonded in accountability and confidentiality, though we are also very different from one another. My counterpart at the Episcopal seminary in Austin, a former Jesuit who runs a nonprofit organization, two Baptist pastors, and I are brothers now. Each has permission to push and challenge the others. Sometimes we snap the rattail with one another, like middle school kids in a locker room, and other times we weep out loud. Our former Jesuit is often like the coach in the room, saying the right thing at the right moment, and sounding a bit like Jesus in the guise of a drill sergeant. Early on, he suggested a process for us that we have more or less followed for some time now. In the morning, before the busyness starts, he tells each of us to go to a quiet

2. From the presentation "Leadership That Works: A Study of Seminary Presidents and Their Administrative Teams" by Barbara Wheeler, given on December 8, 2009, at the Association of Theological Schools' Presidential Leadership Intensive Week in Santa Fe, New Mexico.

place and rehearse our calendar for the day, to think of the challenges before us, and in our prayer time to ask Jesus for what we will need in each moment to be a vessel of his presence. Then we are to wait for him to answer.

The assignment was initially difficult for me, Calvinist that I am, because, among other things, the image of the vessel felt so passive. If you tell me to build a hospital, to run for a slot on the school board, to organize a mission trip or a beach cleanup, these are things that feel somehow more comfortable for a person living in the middle. But be a vessel? Jesus will tell me what to do? Believing this and acting accordingly takes time, at least for me. I have been more accustomed to just barking quick orders at Jesus, as if I were Colonel Henry Blake and Jesus were Corporal Radar O'Reilly. It's a new thing for me to write down my dreams, to rehearse what the daily calendar promises to be the signposts of my day, and to listen for whatever Jesus may have to say to me about it all. Needless to say, there are some days when I'm more open to such a conversation, and there are other days when I wonder if I'm not in fact just talking to myself. But at the core of this practice, I find the cultivation of a certain mindfulness that enables me more readily to be present to the One who ultimately stands squarely in the middle of life, even as this One's eyes reach knowingly to every margin with the same invitation for all of us: "Come unto me, and I will give you rest" (Matt. 11:28). Obedience to Jesus engenders fear, resistance, denial, suffering, and, once in a while, also joy.

PARADOXICAL JOY

I can't think of another time in my life when such joy has felt more paradoxical. As I write these words, I am reflecting upon the last two brutal years in our economy, in which every academic institution in the country—from Austin Community College to Harvard University—has felt its ravages. Even if the Great Recession is over, at least technically, the way ahead still seems dangerous, and many questions linger. What will these economic uncertainties do to the psyches of maybe a whole generation? How many men and women will remain unemployed, and for how long? How will this affect families? Neighborhoods? Churches? Personal stress levels? How will it show itself in the composition of future entering classes at the seminary I serve? How will it show itself in the upcoming new member classes of our churches? Something tells me we should brace ourselves. In the middle of life, there will be new restlessness, new cynicism, new armies of the idle. Where will the joy be in such a mix? I don't know the answers to any of these questions, caught as I am between the mesh of rope and the net of stars.

Caught with me is an American suspicion of institutions, generally considered—seminaries, universities, city halls, Congress, you name it. Hugh Heclo, a professor of public affairs, writes:

> We are disposed to distrust institutions. That is the basic fact of life we share as modern people. . . . As good pluralists, tolerant multiculturalists, secular or religious moralists, . . . we can be divided on almost any other imaginable subject. But a fundamental distrust of institutions is the one mark we have in common as inhabitants of these times. . . . It is that pervasive, recurrent nod of agreement we have in common as modern, twenty-first century people. We are compelled to live in a thick tangle of institutions while believing that they do not have our best interests at heart.[3]

The fact of the matter, as Heclo puts it, is that "today's institutions have gained our distrust the old-fashioned way. They have earned it."[4] This mistrust has been earned by the church and even the ministry. The antidote, some propose, is a church and a ministry divorced from institutions, somehow unencumbered and "emergent" enough to be as free-flowing as a flag fluttering in the breeze. Throw over these encrusted institutions that weigh us down with their centuries of buildings and memory and tradition! Even Eugene Peterson, the iconic pastor and model for the pastoral life, has argued that ministers should concentrate on preaching and teaching and stay out of such institutional matters as administration.

Alternatively, I agree with Thomas White Currie III, who said in response to such a notion that it "strikes me as more than a little romantic, and perhaps even a bit docetic." He continues:

> The administrative task [of a minister] extends to knowing what the giving patterns in her congregation are like, what financial needs and challenges the congregation faces, and what resources and people can be called upon to help the community meet those needs and challenges. That means meetings and time. This is not the most important thing, but it is far from being the least important. It is hard and often energy draining and time consuming. Still, unless [these matters too] are embraced by the minister, her own ministry will become entirely too "spiritual" and not nearly as intimate as it needs to be. Life is in the minutiae, in the details, as is much of ministry.[5]

---

3. Hugh Heclo, *On Thinking Institutionally* (Boulder, CO: Paradigm Publishers, 2008), 10–11.

4. Ibid., 15.

5. Thomas W. Currie III, "The Theological Significance of Administration in the Pastoral Ministry," in *The Power to Comprehend with All the Saints*, ed. Wallace M. Alston Jr. and Cynthia A. Jarvis (Grand Rapids: Wm. B. Eerdmans, 2009), 279.

Here in the middle, I am called to care about such minutiae and such details. I am called to be a vessel in their midst, praying daily for how I may be attentive to them and, when I'm at my faithful best, waiting for Jesus to direct me redemptively in their direction. Neither faith nor leadership in the middle allow for an unfettered way of living. Rather, both make for profoundly tangled and incarnational ways of living. "We have this *treasure* in earthen vessels," writes Paul (2 Cor. 4:7). He means, I think, that the gospel is never just a pristine thing that hovers safely above the mesh of rope. The gospel is instead that incarnate reality that enters into all of life, even into us—the clay jars and earthen vessels and cracked pots that all of us are—and calls upon us to care, in the name of Jesus Christ, about everything and everybody.

My younger daughter is probably my most effective teacher and coach in the ways of all about our world that is most contemporary. Some years ago, she took me under her wing and began sharing with me as much of her generation's music and film and technology and literature that she dared to share with me. A while back, she sent me an entry she had picked up from somebody else's Facebook page that she thought I needed to know about. It was a popular definition of Christianity making the rounds, and by my lights it seemed sadly too cynical for a college student: "Christianity is the belief that a two-thousand-year-old Jewish zombie can make you live forever if you symbolically eat his flesh and telepathically tell him that you accept him as your master, so he can remove an evil force from your soul that is present in humanity because a rib-woman was convinced by a talking snake to eat an apple off a magical tree in a wonderland."

I e-mailed her back: "Yeah, that's how the faith often looks from the outside."

But here's how the faith looks from the inside. Two members of the church we attend were working in a hospital twenty miles away from Port-au-Prince when the earthquake hit in Haiti in January 2010. They got out from the rubble of their building, and, amid the ensuing chaos, the wife in that couple was finally able, on a borrowed cell phone with just a little juice left in it, to get an e-mail message out that they were okay. That message ultimately got forwarded to a number of us in the congregation:

> At night we sleep in the yard behind the hospital. . . . It has fallen, as has the Episcopal school. There are 200 to 300 people who sleep in that field at night. They sing hymns until almost midnight, and we wake up to a church service, with hymns, a morning prayer, and the Apostles' Creed. The evening sky is glorious. In the field there is a real sense of community. . . . People have shared with us and we are

getting a chance to feel how the Haitians really live. . . . I have never understood joy in the midst of suffering, but now I do.[6]

They were caught, as many of us are caught, in the middle of things. In our various settings, amid being caught, we are invited nonetheless to be vessels attentive to the voice of Jesus. And oddly enough, there *is* joy. We who follow Jesus are embodying not just a good idea but the good news—in the midst of a hellish circumstance—for which the world hungers. Caught between the mesh of rope and the net of stars—this is the life that we are called to live, for God's sake and for the sake of the world—for as long as we have time.

6. From an e-mail message sent from Haiti on January 15, 2010, from John and Suzi Parker, members of University Presbyterian Church in Austin and mission workers in Haiti.

20

Spiritual Integrity

A large crowd had gathered at the railroad station. A benign, fatherly figure stepped off the arriving train to be surrounded and greeted enthusiastically by the people. A lovely blond, blue-eyed little girl came forward with flowers for the man. Taking the flowers, he gathered her into his arms. The scene was filled with love, the love of the people for this man, and the man's love for them and for the child who had brought him the flowers. It was a beautifully spirit-filled moment. The man's name was Adolf Hitler.

In this old newsreel film from the 1930s, he was the *Führer*. To the gathered people, he was the embodiment of hope for the future, the fulfillment of the spiritual meaning of the *Volk*. Later, multitudes would be gathered in a spirit-filled rally at Nuremburg, with thousands singing as one, "*Deutschland, Deutschland über alles.*"

This was a spiritual moment in the life of the nation; of that there could be no question. But seventy years later, the world knows that beneath the surface of this spiritual reality was a dark, demonic force—a profoundly idolatrous worship of peoplehood and murderous hatred of many of God's children, millions of whom were systematically killed in one of the greatest evils in the history of humankind. So we learned afresh that spirit, as such, is not necessarily good. And we are reminded of a scriptural word: "Beloved, do not believe every spirit, but test the spirits to see whether they are of God," to which the writer adds, "for many false prophets have gone out into the world" (1 John 4:1).

Despite the fact that many "German Christians" supported him, Hitler and the Nazi party made no pretense of being a Christian movement. However, many false prophets through the centuries have led spirit-filled movements under explicitly religious auspices. This continues in the present day, when charismatic religious charlatans captivate numbers of people with their own brands of spiritual appeal. Numerous televangelists and other charismatic preachers have been involved in scandals of one kind or another, leaving thousands of disillusioned followers in their wake. So being "spiritual" is not always such a good thing. We do need to test the spirits. We even need to be cautious in criticizing less spirited forms of religious expression. I recall a standard comment by one of the great mid-twentieth-century preachers that the worst sin for a preacher is to be uninteresting. I bought that for a long time, until it dawned on me that a large number of very interesting speakers have had truly evil things to say; Hitler is but one illustration. It is no virtue for a preacher or any other speaker to be uninteresting, but I have come to believe that what we have to say trumps how we say it, at least most of the time.

So we do have to test the spirits. But what is the test? First John continues: "By this you know the Spirit of God: every spirit that confesses that Jesus Christ has come in the flesh is from God, and every spirit that does not confess Jesus is not from God." Put theologically, this means that the test is christological. Does the spirit, the feeling, express the reality of Christ? To push this further, does it express the *love* of Christ? There may be nothing wicked about feel-good religion as practiced in innocuous ways in so many churches and reflected so often in sweet-sounding hymns. But when put to the test of the degree to which the feelings express the depth of God's love in Christ, they don't quite measure up. Again, there's nothing wicked about good but superficial feelings. We can get all excited at a football game, roaring with excitement when the warriors of dear old Siwash U. score again and sinking into dejection when they lose. The moment comes and goes, as do many moments in everyday life when we feel good or not so good, depending on what happens or doesn't happen. Those moments of not feeling good can actually be good, however, if they reset our minds and spirits.

But when we speak of the spiritual life we come back to the ultimate test: Is our spirit attuned to the depth of God's love as expressed through Christ? Are our loves—of family, community, country, nature—grounded in God's love with an openness to love as God loves? When this is the case, one is, in Christian terms, a *spiritual* person. One is spiritual with *integrity*.

Part of my assignment in writing this essay was to speak out of my own experience. Ouch! What is one to say? Am I to say that I pass the 1 John 4 test in my own spiritual life? Maybe once in a while—once in a long while.

As I have reflected on this question, my mind has drifted back to a truly luminescent moment in March 1965. For a few days that month, I was in Selma, Alabama. At one of the pivotal moments in the civil rights movement, demonstrators in Selma sought to gain voting rights for the vast majority of African Americans in that city who had never been allowed to vote (at the time only about 300 out of some 10,000 had that basic right of citizenship). By dramatizing the situation in Selma, the idea was to push for legislation at the national level that would gain the franchise for all African Americans throughout the nation. The movement decided to dramatize the state of affairs by staging a march from Selma to the state capital, Montgomery. But demonstrators were brutally repressed by local and state police as they passed over the Edmund Pettis Bridge leaving Selma. Martin Luther King Jr. put out a call for people of goodwill to come to Selma and join the demonstrations, and I was one of the many who responded.

Our center of activity was the Brown's Chapel African Methodist Episcopal Church in the predominantly African American section of town. For several days we joined in activities, including a march to the local courthouse, where we held a prayer gathering in a torrential rain. (I thought at the time that, indeed, God does send the rain on the just and the unjust alike, but why is it that the police—the "unjust," so to speak—were the ones equipped with rain gear and we were not!) Other activities included a series of simultaneous marches in the white section of the city, during which we were all arrested and herded into school buses. Ordered to keep quiet, we nevertheless broke into the Lord's Prayer. When the buses arrived at the police station, I noted a number of ordinary white men who had evidently been deputized to help the police, including one little man who was carrying a bundle of wooden clubs; he appeared to be the batboy. We weren't booked, but after being lined up for an hour or so outside, we were gathered into a nearby African American recreation building, where the two or three hundred of us spent the night. Jewish rabbis led us in a Sabbath service. Christians read Scripture and offered prayer. Permitted to leave the next morning, we arrived back at Brown's Chapel just as a contingent of Episcopalians was about to celebrate an outdoor Eucharist. Led by Bishop Kilmer Myers, the group had been turned away from the Selma Episcopal Church, so they arranged the outdoor Eucharist, conducted in exquisite high-church perfection.

Each evening we had combination prayer meeting and strategy sessions. During the day, local African American children gathered outside to sing freedom songs, often concocted in the moment. Many of these children had been arrested and held in cold prison cells without bedding and with floors that were hosed down. Yet here they were singing, "We love Jim Clark, in our heart." (Clark was the mean-spirited county sheriff.) One night an elderly African American man spoke of the history-making character of the campaign: "What we are doing here will make stories mothers tell their children for a thousand years." Hyperbole? Probably. But he voiced the deep sense that this was God's work that we were about. Another evening, when a group of newly arrived California college kids showed disrespect for the religious character of the movement, an elderly African American (possibly the same one) looked down at them from the chancel and said, "I don't know why you're here, and we can't prevent you from being here. But if you're not here because of God, you don't belong." That word had an instantly sobering effect on the young people, and it restored the integrity of the movement.

The march to Montgomery then occurred, this time with thousands crossing the bridge under a beautiful Alabama sun and with the court-ordered protection by federalized National Guard units.

As I reflect back on those days and events, this was an extraordinary union of effective action in behalf of social justice, infused with the spirit of love, determination, courage, and lightheartedness. It was a deeply spiritual moment. Participants were virtually transported by spirit, but the spirit was utterly without hatred. The movement was grounded in the truth that justice for the long-suffering African American population was also a new spiritual freedom for their oppressors. I do not want to make too much of this, but that moment in American history has stood the test of time. Its spirit exemplified the love of God; it had spiritual integrity.

Can we cultivate spiritual integrity in our own lives? Most of us have known persons whom we would characterize as spiritual in the best sense. Is this inborn? Is it nurtured in a loving home? Is it the fruit of spiritual disciplines? I'm not sure. I do react with caution when anybody asks me about my prayer life or other spiritual disciplines, not because I disdain regular prayer and spiritual discipline, but because the question invites a sense of guilt if we have little to report or a sense of pride if we have too much. I am persuaded that through self-discipline we can gain better control over feelings that are contrary to love, for example, by pausing on the brink of angry words or hateful deeds. We can cultivate a greater rational mastery of destructive or corrupting impulses. The philosopher Immanuel Kant contrasted the rational will to what he called the "pathological" will; by "pathological" he referred to a will that is governed primarily by feeling, not the present-day connotation of the word. A good deal of self-discipline involves progressively gaining rational control over feelings that are contrary to higher moral purposes. But I wonder whether this exhausts the meaning of spiritual, for spiritual life surely has something to do with our feelings. Perhaps spiritual integrity is when our feelings are in harmony with a rationally formed moral will.

But how do we achieve this spiritual integrity? It seems to me that one of the deepest insights of Christian Scripture is the distinction between grace and works of the law. The former is a gift, the latter, an action to conform our will to moral law. Both are implicit in the life of the spirit, but grace comes first. "We love because he first loved us," to quote again that great fourth chapter of 1 John. Can we love if we have not been loved? I doubt it. We can engage in spiritual disciplines of one sort or another even if we have seldom experienced love, but do those disciplines lead us to love? Do they transform us into spiritual beings? Again, I doubt it. There can be discernible effects from the disciplines, but mostly these are more from conformity to external commandments than from the springs of love within. How then can the two be brought together—love from within and moral response to rationally discerned needs?

Perhaps one thing we can *do* is open ourselves up to the resources of love that are readily at hand. To cultivate feelings of empathy for others, we can get to know other people in their vulnerabilities. In my teaching of Christian ethics through the years, I have often discovered that students become more enlightened as well as more loving when they have opportunities to meet, talk, and work with those who are less privileged or who are socially stigmatized. Hillary Rodham Clinton reports the formative effects of field trips to Chicago from her privileged suburban church that were led by her youth minister. She was able to see some things firsthand that could no longer be distanced as abstractions. I will confess to a similar experience in transforming my attitudes toward gay and lesbian people. In my early years as a teacher of Christian ethics, I viewed homosexuality as either an emotional disease or a sin, and I had a tendency to define homosexual persons by their sexuality and not by their humanity. Later, as I had occasion to become better acquainted personally with gay and lesbian persons, both as a pastor and as a member in a churchwide study commission, I was able to see beyond the stereotypes and misassumptions.

One spiritual resource that we might not think of in these terms is great literature. Charles Dickens created new spiritual openings for the English-speaking world with novels featuring the English underclass suffering in the crowded cities of the Industrial Revolution. By being drawn into the lives of particular people, one gained new empathy for them and others like them. Poverty could no longer be distanced as a statistical abstraction, affecting people, to be sure, but far enough removed from our own experience to become spiritually irrelevant. In the past year or so my reading has included novels and memoirs related to the Holocaust, which has helped me recognize that its deep evil was not just the raw numbers of people murdered but the actual lives and experiences of real persons, like myself. A book like Daniel Mendelsohn's *The Lost* brought me into the awfulness of the killing by its careful exploration of the lives of only six of the six million Jewish victims. This literature is an invitation to hate the perpetrators of such cruel deeds, but the stories of some of the caring people who risked their lives to hide Jews from the Nazis draw one into deeper love. We need to choose our reading with care, for it helps nurture a life of spiritual integrity.

I personally find such literature more helpful than some of the devotional manuals, but insofar as the latter open us to the human world about us, they can also be helpful. For example, the work of a Thomas Merton or a Dorothy Day can lure us into our better selves.

What, then, about God? God can either be the grandest abstraction of all or the greatest living presence. I write these words from a place of retreat in the Adirondacks of northern New York. Here, surrounded by beautiful forests, sparkling lakes, graceful mountains, and brilliant night skies, it is easy to contemplate the presence of a creator of such beauty. Yet I also recall the wealthy few who built their "great camps" by the lakes so they could be next to nature and enjoy all this beauty. Were they challenged by this beauty to care much for the workers whose labor enabled their great wealth? Or did they rather gain new energy to implement a gospel of wealth remote from the God of love? I love the beauty of this place and other beauties of sight and sound, owed to hands other than our own and to which we are indebted. But I am reminded once again that the test of this spirit, this aesthetic spirit, must finally be christological. Do we see and hear this spirit through the love of Christ that we take to be the love of God? The beauty of nature comes to us largely refracted through the love we find in human beings. By virtue of our humanity, we can find beauty in other sentient beings.

And what, then, about the life of prayer? Can we speak to God in prayer? Can God speak to us? Surely we can speak to God, in the hope and faith that there is a listening ear. And as we open ourselves to the gifts of love, surely God can speak to us. Intellectually, I have no problem in believing that God, the center and source of all being, infuses all of reality. God is *everywhere*. For many people, regular times set aside for prayer are channels of openness. I have not found this terribly useful myself. For me, prayer is more natural at odd, sometimes unexpected times—for example, upon awakening or confronting special opportunity or temptation, or when doing some of that reading I've referred to above. All of us can pause occasionally to voice our deep gratitude for the gift of life itself. Think of the odds against us having been born—the vast number of ancestral decisions that predated our birth, multiplied by countless billions of sperm cells and ova that never united. Each of us represents the one in trillions of possibilities that actually got born! Each of us was gifted with a world and our own little window on eternity! Sometimes I think gratitude itself must be close to the heart of the spiritual life when it is infused with love and expressed with integrity.

Let us also consider the practical value of regular worship and church attendance. It can become very routine, of course, and even dull. Still, in worship and church life the great traditions of spirituality are an ongoing presence through prayers, hymns, sacraments, and sometimes, by the grace of God, even the word as preached.

Encountering such traditions may bring spiritual breakthroughs. Let me illustrate. When serving as pastor of a church in Washington, D.C., I participated in a midweek healing and Communion service in our small chapel. It wasn't the kind of healing service that one often associates with some charismatic faith healers; most of the healing was at a spiritual or emotional level. One evening a young man knelt at the altar and asked me to pray for him as he poured out his deep sense of personal failure. I had not wanted to be there that night; I just didn't feel up to it. But somehow this man's need got to me, and I confess that something like the Holy Spirit led me to take him by the shoulders and speak of God's love for him. It was something like that spirit I had felt at Selma years before, but in a very different setting.

So we come full circle. What is spiritual integrity in this time and place? We live in a materialistic society, suffused with corruptions of the spirit and yet teased by national traditions and church traditions of a higher sort. Our history is not all lovely, but it nevertheless contains so many reminders of how God is brooding over this world, inviting us into new dimensions of spiritual integrity.

21

Table Grace

DEBORAH A. BLOCK

My job was to set the table. A place for everyone in the family. Forks, knives, spoons, and plates for five. Bread on a plate, milk in a pitcher. My mother didn't allow wrappers or bottles on the table, and she always insisted on candles. The meals were simple fare, nutritious and plentiful. Meatloaf, chicken, liver, pork chops, vegetables from the garden in season, and mashed potatoes from a box. Transforming the dried flakes with water and milk and butter was my job too. Toward the end of the month the simple fare was even simpler, but we thought breakfast for supper was a treat. Pancakes! Even oatmeal. And always, there was table grace.

"For all Thy good gifts, we thank Thee, our Father, and ask Thee to bless us this day. Amen." Sometimes we said it together; sometimes one member of the family would say it for us all. My twin brothers would wiggle and giggle, so I was the preferred pray-er.

One evening when the nod to pray came my way, I was wallowing in one of childhood's "horrible, terrible, no good, very bad" days and grumped that I had nothing to be thankful for. My father came right out of his chair, took me out of mine by my braid, and in a moment I was down the hall and into my room, there to contemplate the error of my ways and the things I did, indeed, have to be thankful for. When I shared that memory with my parents as an adult, they didn't remember the incident at all. I was afraid they'd never forget. What was important is that I never did.

To this day I say that grace before meals, alone in my kitchen, with my colleagues over lunch in the office, with my father in the dining room of his retirement community. Mom is gone now, but we still say the revised version she gave her blessing to when a young feminist brought her concerns

about inclusive language to the family table: "We thank Thee, our God . . ."
Thanks, Mom.

Spiritual life was nourished at the table, but a variety of graces edified the
family. Daily bread was shared with daily news, ideas were dished up and current events were digested, questions were chewed, any appetite for selfishness
was suppressed, and any taste of discord was seasoned by understanding. Bad
manners were rectified by second chances, and good stories got requests for
second helpings. The art of conversation was force-fed to monosyllabic adolescents. Skills of diplomacy were served family style. An ethic of gratitude
was fed by prayer and parental love. All of life was nourished at the table.

Life happened around other, nondomestic, tables. Over years of formal
education, library tables were sacred spaces, oases of quiet for reading and
thinking. The mind feasted at classroom tables. A steady diet of theology
and Bible strengthened a call to ministry. I had little interest in laboring at
a kitchen table, and although I had no images of women at the Communion
table, in my heart I knew I was being called to take my place there.

The assignment for this book, to reflect on the spiritual life, was challenging, but as I pondered and wandered, my family story of saying grace (and
not) was the recurring starting point, revealing the central place of life at the
table. In literature it would be a "controlling metaphor." In my life the table
is an integrating reality. Life at the table has been challenging, and it has been
my calling. Consider the life of the church and how much of it happens at
tables. We meet, eat, bond, commune, communicate, commit, confer, and
connect there.

Seminary was a difficult experience. My sense of call met with resistance
that, in retrospect, focused and strengthened it. I had encountered the apostle Paul in college religion courses, worked to understand him on his terms
and in his times, and befriended him. I felt equipped to counter the noise
about women needing to be silent in churches (1 Cor. 14:34). The Word
that was calling me had to be reclaimed. The words that were teaching me
had to be renamed. I was not part of the brotherhood or the fellowship.
Inclusive language was a new thing in the mid-1970s; it was ridiculed and
opposed. A handful of women students gathered regularly in a "caucus" that
worked on things like financial aid equity, gender diversity on the faculty
(there were no women), and nondiscrimination in field education place-
ments. We organized and strategized for institutional change, and in doing
so we were graced with sustaining personal relationships and experienced
the power of community. Internally the caucus was sometimes more like a
house church. We lamented and we laughed. We ate and drank. We sang old
hymns with new words and new songs with no "hims." We prayed together
in our mother tongue. We communed.

I grew up going to church, but in those years at seminary I drew away. Preparing for the ministry of the Word had too many words, and Sunday worship was just one more sermon critique. So I sought refuge with the Quakers for a while, fed by their Sabbath silence and challenged by their weekday activism. I was also fed breakfast every Sunday morning I attended! Quaker oats held the promise both of lower cholesterol and the Inner Light. God was indeed in that healing silence, calling me back to words and the ministry of the Word and Sacrament. The meetinghouse was simple and beautiful, but I missed the cross, the font, the table. The oatmeal fed my body, and the welcome filled my heart, but I hungered for the bread and wine.

What did I know when I was twenty-five? My mother and I sat together at the dining room table and designed the invitations to my service of ordination, which included a grapevine border and a text: "Live by the Spirit. . . . The fruit of the Spirit is love, joy, peace, patience, kindness, generosity, faithfulness, gentleness, and self-control" (Gal. 5:16, 22–23).

Life in the Spirit is nourished by the study of Scripture, and after many years there are some phrases and images that are staples for living this life. I have lived with this text. I see it in still-life paintings of fruit held in beautiful bowls, as if cupped in God's own hand—varied graces tumbled together or carefully arranged, on a table. Paul's "fruit" is singular. I try to make this point annually to children as we enjoy a long-time custom of "fruit of the Spirit salad" at our Pentecost meal, when an attempt is made to allegorize the ingredients. The Spirit creates a unity characterized by love, joy, peace, patience, kindness, generosity, faithfulness, gentleness, and self-control. Paul would insist that the greatest of these is love, and so all of these other fruits are love's various facets and expressions, or what God produces in human lives and how God's Spirit equips us to live in the world. I love this text because it pushes spirituality out of the narrow confines of personal practices and qualities into the Spirit's realm of community building. God gives the growth, Paul would say, and so this text also reminds us that the spiritual life is not our achievement, no matter how perfect our practices. Like the bread and the fruit of the vine, the fruit of the Spirit is the gift of God for the people of God. Like the bread and the fruit of the vine, the fruit of the Spirit is a sign of the real presence and power of Christ.

Living by the Spirit takes us to the Communion table. We set the table and serve this fruit. God's *love* calls us to this joyful feast. *Peace* is offered and prayed for. In the ancient practice of the church, the *Agnus Dei* was sung at the breaking of the bread: "Lamb of God, you take away the sins of the world. Grant us peace." The Lord's passion is remembered; "patience" comes from the Latin word for suffering. God's *kindness, generosity*, and *faithfulness* are celebrated in the Great Thanksgiving. There is *gentleness* in the invitation

"Come to me, all you that are weary and carrying heavy burdens, and I will give you rest. Take my yoke upon you and learn from me; for I am gentle and humble in heart." *Self-control* is exercised; no matter how deep our hunger, we serve one another and wait to eat together.

I sit at the table and watch as the gifts are served. There are three large chairs at the back of the chancel in the sanctuary, behind the table—a visible proclamation that this is a Communion table, where people are fed, and not an altar, where sacrifices are made. I recede into those few minutes, immersed and swallowed in sacred "surround sound." I look at the table, set with gleaming silver trays or earthenware chalices and African baskets. I look past the table at the panorama of persons in the pews. They are serving one another, praying, listening; there are tears and smiles. Sometimes they come forward to commune by intinction, receiving bread like those Emmaus disciples and dipping it like the guests in the upper room. I look past the table at the parade of persons in the aisles. They are walking together, helping the old ones and the little ones, coaching the new ones by example, saying thanks. I watch this church family come to the table. If John Calvin was in fact cranky, this scene would touch even his heart. At this table, believed Calvin, we are "family . . . children . . . offspring," and a concerned and dutiful Parent nourishes us "throughout the course of our life." Bread and wine are "destined as food for our spiritual life"—bread to invigorate, wine to refresh, strengthen, and gladden.[1] I serve at this table, and I am fed. I am thankful for the best seat in the house, and for a taste and a glimpse of table grace. Great is the mystery of faith.

"For all Thy good gifts, we thank Thee." The Great Thanksgiving is our family grace at this table. It tells our whole story as an expression of gratitude, even when we rebelled in ingratitude. "Send us out to be the body of Christ in the world," we pray. "Send us out in the power of the Spirit to live for others, as Christ lived for us."[2] The Great Thanksgiving is also the great commission. Calvin instructed, "When the supper is finished, there should be an exhortation . . . to love and behavior worthy of Christians."[3] What happens at the table shouldn't stay at the table! Sitting at the table is an occasional spiritual banquet. Walking by the Spirit is daily life. The etiquette of the table yields a sacramental ethic:

> None of the [brothers and sisters] can be injured, despised, rejected, abused, or in any way offended by us, without at the same time, injur-

1. John Calvin, *Institutes of the Christian Religion*, ed. John T. McNeill, trans. Ford Lewis Battles, 2 vols. (Philadelphia: Westminster Press, 1960), 2:1359-61.

2. Book of Common Worship, PCUSA. Variations of the Great Thanksgiving (Louisville, KY: Westminster/John Knox Press, 1993), 72, 132.

3. Calvin, *Institutes*, 2:1422.

ing, despising, and abusing Christ by the wrongs we do. . . . We cannot disagree with our [brothers and sisters] without at the same time disagreeing with Christ. . . . We cannot love Christ without loving him in the [brothers and sisters]. . . . We ought to take the same care of our brothers' and sisters' bodies as we take care of our own; for they are members of our body.[4]

"Spirituality" has always been a word with little resonance for me. First, it is too vague and too varied in meaning, and what it lacks in definition it gains in overuse by church and culture. The preface "spirituality of" is current and rampant; we baptize just about everything from *Avatar* to yoga with the word (check the titles in your local bookstore) in an attempt to imbue transcendent meanings without invoking traditional religious language. If this evidences a desire for depth and purpose, it also relegates spirituality to an expendable dimension of meaning, an add-on, frosting on a cake. Then the thing itself— *Avatar* or yoga or art or baseball or cats or work (I have all of those books)—is not in essence spiritual, but rather superficially and optionally spiritual. Is there a spirituality of everything, a layer that can be applied or removed? Or is what we are seeking an inherent transcendent meaning in all of life?

A personal reservation about spirituality is rooted in deep conviction about the unity we are given in Christ. The gift of salvation—wholeness—as reality and mystery, as experienced and promised, works toward the integration and connection of self, relationships, church, and world. I believe that one of the corrective influences women have brought to theology is the recovery of wholeness as God's intention for creatures and creation. By rejecting dualisms of body and mind, spirit and matter, by bridging dichotomies of contemplative and active, by making permeable the boundaries between domestic and public life, and by refusing to compartmentalize personal and political, the unity of life in Christ is affirmed, and a vision of integrity is restored. I don't want an emphasis on spirituality to have a countereffect, resegregating that wholeness. I don't want a new version of soul-superiority to body realities, and by "body" I mean the physical, organic, organizational body of human community. I've worried that spiritual practices reinforce individualism rather than edifying the whole body of Christ. I'm concerned that the spirit of spirituality is captured by the search for centeredness, by a desire to negotiate the maze-of-life invitation of the labyrinth, and by blessing a retreat from the realities of a broken and fearful world and the pursuit of God's horizons. I'm wary of any use of "spirituality" as a synonym for a calling Paul so emphatically insisted is diverse and yet one: "There is one body and one Spirit, just as you were called to the one hope of your calling,

4. Ibid., 38.

one Lord, one faith, one baptism, one God and Father of all, who is above all and through all and in all" (Eph. 4:4–6).

Spirituality or religion? The current assertion "I'm spiritual but not religious" leaves me puzzled at best, wondering what distinctions the claimant makes between the two terms. This phrase is usually conveyed as dismissive of "organized religion" and defensive about the absence of church affiliation. "Spiritual but not religious" is even the credo of some agnostics and atheists. There is a thoroughly secular spirituality alive and well in our culture. "Believe!" enjoin the door signs and kitchen plaques, bumper stickers, and Christmas kitsch. And don't you think to yourself, "Believe in what?" This "spirituality" is merely an outlook that is cheerful and hopeful, with a dash of the mystical. Too often, its proponents prove worthy of Peter de Vries's immortal verdict: "On the surface he's brilliant, but way deep down he's shallow."[5]

The desire for integrating personal and social centeredness inclines me to religion. I doubt that etymology can rescue "religion" from its pejorative use, but I trust that in this community of readers words do matter. The origin of "religion" persuades a new look: "*Religare*, to bind back < *re-*, back + *ligare*, to bind, bind together . . . *leg-* , to collect."[6] To bind together, to connect, to collect; the same as "ligature" and "ligament." Did Paul know this? We mature in the unity of the Spirit, we fully grow up into Christ, "the whole body, joined and knit together by every ligament with which it is equipped" (Eph. 4:16). So I'm religious and not just spiritual. I believe that we are bound together in our full and common humanity despite all attempts to repudiate that fullness and that commonness. Jesus' ministry was to bind back and bind up and bind together, bringing the marginalized into full communion with him and others, collecting persons to follow a common vision of a compassionate and just God, connecting heart, soul, mind, and strength. The Spirit continues that work of "religion" in the church and in the world, and the Spirit has called me to this ministry.[7]

In the church I serve as pastor, the recurring theme in new member classes is the search for community and the importance of "belonging." For most of the men and women considering membership, "spiritual but not religious" has proven inadequate, and again or for the first time they feel they are being called to a different sort of life—what Dietrich Bonhoeffer referred to as "life together." They sound the notes of "connecting personal faith to community

5. Quoted in Robert McAfee Brown, *Speaking of Christianity: Practical Compassion, Social Justice, and Other Wonders* (Louisville, KY: Westminster John Knox Press, 1997).

6. Victoria Neufeldt and David Bernard Guralnik, *Webster's New World Dictionary of American English*, Third College Edition (New York: Prentice Hall, 1994).

7. This language comes from the Presbyterian Church (U.S.A.)'s "Brief Statement of Faith."

service," "needing others in order to be a Christian," "belonging to a community of questioners," and gratitude "for a place at the table." The testimonials are often emotional; the refrain is "I am home."

As a minister, I preside at the Communion table, but more routinely I reside at conference and committee tables in my congregation, community, and denomination. My job is to set various tables. Life in the Spirit means setting an agenda for love, joy, peace, patience, kindness, generosity, faithfulness, gentleness, and self-control. Sometimes the fruit of our labor produces none of that. If these tables could talk they would tell tales of disagreement, division, strained relationships, sharp words, and awkward silences. They would speak of Presbyterians on two sides of an issue, struggling with Scripture and theology and polity; of persons on the same side of an issue struggling to agree on strategy; of neighbors arguing about preservation versus development; of Christians and Jews uniting on shared tradition and dividing on Middle Eastern politics; of a college board of trustees alienated from faculty and distrusting of leadership. The ministry of the Communion table happens amid the echos from other tables. Life in the Spirit calls me to be the same person and leader at these tables as I am at the Communion table. That Spirit commissions me, in Calvin's words, "to love and behavior worthy of Christians."

Life in the Spirit is living the liturgy of the Communion table. While sitting and working around various other life and ministry tables, life in the Spirit calls for bringing ourselves and our gifts as an offering and putting them on the table. This life prompts us to extend a genuinely gracious invitation, remembering that Jesus collected all sorts of people. When living this life, we lift up our common story with thanksgiving, breaking bread, literally, and experiencing the inherent bond of eating together. In the work of the Spirit and in God's time, there is communion, reunion, unity—even if inchoate and imperfect. When it happens, and it does, it's a religious experience. If those tables of life and ministry could talk, they would also tell of table grace.

If I could illustrate this essay with images that tell stories of table grace, I would do so with a sculpture and three paintings.

One of the foremothers who has nourished me in life, faith, and table grace is Susan B. Anthony. Formed by her Quaker tradition to believe in the equality of all persons, she became an ardent supporter of the abolition of slavery and the enfranchisement of women. She and Frederick Douglass, the former slave and antislavery leader, were close friends over many years. When tensions emerged between the antislavery and the women's suffrage movements, longtime allies were estranged by the language of the Fifteenth Amendment, which was restricted to "race, color, or previous condition of servitude," with women of any color being omitted. Douglass argued that the inclusion of women in the language of the amendment was not as urgent, and to insist on its being included would make passage of the amendment more difficult and perhaps impossible. The two movements split. Although the relationship between Anthony and Douglass was seriously strained by disagreement, it never broke.

Just down the street from the Anthony home in Rochester is a small park featuring a larger-than-life sculpture of Susan B. Anthony and Frederick Douglass. The sculptor, a Laotian refugee named Pepsy Kettavong, lives in the neighborhood. His design very deliberately put the two at a table, having an animated conversation over tea. For this refugee from political and religious repression, their bond of faith and friendship is a model of hope.

Three women depicted in paintings surround me at work and at home. In each place I have the same framed prints by Johannes Vermeer, the seventeenth-century Dutch painter. I first saw *Woman Holding a Balance* at the National Gallery of Art on a visit with my mother over ten years ago. We were both drawn into the woman's serene contemplation as she waits for the balance she is holding in her hand to come to rest. I met *Young Woman with a Water Pitcher* at the Metropolitan Museum of Art, a place that has afforded inspiration and refreshment. The painting is exquisite in color and composition, light and harmony; the woman is standing at a table, with one hand opening a window and intently looking out of it, and the other holding a pitcher that looks like the ewer on our Communion table. She looms large on my living room wall, a focus of meditation and an affirmation of faith. The third image is a recent addition. Last year I saw *The Milkmaid* on her U.S. visit, and she too came to live with me. She also stands at a table, working and looking purposeful. Turned to the light, she pours milk from an earthen vessel. The table is laden with bread, a whole loaf and many smaller pieces. Her eyes are downcast but not angled toward what she is doing with her hands. Is she praying? "For all Thy good gifts . . ."

Life in the Spirit. My job is to set the table.

22

Impractical Christianity

Why Salvation in Jesus Christ Is Better than a Practice

WILLIAM H. WILLIMON

Few things are more humbling for a professor than to have your profound classroom assertions parroted back to you by some undergraduate taking your exam. In his puerile response I hear an echo of my pronouncement, but on undergraduate lips it sounds unbearably stupid. I've come to feel a bit that way upon a recent rereading of *Resident Aliens*.[1] While I still believe just about everything that Stanley Hauerwas and I said there, in the intervening years I've come to have a few regrets.

In *Resident Aliens* we stressed Christianity as inculcation into a communal tradition whereby we are given the skills, habits, and practices that enable us truthfully to know the world in the way of Christ and subversively to resist the toxic pressures to conform to the world's godlessness. We got more specific about how the church does that in our sequel, *Where Resident Aliens Live*,[2] which bore the revealing subtitle *Exercises for Christian Practice*. A constant theme in that second *Aliens* book was the necessity for Christians to develop practices commensurate with the peculiar demands of Christian discipleship in North American culture. In a chapter titled "Practice Discipleship," we even quoted from a *Wall Street Journal* article in order to praise the U.S. Marines for demonstrating that if one desired totally to transform the characters of inner-city, drug-dealing, racist young adults, one could do so only by

---

1. Stanley Hauerwas and William H. Willimon, *Resident Aliens: A Provocative Christian Assessment of Culture and Ministry for People Who Know That Something Is Wrong* (Nashville: Abingdon Press, 1989).
2. Stanley Hauerwas and William H. Willimon, *Where Resident Aliens Live: Exercises for Christian Practice* (Nashville: Abingdon Press, 1996).

teaching them practices that made them better than they would have been if abandoned to the practices of modern American culture.

We cited philosopher Alasdair MacIntyre's definition of a "practice":

> Any coherent and complex form of socially established cooperative human activity through which goods internal to that form of activity are realized in the course of trying to achieve those standards of excellence which are appropriate to, and partially definitive of, that form of activity, with the results that human powers to achieve excellence, and human conceptions of the ends and goods involved, are systematically extended.[3]

Note anything missing in MacIntyre's thick definition of "practice"? *God.*

While Hauerwas and I were not the originators of the notion that Christianity is best defined not as a set of beliefs or a type of experience but as a "socially established cooperative human activity," judging from the rapid widespread usage of the parlance of "practice," we certainly gave a strong shove to the idea that there is nothing wrong with the church that can't be cured by a recovery of the church as a place of practice. Thus bearing some responsibility for the now popular conviction that Christianity is a practice and that Christians are best described as people who have adopted certain practices that make them and keep them Christian, I feel I should share why I now am having grave doubts about describing Christian spirituality as a "practice."

That "practice" has become a primary way of speaking about not only Christianity but any religion in general is well documented by the large number of books that pay homage to this construal of the faith. That it is acceptable to speak of Christianity as a "practice" in company that would not tolerate a conversation about "Jesus Christ as Lord" should tip us off to the theological hazards of thus speaking of Christianity.

Resident Aliens did not introduce the idea that Christianity is a countercultural way of life. Søren Kierkegaard wrote *Practice in Christianity* (also titled *Training in Christianity*) in 1850, calling it his "most perfect and truest book." Adopting an antirationalist position similar to Kant's, Kierkegaard attacked the idea, popular in his day in Protestantism, that one becomes a Christian by simply accepting intellectually a supposedly rational set of proofs for the validity of Christianity. Kierkegaard asserted that the challenge of Christ was not to understand him or to attempt to devise some (Hegelian) system out of him, but rather to obey Christ, to follow him, to put one's trust into practice. Kierkegaard based his arguments on the peculiar nature of Christ himself and

---

3. Alasdair MacIntyre, *After Virtue* (South Bend, IN: University of Notre Dame Press, 1984), 187.

on the way that Christ taught—through parables rather than abstract ideas, through his own miraculous actions rather than metaphysical speculation. As Kierkegaard says, Christ calls people not to admiration but to discipleship.

While Kierkegaard's thought has something in it that presages our current infatuation with Christianity as a practice, the striking thing is that his practical Christianity is based upon the strangeness, the "infinite qualitative distinction" between God and humanity that is seen in Jesus Christ. Much contemporary talk about practice appears to be based on certain vague anthropological (rather than strictly theological) assertions about the way human beings behave; our lives are said to go better when we inculcate certain allegedly salubrious habits like Sabbath keeping, prayer, meditation, hospitality, balance, and community. Kierkegaard, on the other hand, is fairly clear in *Practice in Christianity* that we ought to live in a certain way because of the odd God we've got in Jesus Christ. Discipleship has few intellectual allies. It is counter to the way human beings are wired. Jesus is against our natural inclination. Therefore practices, as I read Kierkegaard, are those ways that one must live if one is convinced that Jesus Christ is the full revelation of God.

Against Kierkegaard, now we have an entire genre of literature that has arisen to extol the virtues of Christian practices and that, in some cases, is too closely tied to anthropological perspectives. My worry is that this may set the stage for "practices" that do not finally require the God who makes *Christian* practice interesting in the first place. Recently a pastor of my acquaintance applied for a grant at a church-related foundation and was told by another friend who had received a grant, "Whatever you propose to them, you need to be sure that the word 'practice' is in the application. That's the only way you'll get the money."

One of the things that first appealed to me about the discovery of Christianity as a practice was that the practices of any faith are so wonderfully particular, specific, and odd. They tend to be incomprehensible without reference to the specific experience of God that has occurred in that faith. This fact seemed to me a wonderful corrective for the now discredited liberal construal of "religion" as a set of rather vague ideas ("beliefs") about the divine.

I recall the Hindu sophomore who made an appointment to complain to me (as the Christian chaplain of the university) about how she felt that her faith had been garbled and misrepresented by a professor in a world religions course at Duke. She said that his presentation of Hinduism spoke of her faith as a set of ideas, desiccated and dull. "Everybody knows that Hinduism is mainly about the way we eat," she countered. "It's things that you smell, stuff that you do that anybody who is not a Hindu would find dumb but we think is the key to everything."

Yet nineteenth-century German liberalism is a hard habit to break. A warning sign of the possible error of construing Christianity primarily as a practice is the propensity of these books to describe the Christian faith in general. Christianity, generally conceived, shares much with other faiths, generally conceived. I'm discovering that generic conceptions of Christianity, or any other religion for that matter, as a practice are as intellectually misleading as conceiving of Christianity as a system of general beliefs. When Christianity is conceived as a practice, a set of paths toward God that some people have found helpful but that lead in much the same direction as every other path, then Christianity has been misconstrued.

For instance, a number of Christianity-as-practice books extol the virtues of the recovery of "Sabbath" as a salubrious practice. Yet I search in vain in these descriptions for a theological grounding of a peculiar activity like keeping Sabbath; nor is there any recognition of the ways in which Jesus Christ (well documented Sabbath-breaker) was presented by the Gospels as inimical to the Fourth Commandment. In *The Truth about God: The Ten Commandments and the Christian Life*,[4] Hauerwas and I commended the keeping of Sabbath as a Christian discipline, but only in the light of Christ. We were trying to indicate the tension within the notion of Sabbath after the advent of Jesus. When Sabbath is commended apart from the story of the salvation and sustenance of Israel as God's people—as a means of helping us achieve balance in life, of helping us stay centered, as a mode of resistance against the clutches of consumerism—then Israel's Sabbath becomes degraded and incomprehensible.

Nowhere is Sabbath asserted in the faith of Israel as a practice that is good for us or as something that would be good for everybody, no matter which god you worship. Sabbath is what Yahweh commands Israel to do. Sabbath keeping is not something akin, spiritually speaking, to a high-fiber diet. Sabbath is what we are compelled to do on the basis of our attempt to love the curious God who has loved us.

Nowhere do I find in any of the current commendation of "keeping Sabbath" any awareness of the great significance that, just a short time after Jesus' death and resurrection—according to Luke, Paul, John, and Ignatius—a mostly Jewish group of believers, living close by the temple, had shifted the major focus of their worship from the last day of the week to the first. That which had kept Jews as Jews—the Sabbath—was being radically reworked, eventually even abandoned. Only something extraordinary could have made them let go of a major defining practice and assume a new one.

For some time now, Hauerwas has engaged in a polemic against "practices

---

4. Stanley Hauerwas and William H. Willimon, *The Truth about God: The Ten Commandments and the Christian Life* (Nashville: Abingdon Press, 1999).

based on atheism."[5] I worry that our infatuation with practice could be but the latest phase of our a-theism. Since God is now mute and absent, follow this set of habits and you will feel better about our situation post–*Deus absconditus* (the hidden God). The most important test of any practice is theological—not "Is this helpful?" but rather "Is this practice commensurate to the God who has met us in Jesus Christ?"

For instance, Karen Armstrong, who says that she "had to give up hope for salvation coming out of myself"[6] before she could put up with the church, says in her book *The Case for God*, that "religion is a practical discipline that teaches us to discover new capacities of mind and heart."[7] Apparently, the God that Armstrong is making the case for is the innocuous God within, the "god" that most North Americans already believe in. Once again, by defining "religion" as "a practical discipline," that is, a set of practices, advocates like Armstrong seem to feel that they can sidestep the tough theological decision required when one is confronted with the question "Is this god whom you are following actually God or not?"

I fear that a practice is what we sometimes do when our attention has been displaced from the living God. This leads to a domestication of Christianity, in which Christianity quietly morphs into a species of unbelief, and revelation is taken into our own hands. All Christian practices are modes of worship. The most relevant commandment to a proper placement of the notion of practice is not the Fourth Commandment but rather the First. The question to ask of any allegedly Christian practice is "Who is the God who is being served through this practice?" Pelagianism is a tough thing to shake. I ought to know. I'm a Methodist. The Arminian idea that we must do something for God before God will do anything for us, the concept that my relationship with God is sustained by my actions or feelings or inclinations, the notion that "religion" is something I do rather than God's effect upon me, all appear to be lurking behind many contemporary discussions of practice.[8]

---

5. Hauerwas and Willimon, *Where Resident Aliens Live*, 90.

6. Karen Armstrong, interview on *Speaking of Faith*, American Public Media, September 21, 2009. She now calls her religious posture (I think quite appropriately) "freelance monotheism."

7. Karen Armstrong, *The Case for God* (New York: Knopf, 2009), xiii. Armstrong makes a valid observation that "Judaism is essentially about doing." But then she says that Christianity is too much about "believing." While there are Jews who might differ with her generalization, I find this helpful in distinguishing Christianity as (like Judaism) much "about doing" but also "about believing" what has been revealed to us as the truth about what's really going on in the world, where the world is headed, and who is in charge. Whereas Armstrong is forever arguing that religious practices are "helpful," Christians believe that our beliefs are truthful, whether those beliefs turn out to be helpful or not.

8. Barth said that "religion is the attempted replacement of the divine work by a human manufacture." Karl Barth, *Church Dogmatics*, I/2, *The Doctrine of the Word of God*, ed G. W. Bromiley and T. F. Torrance, trans. G. W. Bromiley et al. (Edinburgh: T. & T. Clark, 1960), 302.

John Wesley could be justly regarded as a father of the Christian practice movement. Deeply influenced by William Law's *A Serious Call to a Devout and Holy Life*, Wesley pioneered and perfected a number of spiritual disciplines—such as small accountability groups, lay Bible studies, and methods whereby Christians could "grow in grace"—that have wonderful resonance today. Yet toward the end of his life, after his movement of spiritual discipline had spread throughout the English-speaking world, Wesley wrote ominously:

> I am not afraid that the people called Methodists should ever cease to exist either in Europe or America. But I am afraid lest they should only exist as a dead sect, having the form of religion without the power. And this undoubtedly will be the case unless they hold fast both the doctrine, spirit, and discipline with which they first set out.[9]

Typically, Wesley mentions "doctrine" before he says "discipline."[10] He worries about the "form of religion without the power."[11] I think he is pointing here toward that which bothers me about current talk of Christianity as a practice.

Worship's object determines the nature of worship. Some of the "spiritual practices" being urged upon us today seem effete, too tame for a people who are evoked by the wild, untamable Word. Speaking as a preacher, the spiritual practices needed by faithful Christian preachers tend to be those that give us the guts to be in conversation with and to speak up for a true and living God who loves to meet people through the Word. The great P. T. Forsyth emphasized that preachers require a peculiar kind of prayer life. Prayer for the preacher, he said, "is only serious searching prayer, not prayer as sweet

9. John Wesley, "Thoughts upon Methodism," in *The Works of John Wesley*, vol. 9, *The Methodist Societies: History, Nature, and Design*, ed. Rupert E. Davies (Nashville: Abingdon Press, 1989), 527.

10. Particularly troubling is the implication in some of the presentations of Christian practice that the construal of Christianity as a practice gives us a way around our contemporary theological impasse. In response to a debate in the *Christian Century* concerning some theological distinction within Christianity, Patricia A. Conley cites Marcus Borg's *The Heart of Christianity: Rediscovering a Life of Faith* as a way of framing the discussion in such a way that beliefs, after all, don't really matter: "Clearly predominant for Borg is the understanding of Christianity as a tradition of practice not predicated on right belief. Throughout the book he presents Christianity as a path, a way of life." "Books to Start With," *Christian Century*, May 5, 2009, 29.

11. Wesley insisted that spiritual disciplines or practices do not work from their inherent power but only as through them God's grace is conveyed (see Sermon 16, "The Means of Grace," in *The Works of John Wesley*, vol. 1, *Sermons I (1-33)*, ed. Albert C. Outler (Nashville: Abingdon Press, 1984), 396). While Wesley was equally critical of those who wanted the "end" (renewal by the Spirit) without the "means" (God's appointed means of grace; see "Letter to Count Zinzendorf and the Church at Herrnhut (5–8 Aug. 1740)," in *The Works of John Wesley*, vol. 26, *Letters II, 1740-1755*, ed. Frank Baker (London: Clarendon Press, 1982), 27; and Sermon 16), Wesley always managed to speak of his disciplines as evidence of the miraculous grace of God in the lives of ordinary people. In our own time, Wesley's practices are not as interesting as Wesley's God.

and seemly devotion at the day's dawn or close, but prayer as an ingredient of the day's work, pastoral and theological prayer, priest's prayer."[12] I recall the preacher who, in a discussion of "necessary homiletical disciplines," said that for him the important step in sermon preparation was a two-mile jog at dawn on Sunday. Why? "God uses that time to get me pumped up enough to have the guts to stand up and preach at eleven o'clock to people who mostly don't want to hear what I feel compelled to say."

If Sabbath is mainly about taking time to be spiritual, then Islam, as well as any faith I know, has marvelous spiritual disciplines for taking over time in the name of God. The faithful follower prays to God throughout the day—stops everything and prays. It must be a marvelous way of taking time for God. Similar disciplines are practiced in monastic spirituality as the Psalms are prayed through in the course of a day.

Mainstream Christianity has generally taken a different view. We do not, perhaps we cannot, take time for God. God in Christ takes time *for us* and interrupts, throughout the day, if we have the eyes of faith to see it. God takes time *from us*. God does not wait, thank God, for us to fine-tune the spiritual disciplines to the point where we are praying all day long. Rather, God grants us the freedom to be about our vocations in the world, doing what we have to do in this life. Then while we journey (see Acts 9, the call of Saul), God suddenly shows up, unexpectedly becomes an event in our time, takes our time, and disrupts our lives for God. While we are busy planning a wedding, God interrupts, impregnates, and enlists a young woman in a revolution (Luke 2). Eventually, God promises really to take all time from us—that is, all of us shall die and be subsumed into God-determined time, like it or not. Any hint of eschatological concern is only one of the basic Christian affirmations that tend to be absent from discussions of Christianity as a practice.[13]

We have learned from bitter experience that so many of our allegedly helpful means of climbing up to God are easily perverted into ways of defending ourselves against God.[14] We're always in danger of making the Schleiermacherian move that reduces Christianity to mainly a matter of our experience. The true God can never be known through our practices but comes to us only as a gift of God, only as revelation. This is how I can say (as a Wesleyan) that Christian practices are not primarily what we do. Rather, our practice of the faith is something that God does for us, in us, often despite us. Today's talk

12. P. T. Forsyth, *The Soul of Prayer* (Grand Rapids: Wm. B. Eerdmans, 1916), 91, found at http://www.ccel.org/f/forsyth/prayer/soul_of_prayer.htm.

13. For more of this sort of polemic, see William H. Willimon, *Undone by Easter: Keeping Preaching Fresh* (Nashville: Abingdon Press, 2009).

14. Thus, Karl Barth could "humbly" ask Cardinal Joseph Ratzinger (after a brilliant lecture in Tübingen) whether his "magnificent church" and its glorious practices were "not a clever escape from the Holy Spirit." Eberhard Busch, *Barth* (Nashville: Abingdon Press, 2008), 20.

about "spiritual practices" could be just one more in our long line of attempts to take time on our terms. Thank God that we don't have to cultivate a tedious set of practices in order to live in God's time. God takes time.

I write as a Christian in Alabama. We have the distinction of being the state with the second-highest percentage of church attendance in the country (only Mississippi outdoes us). We therefore have excelled beyond all of the rest of you (except for Christians in Mississippi) in the most basic Christian practice of all—attending Sunday worship.

It grieves me to admit this, but it is true: if following Christian practices could save us, Alabama would look a great deal more redeemed.

I write this deep in Eastertide, fifty days of shock when we attempt to regroup and recover some semblance of balance after being assailed by the risen Christ. The Christian faith is that set of practices appropriate to a group of people who have been caught off guard, blindsided by a living God. Otherwise, Christian spirituality is boring.

23

Sanctification and Proclamation

Walking with God

BRAD R. BRAXTON

THE CONNECTION BETWEEN "SACRED TALKING" AND "SANCTIFIED WALKING"

Maria Stewart, a nineteenth-century abolitionist, offered a stirring petition for moral purification. With poetic imagery alluding to the call of the prophet Isaiah, she invoked God's sanctifying presence upon her life, her church, and her preacher:

> O thou King eternal, immortal, invisible, and only wise God, before whom angels bow and seraphs veil their faces, crying holy, holy, holy, is the Lord God Almighty. True and righteous are thy ways, thou King of Saints. Help me, thy poor unworthy creature, humbly to prostrate myself before thee, and implore that mercy which my sins have justly forfeited. O God, I know that I am not worthy of a place at thy footstool; but to whom shall I go but unto thee? Thou alone hast the words of eternal life. . . .
>
> Bless the church to which I belong, and grant that when thou makest up thy jewels, not one soul shall be found missing. Bless him in whom thou hast set over us as a watchman in Zion. Let not his soul be discouraged. May he not fail to declare the whole counsel of God.[1]

Stewart recognized that sanctification was indispensable for authentic discipleship and an effective ministry of proclamation. Pulpit power was linked

---

1. Maria W. Stewart, "A Prayer for Purification (1835)," in *Conversations with God: Two Centuries of Prayers by African Americans*, ed. James Melvin Washington (New York: HarperCollins, 1994), 30.

to the quest for holiness for many of our foremothers and forefathers in the faith. Yet in contemporary Christianity, I wonder if we have neglected the wisdom of the ancestors and need to reclaim some timeless truths.

One timeless truth is that the quest to embody the holy attributes of a holy God provides power for the holy act of preaching a holy word, so that we become holy people prepared for holy living, now and later, in that holy city that some call the "New Jerusalem." In this essay, I pursue a straightforward theme: the sanctification of the messenger is a crucial aspect of the proclamation of the message. Homiletics and holiness are inextricably linked, and by exploring the link in a robust manner, preachers avail themselves of valuable resources for pulpit excellence. While my reflections are aimed primarily at preachers, persons from many different walks of life can benefit from this conversation about the spiritual life and walking with God.

Homiletics is the art of sermon creation, proclamation, and evaluation. The term "homiletics" comes from the Greek verb *homileō*, which means "to talk." Thus, homiletics deals with "sacred talking." I contend that "sacred talking" must always be connected to "sanctified walking." When sacred talking divorces itself from sanctified walking, preachers open themselves up to homiletic flunking and moral failing.

The brief story of Enoch in Genesis accentuates the centrality of sanctified walking: "Enoch walked with God after the birth of Methuselah three hundred years, and had other sons and daughters. Thus all the days of Enoch were three hundred sixty-five years. Enoch walked with God; then he was no more, because God took him" (Gen. 5:22–24). Enoch is noteworthy not because of the *quantity* of his years, but rather for the *quality* of his life. Enoch receives a stellar compliment. The writer says twice that Enoch "walked with God." The verb "to walk" (*halak* in Hebrew) connotes a way of life or a person's conduct in the world. To say that Enoch "walked with God" is to say that he conducted his life in ways that pleased God. Enoch had an intimate connection with God.

Can the same be said of many preachers? A master of divinity degree, required for ordained ministry in many Christian traditions, does not necessarily ensure a sanctified life. Noel Schoonmaker, a ministerial colleague, says it well: "It is possible to have a master of divinity without being in relationship with *the* Master of Divinity."

Public victories in the pulpit usually have some grounding in the preacher's quest to embody God's amazing work of sanctification. In the pulpit, God uses us in spite of us. However, by pursuing a vibrant spiritual life, we ensure that God has the sharpest tools with which to work. Charles Spurgeon, the

nineteenth-century British prince of the pulpit, emphasized the importance
of giving God sharp tools:

> It will be in vain for me to stock my library, or organize societies,
> or project schemes, if I neglect the culture of myself; for books, and
> agencies, and systems, are only remotely the instruments of my holy
> calling; my own spirit, soul, and body, are my nearest machinery for
> sacred service; my spiritual faculties, and my inner life, are my battle
> axe and weapons of war.[2]

Spurgeon's phrase "the culture of myself" deserves further exploration.
Effective preachers pay as much attention to their interior culture as their
exterior culture. In recent years, there have been numerous preachers' conferences highlighting the need for "prophetic preaching." Prophetic preaching involves intense critique of the social order. However, some preachers
fail to examine their interior culture, much less to critique it, with the same
probing intensity.

A holistic prophetic ministry involves investigation of the exterior culture
in which a preacher lives and a cultivation of the interior culture within a
preacher's soul. Too often, prophetic preachers talk about the devil in the
exterior culture while giving consent for the devil to preside at the altar in
their souls. As preachers and pastors, we tend altars in our public sanctuaries. The question is: who is tending the private altar in our souls? A failure
to set proper boundaries in the interior world can quickly contribute to a
transgression of boundaries in the exterior world. Consequently, conversations concerning prophetic preaching are incomplete apart from a prophetic
spirituality. Prophetic spirituality keeps in creative tension the external culture in the street and the internal culture in the soul.

In spite of our failures, God still uses us. If that's not grace, I don't know
what is. God's willingness to use us in spite of us calls to mind a comment from
William A. Jones Jr., the late, legendary pastor of Bethany Baptist Church in
Brooklyn, New York. He once suggested that some ministers have such marvelous preaching gifts that you hope they will never leave a pulpit once they
enter one. And some of these same ministers have such messy lives that you
hate to think they will ever enter a pulpit when they are outside of one.

In these difficult times, the world desperately needs a newfound commitment to integrity among preachers, an earnest attempt to close the gap
between our marvelous gifts and our messy lives. What would happen to
our preaching if we spent as much time cultivating our spirituality as we did

---

2. C. H. Spurgeon, "The Minister's Self-Watch," in *Lectures to My Students* (Grand Rapids:
Zondervan, 1955), 7–8.

preparing to preach? God would be pleased, the church would be stronger, and the world would be more loving.

COMING TO TERMS WITH SPIRITUALITY, HOLINESS, AND SANCTIFICATION

Spirituality

The Latin word *spiritus* means "breath" or "wind," and by extension "life force."[3] *Spiritus* is the life force existing in individuals and communities. The creation story in Genesis 1 emphasizes the life force that hovers over the unruly waters, transforming chaos into creation. In Genesis 1, the Hebrew word for divine breath is *ruach*, and the Latin word is *spiritus*. If *spiritus* is the divine breath animating creation and all its creatures, then *spirituality* is an acknowledgment that breath comes from God and that breath will lead us back to God.

In other words, spirituality entails personal and communal stewardship over the breath—the life force—that God has breathed into us. To preachers, matters of breath should be of utmost concern, especially since preaching is heavily dependent on breath. No matter how melodic your voice or poetic your prose, preaching is impossible without breath. Spirituality involves giving an account to God and others concerning the use of our breath, our life force, both inside and outside the pulpit.

Ethicist Emilie Townes presents a definition of spirituality worthy of embrace:

> Womanist spirituality is not grounded in the notion that spirituality is a force, a practice separate from who we are moment by moment. It is the deep kneading of humanity and divinity into one breath, one hope, one vision. . . . It is a style of witness that seeks to cross the yawning chasm of hatreds and prejudices and oppressions into a deeper and richer love of God as we experience Jesus in our lives. This love extends to self and others. . . . This understanding of spirituality seeks to grow into wholeness of spirit and body, mind and heart—into holiness in God.[4]

Spirituality involves an assortment of attitudes and actions—some as regular and unnoticeable as breathing—that propel us toward God's holiness.

3. I am indebted to my colleague Samuel Weber, OSB, for this insight.
4. Emilie M. Townes, *In a Blaze of Glory: Womanist Spirituality as Social Witness* (Nashville: Abingdon Press, 1995), 11.

Holiness

When considering spirituality, Emilie Townes ultimately locates holiness in God. This is instructive because all understandings of holiness will miss the mark until we realize that holiness is primarily not something we do; it is who God is. Holiness, first and foremost, is an attribute of God, not a human action.

One task of prophetic ministry is reasserting the centrality of God's holiness in our conceptions of prophetic preaching. For evidence, I summon the prophet Isaiah to the witness stand. In his unforgettable call story, Isaiah receives a glimpse of God's glory in the heavenly temple, and this prophet is confronted with the chief characteristic of God—holiness: "In the year that King Uzziah died, I saw the Lord sitting on a throne, high and lofty; and the hem of his robe filled the temple. Seraphs were in attendance above him. . . . And one called to another and said: 'Holy, holy, holy is the LORD of hosts; the whole earth is full of his glory'" (Isa. 6:1–3).

A redemptive rendezvous with a holy God was the precursor to Isaiah's prophetic ministry. God is so holy that seraphs had to hit the repeat button on their celestial soundtrack: "Holy, holy, holy." Their repetition was a rhetorical attempt to plumb the unsearchable sanctity of God.

Holiness is a significant attribute of God's character. The biblical scholar Walter Brueggemann observes, "The term *holiness* . . . refers to the radical otherness of Yahweh, who may not be easily approached, who may not be confused with anyone or anything else, and who lives alone in a prohibitive zone where Israel can enter only guardedly, intentionally, and at great risk."[5] Thus, the term "holiness" expresses the unique nature of God. The difference between God and humans is more than quantitative. God is not simply a supersized version of us. To speak of God as holy is to affirm that there is an infinite qualitative difference (to recall Søren Kierkegaard's observation) in God's being. Holiness is an attestation of God's difference from us.

However, theologian Kelly Brown Douglas reminds us that alongside the radical otherness of God there exist other radical impulses: divine love and passion, which create an "insatiable desire to foster life" and an "unquenchable thirst for that which is not yet."[6] Douglas enables us to perceive more clearly the marvelous mystery of God's holiness. Simultaneously, holiness involves God's *infinite difference* from us and God's *insatiable desire* for us. God

5. Walter Brueggemann, *Theology of the Old Testament: Testimony, Dispute, Advocacy* (Minneapolis: Fortress Press, 1997), 288.

6. Kelly Brown Douglas, *Sexuality and the Black Church: A Womanist Perspective* (Maryknoll, NY: Orbis Books, 1999), 120.

is so dramatically unlike us, and yet God so desperately wants to be with us. Even though God is radically other, there is a quality in God's character that compels God to be in relationship with us. Holiness encapsulates divine difference and divine desire.

God's *difference* sets the standard for the relationship, reminding us that God is God and beside God there is no other god. God's *desire* invites us into relationship with God, reminding us that God passionately seeks to bestow on us love and life. Thus, holiness is God's insatiable desire to transform our relationship with God and all other relationships in our lives. A radically other God seeks to initiate with us radically transformed relationships so that all our relationships lead to life.

Holiness is not an outdated puritanical concept. Holiness is the ultimate social justice category. Holiness encompasses God's relationship with us. Yet God does not allow holiness to remain solely on the vertical register. Holiness becomes horizontal when God says to Israel, and to us by extension, "Sanctify yourselves therefore, and be holy, for I am holy" (Lev. 11:44). At the horizontal level, holiness is our attempt, made possible by God's Spirit, to seek right relationships with others because God has graciously decided to seek right relationship with us.

Since God is holy and desires transformed relationships, we should be holy and seek transformed relationships. Holiness is not simply a priestly concept; it is also a prophetic concept. Anyone who would dare to preach prophetically must come to grips with God's command for us to be holy.

Sanctification

Ethicist Barbara Holmes recasts sanctification in a compelling fashion: "The holiness that Jesus describes has less to do with pious character traits and more to do with the hosting of God's abiding presence. It is not effort but invitation that opens the human spirit to the possibility that God may sojourn with us."[7] If God chooses to abide with us, even for a little while, the anointed aroma of God—the same aroma that overflowed in the temple with Isaiah—surrounds us. This aroma is so thick and pervasive that even on some of our worst days it covers us, and we appear to the world as much better people than we are.

Sanctification is not the onerous effort to avoid scarlet-letter sins. Sanctification is the ongoing invitation to host God's presence—a presence that radically transforms all our relationships, if we would only submit to it and let it have its way. Sanctification is ultimately not asceticism, denying ourselves

7. Barbara A. Holmes, *Joy Unspeakable: Contemplative Practices of the Black Church* (Minneapolis: Fortress Press, 2004), 26.

to death; nor is it athleticism, working ourselves to death. Sanctification is acceptance, allowing God's Spirit to love us into new life, abundant life, and finally everlasting life!

PRACTICE, PRACTICE, PRACTICE: RESTING, EMBRACING, MEDITATING

Some skeptics might ask, "What does all this have to do with preaching?" My response is, "Everything." More ministers need to prioritize the Holy Spirit and sanctification in their overall discipleship and in their preparation and delivery of sermons.[8] In a recent essay on preaching that I coauthored with Martha Simmons, we contend that "the Holy Spirit must constantly remind each proclaimer of the gospel . . . that to preach a *life-changing* word requires a preacher with a *changed life*."[9] Thus, I now explore three practices than can help preachers (and many other people too) change their lives and become better conduits for God's life-changing power.

Resting

Walking with God involves resting. Exodus 20:8 clearly commands us to remember the Sabbath day and keep it holy. Yet instead of following that biblical commandment, too many preachers read the noncanonical books of "First and Second Hesitations" as it relates to Sabbath keeping.

In his book *Rest in the Storm: Self-Care Strategies for Clergy and Other Caregivers*, ethicist Kirk Byron Jones chronicles why preachers hesitate and eventually fail to keep Sabbath. First, some preachers succumb to the myth of indispensability. We feel that the ministry or the church service will not run effectively unless we are there all the time. The myth of indispensability fosters a "messianic complex," the idolatrous belief that we are omnipotent and omnipresent and must do what everyone asks and make every appointment.

The need to be needed can be dangerous and addictive, and it leads us to believe the myth of indispensability. The myth often sounds like this among some pastors: "I can't take a vacation because if I go away for a couple of

---

8. For reflections on the Holy Spirit's role in preaching, consult, for example, James A. Forbes Jr., *The Holy Spirit and Preaching* (Nashville: Abingdon Press, 1989); Brad R. Braxton, *Preaching Paul* (Nashville: Abingdon Press, 2004), 69–96; and Luke A. Powery, *Spirit Speech: Lament and Celebration in Preaching* (Nashville: Abingdon Press, 2009).

9. Martha Simmons and Brad R. Braxton, "What Happened to Sacred Eloquence? Celebrating the Ministry of Gardner C. Taylor," in *Our Sufficiency Is of God: Essays on Preaching in Honor of Gardner C. Taylor*, ed. Timothy George, James Earl Massey, and Robert Smith Jr. (Macon, GA: Mercer University Press, 2010), 283.

weeks, I may not be the pastor when I get back." Let's be honest—if you won't be the pastor after two weeks of vacation, then you really aren't the pastor now.

Second, some preachers confuse activity for productivity. We live in a world of constant motion. The culture coaxes us into doing many things, and we rarely pause to ask if the activity is worth doing in the first place. Catholic contemplative Thomas Merton challenges our holy hyperactivity:

> There is a pervasive form of contemporary violence . . . [and that is] activism and overwork. . . . To allow oneself to be carried away by a multitude of conflicting concerns, to surrender to too many demands, to commit oneself to too many projects, to want to help everyone in everything, is to succumb to violence.[10]

Self-neglect is a form of violence. Irrespective of the size of our church memberships and annual budgets, if we are not able to cultivate other congregational leaders such that we can take off twenty-four or forty-eight hours each week and rest from our labors, we have been professionally negligent as it relates to equipping the saints (Eph. 4:11–13).

As Rabbi Abraham Heschel suggested, we should keep Sabbath as a continual reminder that God created the world and that God can handle the world for twenty-four hours (or maybe even forty-eight hours) without our help.[11] Furthermore, my wife Lazetta insists that I should keep Sabbath since there has been no expansion in the Trinity. God is God, and God can handle things while we rest.

Embracing

Walking with God involves embracing our shadow side. For this wisdom, I am indebted to Gardner C. Taylor, the venerable dean of American preachers and pastor emeritus of the Concord Baptist Church of Christ in Brooklyn, New York. In 2007, I sat for nearly two hours in his living room gleaning homiletic wisdom from him and learning great lessons about life. Toward the end of the conversation, he said that preachers, and all of us, are like a coin being held up to the light. One side of the coin is in the light, and the other side is in the shadows. It is important, he said, to recognize the shadow side as well.

10. Quoted in Kirk Byron Jones, *Rest in the Storm: Self-Care Strategies for Clergy and Other Caregivers* (Valley Forge, PA: Judson Press, 2001), 12.
11. Abraham Joshua Heschel, *The Sabbath: Its Meaning for Modern Man* (New York: Noonday Press, 1951), 13.

We are genuinely on the path to sanctification and walking with God when we recognize and embrace our shadow side. On the underside of the coin of our character are impulses, tendencies, and memories that are not in the best interests of anyone, including our families, our congregations, and ourselves, and certainly are not in the best interests of the commonwealth of God. Yet to deny the shadow side is to eventually set up circumstances where the shadows can be overcome by dense darkness.

I am no physicist, but I believe that shadows only exist where light is present. So embracing our shadow side means acknowledging those disturbing aspects of our character and keeping them in some modicum of light. As long as the underside of our character is somewhat in the light, the possibility for further conversion exists. When we fail to embrace our shadow side and turn the underside of our character away from the light, our demonic impulses will devour us in the deep darkness.

Embracing the shadow side requires a willingness to examine the depths of our character. It is serious work, not for the fainthearted. Poet Annie Dillard underscores the diligence required:

> In the deeps [of our personality] are the violence and terror of which psychology has warned us. But if you ride these monsters deeper down . . . you find what our sciences cannot locate or name, the substrate, the ocean or matrix of ether which buoys the rest, which gives goodness its power for good, and evil its power for evil, the unified field: our complex and inexplicable caring for each other, and for our life together here.[12]

Dillard is right. In order to care for ourselves and others, we must embrace our shadow side and travel into the depths of those parts of us that disturb us. By communing with them, we will prevent those parts of us from destroying us.

Meditating

Walking with God involves meditating. Meditation is a practice by which we embody the words of Psalm 46:10: "Be still and know that I am God!" There is a connection between stillness and the proper acknowledgment of God. As long as we are constantly moving, we can fool ourselves into believing that our activity is ultimately what matters. But stillness, the distant cousin of death, reminds us that some cemetery will eventually bring all our movement to a halt.

Stillness moves us to consider our mortality and God's eternity. In stillness, we realize afresh that we are simply walking dust. Theologian Howard

12. Quoted in Parker J. Palmer, *Leading from Within: Reflections on Spirituality and Leadership* (The Servant Leadership School: Washington, D.C., 1990), 9.

Thurman creatively described the process of meditating: "How good it is to center down! To sit quietly and see one's self pass by!"[13] When was the last time you were still enough to watch yourself go by? And when you saw yourself, did you like what you saw? To meditate is to gather all our emotional and intellectual faculties to a point of "holy focus."[14] When there is holy focus, our "third eye" will be blessed with homiletic sight, moral insight, and prophetic foresight.

So meditate. Take a walk and meditate. Pray and meditate. Sit by a body of water and meditate. Shut off your cell phone and meditate. Stop texting and e-mailing and meditate. Let some of those deacons, trustees, and elders handle their own meetings, and go meditate. Recommend someone else to do some of those speaking engagements you are offered and go meditate!

RESTING, EMBRACING, MEDITATING—SPIRITUAL REM

REM, which in medical terminology stands for "rapid eye movement," is the creative, restoring form of sleep. Scientists believe that REM sleep is important for declarative memory, which is the memory that stores facts. REM sleep is also important for memory consolidation. By memory consolidation, scientists mean the removal of "certain undesirable modes of interaction in networks of cells in the cerebral cortex," a process called "unlearning." Consequently, during REM sleep "those memories which are relevant . . . are further strengthened, whilst weaker, transient, 'noise' memory traces disintegrate."[15] If our REM sleep is disturbed, our creative capacity is diminished.

Preachers without "spiritual REM" (resting, embracing, meditating) are not really walking with God; we are sleepwalking on the job because our creativity has been dulled. When we are deficient of spiritual REM, our words come out slow and stagnant. We get a great idea but can't turn it into a great sermon. We find an amazing sermon illustration, but we can't make it fit. We want to be more prophetic but end up throwing up our hands and feeling overwhelmed.

But when we get enough spiritual REM, the eyes of our souls are wide open. Our senses are heightened. Our creativity crescendoes, and people know. When we are in the grocery store, people know. When we are at the airport, people know. When we are at the barbershop or the beauty salon,

13. Howard Thurman, *Meditations of the Heart* (Richmond, IN: Friends United Press, 1953), 28.
14. Ibid., 31.
15. "Rapid Eye Movement Sleep," Wikipedia, http://en.wikipedia.org/wiki/Rapid_eye_movement_sleep, accessed June 19, 2010.

people know. When we are on the phone, people know. When we are in the pulpit, people know. What do they know? They know that they are in the presence of a preacher who has been in the presence of "the Presence."

To walk with God ultimately is to be in the presence of the Presence. When we as preachers walk with God, people will walk by us and say, "The presence of the Lord is here, the presence of the Lord is here, I feel it in the atmosphere, the presence of the Lord is here!"[16]

16. These lyrics are from Byron Cage's popular 2003 gospel song "The Presence of the Lord Is Here."

24

Spiritual Ill-Discipline

MICHAEL L. LINDVALL

A SPIRITUAL PREAMBLE

Before I explain the implications of my title, I feel I must offer a digression on the vocabulary used to speak about Christian faith when it is seriously and intentionally practiced. The adjective "spiritual" and its noun partner, "spirituality," are problematic. That being said, I chose the former for the title of this essay, and were I the editor of this book I probably would have chosen the very title on its cover. Let me explain the dilemma.

A number of adjective-noun word pairs have been used in Christian discourse over the years to talk about the serious and intentional life of faith. Common examples include *holy-holiness, righteous-righteousness, pious-piety, devout-devotion, religious-religion*, and more recently, *spiritual-spirituality*.

At one time or another, any of the adjectives in these pairs would have been the logical choice for the first word of the title of this book. A title like *The Holy Life, The Pious Life*, or *The Devout Life* would have served well in earlier days—indeed, any number of such titles have doubtless been penned. Today, the use of any of the first five adjectives in the above list in the title of a book like the one in your hands would surely be challenged by the publisher's marketing division. Savvy marketers know that in common parlance, to name a life or a person "righteous" (except in the radically colloquial and redefined sense in which trendy adolescents used the word a few years ago) does not ring as a compliment in most modern ears. Marketing offices know that even though you may *say* "righteous," most people *hear* "self-righteous." They also understand that to many hearers, the word "holy," when applied to persons, inevitably sounds like "holier than thou." They understand that "pious," once

243

a positive term, has picked up an elitist and archaic edge. Even "religious" and "devout," probably the least tainted of the words on the list, come with rumors of arrogance. Which leaves us (and the editor and publisher of this book) with the words "spiritual" and "spirituality," a pair of relative newcomers with their own peculiar problems. But mark my words—the same fate that befell their precursors will come to this last pair as well. One day, to name someone "deeply spiritual" will sound like calling someone "really holy" would today. There will come a day when "spirituality" will mean something like what "piety" does today.

One can only speculate as to why the terms used to speak of a serious and intentionally practiced faith fade to altered connotation and then pass from fashion. You might guess that a secular culture suspicious of any serious faith might use the words describing such faith in a mocking way. You might speculate that Christians who sensed elitism or pride in other Christians who were deeply engaged in some discipline or practice would come to use the terms denoting that discipline or practice in a subtly pejorative way—returning the rejection with rejection. And finally, words used to describe a life lived close to God become hollow when that life is not clearly lived in obedience to God's call to love, justice, and compassion for others. The holiness of those who do not clearly love others degrades the word "holy." The piety of those who care little about justice for others degrades the word "pious." The righteousness of these who experience little compassion for others degrades the word "righteous."

But this is not the problem with "spiritual" and "spirituality," at least not yet. The first of several present problems with these two terms is that though "spirit" is a thoroughly biblical term, its derivatives are not. (But then, the only two pairs in the list above that actually are central to the biblical vocabulary are *holy-holiness* and *righteous-righteousness*.) Second, one could argue that the terms "spirit" and "spirituality" skew a balanced understanding of God-as-Trinity by focusing too much or even exclusively on the work of the Third Person of the Trinity, the Holy Spirit. But finally, and most detrimentally, "spirit" and "spirituality" carry on their clothes the strong odor of something like neo-gnosticism—an individualized, anti-institutional, even anti-corporal faith that emphasizes special wisdom, "spiritual" technique, private practice, even a division between "spirit" and "body."

As many commentators have noted, it is commonplace to hear modern Americans and Europeans say things like, "I am spiritual, but not religious." They mean at least two things by this statement. First, they mean that they do not identify with the negative stereotypes evoked in their minds by the term "religious" (or for that matter, "pious," "holy," "righteous," or "devout."). Second, they mean to communicate that their faith is essentially personal and not communal, that they do not wish to be identified with the church—the essential Christian institution. They may even mean that they do not wish to identify with any historic religious tradition, perhaps especially Christianity. They may also mean that their faith and practice are essentially a means to temporarily escape the world and perhaps be "spiritually" strengthened in that escape in order to return to and manage better in an earthly world that they understand to be essentially unspiritual.

Many of the assumptions that permit the word "spirituality" while disallowing older vocabulary participate in the vague religious ethos that Thomas G. Long rightly identifies as neo-gnosticism. It is, he argues, the contemporary manifestation of a venerable religious impulse that has surfaced time and again in history.[1] Today's neo-gnosticism is indeed characterized by many of the marks of the second-century original: an affection for spiritual wisdom and technique, an emphasis on the personal and private over the communal and institutional, a dichotomy between "spirit" and "body" (understanding the essential religious quest as an escape from the latter to the former), and finally, a tendency toward intellectual and spiritual elitism that tends to view the routine churchly practice of the *hoi polloi* (the majority) with kindly disdain. By no means do all, or even most, of those who call themselves "spiritual" and who practice what they would name "spirituality" slide into anything like the new gnosticism. My point is simply that this strong strand of contemporary religious thought has often allied itself with and co-opted the vocabulary of "spirituality." My purpose in this preamble is simply to express a measure of frustration about the vocabulary that must be used to discuss the topic of this book and the subject I presently want to reflect upon more personally. There are seldom perfect words for anything, especially for talking about what I must relent and call the "spiritual life." I use these words only for want of other words that can be heard accurately. Perhaps one day we might redeem words like "holy" and "righteous" for common parlance.

A SPIRITUAL CONFESSION

My brother-in-law, whom I count as one of my favorite people in the world, almost never goes to church, yet he is both deeply spiritual and much more disciplined in his spirituality that I am. An addict nearly ten years into recovery, he begins every day, *every* day, with at least a half hour of reading and prayer. His copy of Alcoholics Anonymous's *The Big Book* is crammed with

---

1. Thomas G. Long, *Preaching from Memory to Hope* (Louisville, KY: Westminster John Knox Press, 2009), 55ff.

margin notes written to himself over the last decade. The first time I saw it, it reminded me of my devout late grandfather's onion-skin King James Version New Testament with a thousand little thoughts that he had lovingly penned into the margins over the years of his life. If my brother-in-law and I happen to be together, he often invites me to read and pray with him in the morning. The readings from *The Big Book* and a smaller Nar-Anon volume are down to earth, almost gritty in their spiritual honesty. My brother-in-law's morning reflections and prayers are honest and true, with no whisper of pretense. He is leagues more disciplined in his spirituality that I am. He never misses a morning. It has changed his life.

He is a successful attorney leading a very busy life, so I can hardly excuse my relative spiritual ill-discipline by telling myself that my minister life is more demanding than his lawyer life. It's not. In my own life, I have occasionally tried to rise extra early in the morning and begin every day with thirty minutes of Bible study and prayer. But my resolve is soon sunk by late nights, early meetings, plain laziness, or all three. I have finally come to confess that I am not wired for a spiritual life shaped by a segmented, disciplined time of day set aside for Scripture and prayer. I deeply respect people like my brother-in-law who can do it. I have the highest regard for Benedictine monks who tithe the hours. But I cannot do what they do. No excuses—it's just how it is.

I have finally forgiven myself for my spiritual ill-discipline. At the same time, I have come to affirm that I do nevertheless have a spiritual life. It is differently shaped, and though it would perhaps appear ragged and lazy to some, it has become fulsome and rewarding. In these few pages, I would simply describe my ill-disciplined spiritual practice and suggest how it brings me closer to God. Haphazard as it may be, it leads me into a life of fuller obedience to God. Woven into my workaday routine, not separate from it, it helps me to better live in love, justice, and compassion toward others.

WORK AND SPIRITUALITY

Somewhere, perhaps in seminary, I was told that leading worship cannot really be worship for the worship leader. Somewhere, perhaps in seminary, I was taught that preparing to lead a Bible study or preach a sermon did not count as actual Bible study for the one doing the preparation. Somewhere I got the impression that leading prayer at committee meetings did not count as prayer life. None of the spiritual matters I labored at *as a minister* counted as spiritual practice. It was all, I had been told, "professional," not personal or spiritual. My eventual realization that this was untrue has brought me great relief, even joy.

When I sit down to write a sermon on Friday morning, as is my routine, I pray before I read the passage I plan to preach about. I pray what the Reformed tradition would name a "prayer for illumination of the Word." Later, I pray at my word processor. In the early afternoon, I pray as I pace my study struggling to imagine how I can tune this sermon to the ears of my congregation. I sometimes pray when the printer spits out the first draft: "Dear God, these words lay flat on paper; raise them up; transform them from ink into truth that matters." I pray Sunday morning early as I do those final changes—nips and tucks, sanding rough dependent clauses smooth. I pray as I read the thing over and over till I know it nearly by heart and labor with those late doubts, "Does this *really* make sense, Lindvall?" And then, just before the choir sings the introit and I find my place in the procession, I settle for a minute in the back pew and pray yet again that the Holy Spirit may bear these mortal words of mine from lip to ear and make them something like the Word of God to the congregation sitting in the pews in front of me.

These sermon-writing prayers often spill into pastoral prayers for individual members of my congregation whom I had in my imagination as I wrote but who may or may not actually hear what I am struggling to say. Sometimes my Friday prayers become prayers of petition for the tired and empty preacher staring blankly at an equally blank computer monitor. Sometimes they become prayers of thanksgiving for some thought that falls into my head, some tale or wise word that threw itself across my path, wisdom that could hardly be called mine.

Last fall, I prayed for some heavenly assistance with a sermon I was about to preach on prayer. I had offered a few prayers during the week for this sermon, a sermon I would write on Friday. Early that Friday morning, a dream woke me up. In the dream, I was in church. Although I could not say for sure which church, it felt like my wife's home church in Indiana, though not exactly. In the dream, when it was time for Communion, I went forward and got in line. They were serving by intinction (dipping a piece of bread into a chalice of wine), and I was not the minister. The people in front of me were kneeling to receive the sacrament. (They don't do that in my wife's home church, but they were in the dream.) The minister had a plate that was absolutely overflowing with bread, I mean, spilling everywhere, and she was literally tossing bread to people like they were hungry little baby birds. When it got time for me, she tore off an immense piece of bread, way too big to eat, and gently threw it to me.

That's when I woke up and looked at the clock—4:41. As I lay there awake, I suddenly remembered a story about prayer. I hadn't thought of this story for at least a decade. It just slipped into my head. I had heard the story thirty-five years earlier from the former minister of my wife's old church, the one in the dream, I think.

I must, of course, share the story:

> In the early fifties, a young man's appendix ruptured, a medical event that used to be fatal as often as not. They rushed him to the hospital. His wife prayed, his church prayed, they all prayed that he might be spared by some miracle. They operated, found the ruptured appendix, and discovered that infection had spilled into his entire lower abdomen. Not good. Several days after the surgery, the surgeon came into his hospital room. He told the man what he had found when he operated—about the worst he could have anticipated. Then the doctor said that a few days before the operation he had been visited by a pharmaceutical salesman who had left him a sample of a new drug, a powdered form of something called penicillin. The doctor said that during the operation he thought to himself, "Can't hurt," sent to his office for the sample, and sprinkled the entire packet of the stuff inside the man's open abdomen. He lived to tell the tale.

I have discovered that prayer imbedded into sermon preparation, prayer infused into committee work, and prayer inserted into hospital visits leads to a radically incarnational sort of prayer life—the warp of prayer woven into weft of work, the "spiritual" infusing every fleshly hour of my often mundane duties as a pastor.

I have been relieved to find the same to be true not only of prayer, but of the study of Scripture done in preparation for the sermons and Bible studies that are part of my weekly work. One morning a week I lead a men's Bible study that includes ten to twenty bankers and lawyers and doctors, plus one former U.S. senator and a psychiatrist who is a recognized expert on sociopathy. He is semiretired and no longer works with sociopaths; his clients are now Hasidic Jews. He is also a mystic who spends a lot of time in Jerusalem. He knows what the Jerusalem syndrome is—namely, obsession and even intoxication with that city and what it represents, stemming from having spent time there. He also knows that he does not suffer from this syndrome. He goes there to pray and to listen for God. I rise very early on Thursday and spend a couple of hours with the chapters the group is to study at 7:45. This is perhaps my lone act of real spiritual discipline. I begin the class with a quick walk through the text and raise some thoughts for discussion. The discussion is stunningly rich. These bankers and lawyers, doctors and politicians, and the psychiatrist-mystic see things that I would simply never see. They understand things I miss. And I see things they don't. It becomes a journey into the heart of Scripture that goes deeper than I could ever go alone. It is changing all of our lives. It's doing this, even though it's just a part of my job. The study of Scripture as an integral part of my work, not separate from it but incarnate in it, has shaped itself into one of the most transforming spiritual experiences of my "personal" life.

SPIRITUALITY AND THE DAYS AS THEY ARE

I often pray when I get out of bed in the morning, usually for the day ahead of me and the people I know I will be with. I pray at night as well, for my family and the world mostly, though I often slip into sleep before I get out the "Amen." If I have no words, I just say the ancient Jesus Prayer over and over, mantra-like: "Lord Jesus Christ, Son of God, have mercy upon me, a sinner."

Having little discipline beyond such spiritual quickies morning and night, I resort to tucking prayer into the odd moments of the days. I often go to yoga class with my older daughter, an experience I do not find, in itself, to be exactly "spiritual," though I do like the "Om" part, in which two dozen people hum harmonically. I do yoga mostly to stretch old muscles that no longer much want to. But there is a lot of silence during yoga sessions, so I pray into the silence. I also pray in taxi cabs. New Yorkers spend a lot of time in taxis. Most trips are too bumpy and jerky to do anything on my BlackBerry, so I have to pray, usually for the folks in my congregation, the ones I have ritually promised to "keep in my prayers." I also pray in the subway. I get queasy if I try to read, so I often pray for the strangers on the train with me. Some of them appear burdened, others seem venal, some are clearly mad. Sometimes I imagine that one of them might be praying for me.

A SPIRITUAL CONCLUSION

The greatest danger of spirituality is that you might come to be proud of it. It calls to mind the old chestnut about the Franciscan friar who acknowledged that though the Jesuits were doubtless better scholars and the Dominicans surely better preachers, nobody could beat the Franciscans for humility. I have such regard for the spiritually disciplined. I am not pleased with my spiritual ill-discipline. Like everything else about me, it is provisional—the best I can do just now, and not really very good. But it is deeply imbedded in my life, incarnational, woven into my work as a pastor and my days as a harried New Yorker. Planted firmly in the dirt of the days, it is the way it is, and it makes me a marginally better Christian and human being.